Missing the Target

*Why Stock Market Short-Termism
Is Not the Problem*

Mark J. Roe

OXFORD
UNIVERSITY PRESS

OXFORD
UNIVERSITY PRESS

Oxford University Press is a department of the University of Oxford. It furthers
the University's objective of excellence in research, scholarship, and education
by publishing worldwide. Oxford is a registered trade mark of Oxford University
Press in the UK and certain other countries.

Published in the United States of America by Oxford University Press
198 Madison Avenue, New York, NY 10016, United States of America.

CIP data is on file at the Library of Congress
ISBN 978-0-19-762562-0

DOI: 10.1093/oso/9780197625620.001.0001

1 3 5 7 9 8 6 4 2

Printed by Sheridan Books, Inc., United States of America

Contents

Figures and Tables

Figures

Tables

Introduction

How Big Is the Problem of Stock-Market-Driven Short-Termism?

Look at the ten largest US firms by stock value in 2020, shown in Table I.1.

Table I.1. Ten Largest US Nonfinancial Public Firms, by Stock Market Capitalization

Rank	Company Name	Total stock market value (in billions of dollars)
1	Microsoft	1,200
2	Apple	1,113
3	Amazon	971
4	Alphabet (Google)	799
5	Facebook	475
6	Johnson & Johnson	346
7	Walmart	322
8	Proctor & Gamble	272
9	United Health	237
10	Intel	232

Source: Fortune 500, https://fortune.com/fortune500/2020/search/?f 500_mktval=desc (last visited July 9, 2020).

A stock market that accords a value of several trillion dollars to Amazon, Apple, Google, Facebook, and Microsoft is not one that we should worry about being too short-term oriented. These five are quintessentially longer-term companies that do much research and development—anemic R&D is seen as a core cost of a short-term stock market, but it's not short-changed at these companies. Because their current money making cannot justify their stocks' high prices, the stock market is paying for their future earnings and growth—as it has right from when they first sold their stock decades ago. Yes, their power, political influence, and market share are concerns, but their time horizons are not. These companies' longstanding sky-high value contradicts the widespread idea that the stock market is unable to look beyond the next quarter's financial statements.

Yet fear that stock-market-driven short-termism is seriously harming the US economy is pervasive. The venerable business publication *The Economist* reports that "several grand theories have emerged about what went wrong [with the US economy in the past decade]. Economists fret about secular stagnation, debt hangover and . . . demography. [But i]n American boardrooms, meanwhile, a widely held view is that a dangerous short-termism has taken hold."[1] And not just in boardrooms: A widely held view among Washington policymakers, corporate executives, the media, and the public is that frenzied, short-term stock market trading has coupled with Wall Street's unquenchable thirst for immediate results to disrupt US firms and badly hurt the economy. Something must be done to reverse short-termism's impact. Jobs are destroyed and technological progress is stunted, while solutions seem, in the public view, so easy to implement that one is angered at their absence.

Joe Biden, for example, when Vice President wrote under the headline "short-termism saps the economy,"[2] attributing US workers' weakened well-being to two institutional failures—with Wall Street short-termism one of the two.[3] Former President Obama recently laid out the goals that unify most Democrats: universal health care, higher taxes on the wealthy, handling a bloated financial sector, and dealing with "short-term thinking [behind] how our corporations operate because of [the] CEOs' concerns about quarterly reports . . . taking precedence over long-term concerns about investment and jobs and environmental sustainability."[4] And, corporate executives—often Republican—and their allies castigate stock market short-termism for purportedly inducing poor economic performance, which, they say, could be improved if executives and boards had more autonomy from stock markets.

I share Biden and Obama's ultimate goals of a more economically equal, and an environmentally sound, society. But I show in this book first that the evidence for stock-market-driven short-termism is much weaker than is usually thought and then that working to lengthen corporate time horizons will not bring us closer to a fairer and environmentally stronger society. The two issues—the corporation's time horizon and its purpose—are largely separate issues that public discourse often conflates. A long-term factory could keep workers employed and be good for stockholders too over the long run but still

---

[1] *Corporate Short-Termism Is a Frustratingly Slippery Idea*, THE ECONOMIST, Feb. 16, 2017, at 58.

[2] *See, e.g.*, Joe Biden, *How Short-Termism Saps the Economy*, WALL ST. J., Sept. 28, 2016, at A13.

[3] David Brooks, *President Biden's First Day—Imagining Jan. 20, 2021*, N.Y. TIMES, July 17, 2020 ("asked . . . to describe the big forces that have flattened working-class wages over the past decades . . . Biden pointed to two institutional failures—[one being the] broken [character of] Washington and [the other being] the way Wall Street forces business leaders to focus obsessively on the short term.").

[4] Jonathan Chait, *In Conversation with Barack Obama*, NEW YORK MAGAZINE, Dec. 9, 2010.

degrade the environment. And besides that, corporate interests can capture for their own benefit the effort to lengthen corporate time horizons by convincing lawmakers to shield boards and executives from stock markets in a mistaken belief that the former are fundamentally long-term and the latter are not. And so, this book also provides friendly advice on why to avoid this policy path.

* * *

Stock-market-driven short-termism is the rare corporate structural issue that both resonates with the public and has a place in political rhetoric. Most corporate law issues are technical—for experts, for lawyers, and for corporate interests. But especially when businesses are threatened with closure, political leaders react and often justify their response as not just seeking to save a local business with loyal employees who did nothing wrong but also as fighting Wall Street short-termism.

Consider how senators reacted to the shutdown of a major paper mill in Wisconsin. Hedge fund activists were said to have forced the Wausau Paper Company to close its paper mill—throwing lifetime employees out of work and devastating the mill town. In response, Wisconsin's Democratic senator, Tammy Baldwin, joined with Georgia's Republican senator, David Perdue (Georgia also has major paper mills) to sponsor a major anti-hedge-fund bill aiming to reduce the influence of hedge funds on businesses. The sponsors described it as a "bipartisan reform to protect Main St from Wall St hedge funds" so as to "fight against increasing short-termism in our economy."[5] Senators who had proposed a prior version of the bill castigated predatory activists who "demand[] short-term returns and buybacks at the expense of the company's long-term future." This short-termism, they said, must end:

> [T]here is [a] growing chorus who believe short-termism is holding America back . . . . [S]hort-termism . . . is the focus on short time horizons by both corporate managers and financial markets. It results in corporate funds being used for payouts to shareholders in the form of dividends and buybacks rather than investment in workers, R&D, infrastructure, and long-term success.[6]

---

[5] Senators Tammy Baldwin (Wisconsin) and David Perdue (Georgia), Brokaw Act: Bipartisan Reform to Protect Main St from Wall St Hedge Funds, www.baldwin.senate.gov/imo/media/doc/Brokaw%20Act%20OnePager.pdf.

[6] Senators Tammy Baldwin (Wisconsin) and Jeff Merkley (Oregon), The Brokaw Act: Strengthening Oversight of Activist Hedge Funds, www.baldwin.senate.gov/imo/media/doc/3.7.16%20-%20Brokaw%20Act%201.pdf.

The senators' statement shows why stock market short-termism is not just a specialists' issue but also a political one: it's blamed for the Wausau mill closing and other setbacks, and for widespread US economic degradation. That's what I examine in this book: Does stock market short-termism really worm its way in to do major damage to the economy? Was the Wausau closing really the result of a pernicious short-term stock market? Even if it was, does the problem scale up to the economy-wide level to cripple US R&D, investment, and long-term business focus, as the senators argue? Or is the Wausau closing better seen as a local misfortune that's mistakenly categorized as due to a dysfunctional time horizon and then exaggerated as indicating an economy-wide problem?

Political convenience can lead politicians to blame the stock market's purportedly faulty time horizon for economic setbacks for which its responsibility is minor or nil. Faulting Wall Street is politically satisfying and looks like forward-moving action both to voters and to senators trying to do their best. But the evidence is that doing so avoids the hard political effort to address the disruption's root causes and effects. True, many shortcomings could be pinned on the large corporation. But excessively truncated time horizons and a crippling inability to bring forward good new technologies and products or to stick with tried-and-true good ones, to usually do the underlying R&D when needed, and to adapt to new markets and political realities are not among the large corporation's major faults. The evidence, we shall see, does not support the idea that the stock market's time horizon is damaging the economy in any major way.

Dislocations and closings are real problems for those thrown out of work, yes, but lengthening Wall Street's time horizons to more highly value good results years down the road will do little or nothing for the US worker, for greater equality, or for the environment and climate degradation. It's not the best target if there's a major R&D shortfall. Aiming at purportedly truncated time horizons to fix these problems is aiming at the wrong target.

Even the Wausau paper mill result in Wisconsin deserves further thought. Paper manufacturing had been in a *long-term* decline in the United States when Wausau closed its Wisconsin mill, government data tells us.[7] The company was slow to adjust to the country's declining use of print paper. The cause was obvious: computerization changed how businesspeople communicated, emails meant fewer letters and fewer office memos, and online media and

---

[7] Jeffrey P. Prestemon et al., U.S. Dep't of Agric., The Global Position of the U.S. Forest Products Industry 3, fig. 2 (E-Gen. Tech. Rep. SRS-204, 2015).

ebooks meant fewer printed newspapers, magazines, and books.[8] The senators and their supporters viewed the Wausau paper mill as a victim of stock market short-termism, but the workers' and their families' pain was more likely due to the company's excessive *long-termism*. It clung for too long to an outmoded business plan, leading to the company having to abruptly pivot to the realities of declining paper use.

But the political impact is clear: a mill closes, workers lose jobs, and senators blame Wall Street short-termism, extol legislation to diminish Wall Street influence, and paint vivid imagery of Wall Street "wolf packs" hunting down companies to close and jobs to eliminate. If stock market short-termism wasn't central—and it wasn't—to the Wausau paper mill shutdown, other policies are in order.

The senators blamed the financial market messenger bringing an unwanted message. Accelerating technological change, not the stock market, was the real culprit. The senators' action was a symbolic gesture of sympathy for affected constituents. But they were not helping long-term adjustment—and their plans would maybe even slow it down.

They found a scapegoat, not a solution.

* * *

By corporate short-termism I mean overvaluing current corporate results at the expense of future profits and well-being. In recent years, stock market short-termism has also become intertwined in public rhetoric with conceptualizations of corporate social responsibility, corporate purpose, and the need to emphasize corporate attention to the environment, stakeholders, and the risk of climate catastrophe, the so-called ESG issues. There is a widely held view that shifting the large US corporation from its supposed short-term orientation to a longer one is needed to ameliorate a raft of social and economic problems, such as employment, equality, and R&D. According to this thinking, lengthening the stock market's time horizon will release a dammed up investment tide, while also doing much to save the planet from climate catastrophe. It's satisfying to think so, because if the stock market's time horizon is the main culprit and long-term companies are inherently environmentally friendly, then there is less need to do the hard political and economic work to more directly handle these problems. But we'll see that these corporate responsibility considerations are for the most part not time horizon

[8] Alon Brav, J.B. Heaton & Jonathan Zandberg, *Failed Anti-Activist Legislation: The Curious Case of the Brokaw Act*, 11 J. Bus. Entrepreneurship & L. 329 (2018).

issues; making the large firm more long-term focused will have little or no impact here.

Stock market short-termism and lawmaking ideas on how to handle it are also prominent in part because they implicate interests. Their prominence is not just the result of abstract ideas and big picture social policy, but also comes from the boost that two interest groups get from policymakers seeing stock market short-termism as pernicious. Employees with good jobs, along with their policy supporters, see stock market short-termism as degrading employees' well-being and as fostering risky, economically costly policies throughout corporate America. Much of the public rhetoric on short-termism aims to help employees and advance social well-being, but the beneficiaries often end up being executives seeking autonomy and authority. These two interests have differing although overlapping policy goals, but both seek results that would make their jobs and pay more secure from stock market disruption. Liberal-minded judges, policymakers, and political leaders are more likely to accord executives power and autonomy when these leaders see themselves as helping the economy, employees, and the environment; they support corporate structure outcomes—more power and more autonomy for executives—that if presented to them directly and starkly, would induce more skepticism.

In corporate policymaking circles, executives and their allies often see stock market short-termism as hurting the economy. They seek and often obtain more autonomy from the stock market by insisting that insulating management from the stock market's purported short-termism would bolster the economy. Such executives benefit directly because their jobs are thereby made more secure, their pay less likely to be questioned, their day-to-day autonomy enhanced, and one source of their day-to-day stress somewhat relaxed. Yet executives' public-spirited resistance to accountability for short-term performance—to do more for the economy and the public good—could at times morph into less accountability for performance, period. That many executives genuinely believe that the stock market hurts the economy does not undermine the fact that these beliefs align with their interests.

Misdiagnosis—attributing too many societal problems to a stock market time horizon problem—leads to stock market rules that insulate executives and boards from feedback, allowing some strategic mistakes to persist unnecessarily. Misdiagnosis can also facilitate outsized compensation, if a main remedy is to accord executives more autonomy overall. Whether this insulation contributes in a major or minor way to the inequality that afflicts the US body politic could be investigated.

* * *

Getting this right is important because misdiagnosis leads us to policies that fail to cure real problems. The real target is a better-performing, more equitable economy. Aiming at the purported damage emanating from a purportedly excessively short-term stock market will miss that bigger and better target for something small and not particularly problematic.

Consider government support for R&D and for better climate and environmental policy.

Government's declining support for research and development. R&D is weakening in the United States, the critics say, and stock market short-termism is to blame. Stock buybacks, exacerbated by short-termism, starve large firms of the cash they need to invest and to do more R&D. If those diagnoses were correct, a policy of insulating firms and their executives from stock market pressure could have cogency.

But *corporate* R&D spending is *rising*, not falling. Perhaps R&D should be rising more, yes. But a more obvious R&D weakness, as I show in Chapter 4, is the spectacular *fall* in US *government* R&D spending. Government-backed R&D often leads to breakthroughs in basic technology that greatly boost prosperity. If the decline-in-R&D culprit is mostly the sharply shrinking *government* support for basic research, then no amount of new time-horizon-focused stock market rules will fix the problem.

Thinking that stock market short-termism's truncating of corporate time horizons is the primary cause of weakened US R&D leads policymakers astray—to aim at the wrong target. It serves some corporate players' interests for policymakers to think so, but the misdirection does not serve the citizenry and the nation.

Weakened environmental and climate change rules. Critics complain that corporations contribute gravely to climate change and environmental degradation, with stock market short-termism particularly to blame. But weak corporate respect for the environment is not due to individual firms' shortened time horizons but to the ability of firms to push the costs of environmental and climate damage away from themselves and onto others. They can do this in the short-term *and* the long-term, and can profit from offloading environmental costs while others pay. Indeed, maintaining a factory with toxic emissions into the future may look long-term to some and could save jobs but be bad for the environment. The right focus is not on *when* the damage is done— the time horizon problem—but rather on *who* suffers from the damage.

In too much public discourse, the stock market's time horizon is mixed up with what the corporation aims for—profits instead of doing good in and of itself. But these two are largely separate: a firm can be long-term and selfish, or it can be short-term and generous. Thinking that time horizons and purpose are one and the same, or that changing the firm's time horizon will make it less selfish, weakens our resolve for implementing better environmental regulation and climate solutions. What we need are better rules that prevent players—corporate and individual—from externalizing environmental costs to society while keeping the profits and convenience for themselves. No amount of tinkering with stock market *time horizons* will fix that problem. Thinking that tinkering with time horizons can fix it misses the real targets— the corporation's (and our own) warped incentives—and prevents us from reaching the best solution.

Or any solution.

* * *

Consider the following when you think about how plausible it is that the stock market's time horizon is persistently and perniciously too short: Tech companies that had their initial stock offerings in 2018 and 2019 before the Covid-19 slowdown included Dropbox, Survey Monkey, Cloudflare, and Spotify. Not one was profitable;[9] the stock market bought them on a future-oriented view. Similarly, a slew of money-losing biotech companies made their initial stock offerings in 2018. In 2019 seven of the top ten biotech IPOs had *no* approved drug—hence, the market valued those companies for their long-term prospects not their immediate marketing capabilities—and still they collectively raised more than $1.95 billion from the stock market.[10] Future possibilities, not current profits, drove investors, who were betting on the firms' potential successes in drugs that would treat maladies such as autoimmune disorders and cancer.[11]

This is not an accidental or one-time event. Recall the companies that were the largest by stock market capitalization in 2020—listed in Table 1. When Amazon years ago first sold its stock to the public, it had no earnings but still was accorded a half-billion-dollar value by the stock market, while Apple, Facebook and Google obtained a stock price about one hundred times their

---

[9] Ben Eisen, *No Profit? No Problem! Loss-Making Companies Flood the IPO Market*, WALL ST. J., Mar. 16, 2018; Alex Wilhelm, *Over 80% of 2018 IPOs Are Unprofitable Setting New Record*, CRUNCHBASE NEWS, Oct. 2, 2018, https://news.crunchbase.com/news/over-80-of-2018-ipos-are-unprofitable-setting-new-record/; Cloudflare S-1 filing, Aug. 15, 2019, www.sec.gov/Archives/edgar/data/1477333/000119312519222176/d735023ds1.htm. Much of the data on these IPO issues originates with Jay Ritter's IPO database, to be further discussed later in chapters 2 and 6.

[10] Melanie Senior, *The Biopharmaceutical Anomaly*, 38 NATURE BIOTECHNOLOGY 798 (2020); Eisen, *supra* note 9.

[11] Kate Rooney, *More Money-losing Companies Than Ever Are Going Public, Even Compared with the Dotcom Bubble*, CNBC NEWS, Oct. 1, 2018; Joanna Glasner, *While Tech Waffles on Going Public, Biotech IPOs Boom*, TECHCRUNCH, July 2018.

earnings when they first sold their stock—more than five times the stock market's overall ratio of stock price to earnings.[12]

All this indicates the stock market does value the distant future and has been doing so for decades.

Moreover, the logic behind the theory that there is *pervasive* economy-wide short-termism is not strong. For stock-market-driven short-termism to deeply afflict the US economy—as opposed to damaging only some firms, here and there, now and then—normal market processes must fail. When one big firm is too short-term and gives up long-term profit, others can jump in to profit from the short-termers' neglect. The United States' dynamic venture capital and private equity sectors make money from opportunities big firms don't take. Or another big public firm that isn't tied up by the stock market can pick up the slack. They all have the profit incentive to do so.

The Covid-19 crisis opened another window into short-termism. The consensus view among short-term critics is that the stock market overreacts to quarterly earnings changes. A few pennies up in quarterly profit and the stock soars. A few pennies down and the stock price plummets. Surely there's some truth to this; but how seriously detrimental is it? In the first months of 2020, as the Covid-19 lockdown froze more and more economic activity and gross domestic product plummeted, with forecasters then expecting a severe 2020 GDP decline of 5.8%. Unemployment rose to post–World War II highs. The Covid-19 lockdown and resulting decline in much economic activity crushed corporate earnings. By early June 2020, second quarter earnings were estimated to be down by more than 40% compared to the prior year—a swift and steep drop.[13]

Yet during that time the stock market, after a modest decline, recovered strongly. The 40% estimated earnings decline was not matched by a 40% stock market fall, and the stock market reached an all-time high at the end of 2020. The critics who see the stock market as excessively short-run and obsessively quarterly focused need to explain why we did not see Covid-19-induced stock market declines as steep as the Covid-19-induced fall in earnings.

The easiest explanation is that the stock market is nowhere nearly as short-run oriented as critics say it is. The stock market's *long-run expectation* was that the economy would recover in a year or two, when a good-enough vaccine or a cure became available, and it priced stocks for the long-run, *not* the

---

[12] More specifically, the S&P 500's price to earnings ratio was 9, 15, and 19, when the three went public. Microsoft was, comparatively speaking, the laggard, with a price-to-earnings ratio of 25 when the stock market overall was selling at about 16 times its prior year's earnings.

[13] Factset, Earnings Insights, July 10, 2020, www.factset.com/hubfs/Resources%20Section/Research%20 Desk/Earnings%20Insight/EarningsInsight_071020.pdf (last visited July 13, 2020).

immediate short-run. Yes, there is a coldness to a stock market assessing long-term economic value as a medical tragedy unfolded, but the stock market's reaction to the Covid-19 crisis was hardly a short-term stock market at work.[14]

* * *

Broader social and economic reasons help to explain why stock market short-termism is seen as seriously pernicious, as opposed to a small issue that might be better handled. These reasons are rooted in part in rapid economic change and in hard-to-resolve, perhaps irresolvable, conflict.

Economic change is accelerating. New technologies rise, dominate, and then are superseded. Markets open and close. Companies with high-flying stocks find themselves after several years with outmoded technologies, and their stock price falls. Long-established papermakers find people buy less paper than before. Retailers sell books one year and VCR tapes the next until DVD mailers put the VCR rental firms out of business and then online streaming forces the DVD distributors to recede. Newspapers are read on tablets; books are ordered, delivered, and read online; banks become virtual. Physical capital assets become obsolete before they have worn out. All these make the stock market jump, as new technologies change old ways.

The pace of economic change quickens and disrupts more jobs. Both those who are affected and their political protectors react, blaming the stock market for inducing the changes and being too short-term. Even if new technologies make many people better off, those who do not benefit—the employees and executives whose working lives, personal lives, and sense of self are diminished—do not sit still. They act and constitute a sympathetic audience for leaders who blame financial market short-termism for the disruption. Executives who want more autonomy from financial markets applaud, and corporate lawmakers give them a sympathetic hearing.

Even if some important part of what is conventionally seen as stock market short-termism is financial pressure to prepare for the future, that likely reality is of little comfort to those who lose because of change. Thus, we have more than a simple problem of technical data interpretation at hand. We are not

---

[14] Matt Levine, the Bloomberg columnist, sharply analyzes this Covid-19 short-term versus long-term contradiction. Matt Levine, *Stocks Are Trying to Forget 2020*, BLOOMBERG OPINION—MONEY STUFF, June 1, 2020. A *New York Times* story on the stock market's strength despite the Covid-19 hit to the economy reflects the forward-looking nature of the stock market, where—in theory—investors buy stock based on long-term expectation for profits and dividends they expect companies to generate, rather than on how they're faring when the shares are purchased. Matt Phillips, *"This Market Is Nuts": Stocks Defy a Recession*, N.Y. TIMES, Aug. 19, 2020, at A1, A10. The Federal Reserve's low interest policy during the Covid-19 economic setback—which buoys the stock market—cannot be ignored here.

just examining whether the stock market is too slow or too fast, but whether it is the conduit for disrupting too many people's lives and livelihoods. Instead of a pure time horizon problem, we have serious underlying conflict and social dislocation, with the rhetoric of short-termism having become a weapon for criticizing the economy and the corporation. The rhetoric of stock market short-termism has become a means for political, policy, and social combat as much as it is an economic problem for data inquiry and logical analysis.

PART I
LOOKING FOR STOCK-MARKET-DRIVEN SHORT-TERMISM'S IMPACT ON THE ECONOMY

1

The Short-Term Problem Perceived

Activists and stock traders prevent firms from investing for the long run. Employees who do their jobs well are laid off to save shareholders a few dollars. Short-termism seeps through the economy. Big firms burn so much cash in buybacks that they slash employment-boosting investment, jeopardize their own and the economy's future by cutting R&D spending, and fail to think beyond the next quarter's financial results. These problems deeply damage the US economy, and they're getting worse. They justify more laws to weaken shareholders' influence.

That's the core of the widely-perceived stock-market-driven short-termist story. Here, in Chapter 1, I set forth that perspective, often quoting and summarizing corporate, political, and other luminaries to do so. In Chapters 2, 5, 6, and 7, I evaluate this widely-supported stock market short-termism story against the evidence.

A. Frenzied Stock Trading and Activist Aggression Induce Economic Degradation

The view is widespread that a vociferously short-term-focused stock market's demands on corporate executives affect the economy deleteriously.

The predicates are straightforward: increasingly rapid and even frenzied stock trading and rising activist pressure on public firms. Traders and institutional investors buy and sell stock too rapidly—hoping to buy for a few pennies less and sell for a few pennies more and thereby make a profit. Activist shareholders buy up a slice of a company's stock. They seek to change their target company's business strategy by, say, pressing it to drop an unsuccessful product line. Executives who oppose the activists fear being pushed out of their jobs if the activists get enough shareholder support.

These lead in the conventional short-term theory to pernicious economy-wide results: firms drop good R&D projects (which cost cash today but whose benefits come later) or never start them, buy back stock (stripping themselves of cash for investment), and cut back expensive capital expenditures (cheating themselves out of the productive cutting edge they'll want in the future).

Wall Street, looking for a quick profit, impedes corporate executives at public companies from investing for the long-term, it's said. One bad quarter for a sound company leads senior management to lay off loyal, long-term, well-performing employees. Another bad quarter puts the executives' own posts at risk. "[T]here really is widespread consensus among managers, among boards, and even among major institutional shareholders, that . . . short-term pressures . . . are causing boards and managers to manage their companies suboptimally."[1] Law firms that represent major US companies and their executives say so regularly, as does McKinsey, the premiere management consulting firm. And they are all well-positioned to know.

These degradations to the US economy have been pernicious for some time, in the critics' view, and they're worsening.[2] Frenzied stock trading makes stock prices reflect the latest tidbit of information, not the company's long-term prospects. Accelerating trading makes managers manage mainly for this quarter. With R&D slashed, the nation's economic future is being mortgaged for the quick dollar that stockholders demand, one that "loot[s] the future."[3]

Business leaders see the problem as serious. The World Economic Forum, the influential international organization that hosts annual meetings of world leaders in Davos, Switzerland, viewed combatting short-termism as one of its five leadership priorities.[4] Its international council of business leaders resolved in a formal statement to criticize firms and shareholders for being preoccupied with short-term financial gains. These leaders want corporate

---

[1] Steven Rosenblum, *Corporations: The Short-Termism Debate*, 85 Miss. L.J. 697, 708, 710 (2016) (Mr. Rosenblum, a Wachtell Lipton partner, often comments on corporate short-termism).

[2] *See* Andrew Haldane, Patience and Finance: Speech by Executive Director, Financial Stability, Bank of England, at the Oxford China Business Forum, Beijing, Sept. 9, 2010, www.bis.org/review/r100909e.pdf; Alfred Rappaport, *The Economics of Short-Term Performance Obsession*, 61 Fin. Analysts J., May/June 2005, at 65, 66; Richard Davies, Andrew G. Haldane, Mette Nielsen & Silvia Pezzini, *Measuring the Costs of Short-termism*, 12 J. Fin. Stability 16, 20 (2014); Lawrence E. Mitchell, *The Fault, Dear Investors, Lies in Ourselves*, Wash. Post, Mar. 31, 2002.

[3] *See, e.g.*, Edward Luce, *US Share Buybacks Loot the Future: Corporate Leaders Should Put Long-Term Growth Ahead of Quick Gains*, Fin. Times, Apr. 26, 2015.

[4] Klaus Schwab, Five Leadership Priorities for 2017, World Economic Forum Annual Meeting 2017, www.weforum.org/agenda/2017/01/five-leadership-priorities-for-2017/. More precisely, myopic short-termism was seen as the first structural flaw in market capitalism overall.

boards, and not large firms' shareholders, to decide what is and is not good long-term value creation,[5] presumably because the council saw boards of directors as long-run oriented while the shareholders are not.[6]

Prominent business, academic, and labor leaders, working through the influential Aspen Institute, attacked investor-based short-termism as disincentivizing healthy economic growth,[7] as did the Conference Board, an organization of leading corporate executives.[8] Commentators at the Brookings Institution, the important Washington think tank, pushed forward the idea that "incentives [now] favor[] short-term gains over long-term growth. . . . [Those incentives] include: [t]he proliferation of stock buybacks[,] . . . [t]he fixation on quarterly earnings . . . [, and t]he rise of activist investors."[9] "Stock buybacks . . . are rendering firms unable to engage in productive investments because there is no capital leftover for other investment opportunities or for other corporate stakeholders."[10]

Influential business media advocate similarly. Leading business players from the major management consultants, like the recent global managing partner of McKinsey and his colleagues, urge executives to "fight the tyranny of short-termism" in the *Harvard Business Review*[11] and castigate the scourge of short-termism.[12] Both the Business Roundtable—an organization of the largest public companies' executives—and the National Association of Corporate Directors lament the excessive short-term focus that is destroying value.[13] Respected business leaders—Jamie Dimon and Warren Buffett—write

[5] World Economic Forum, The Compact for Responsive and Responsible Leadership: A Roadmap for Sustainable Long-Term, Growth and Opportunity, Nov. 30, 2016, www3.weforum.org/docs/Media/AM17/The_Compact_for_Responsive_and_Responsible_Leadership_09.01.2017.pdf.

[6] Sarah Bostwick Stromoski, The World Economic Forum 2017 Cheat Sheet, http://cecp.co/world-economic-forum-2017-cheat-sheet/.

[7] Aspen Institute, Overcoming Short-termism: A Call for A More Responsible Approach to Investment and Business Management, Sept. 2009, at 3, www.assets.aspeninstitute.org/content/uploads/files/content/docs/pubs/overcome_short_state0909_0.pdf.

[8] The Conference Board, Is Short-Term Behavior Jeopardizing the Future Prosperity of Business?, Oct. 30, 2015, at 3, www.conference-board.org/topics/short-termism/Future-Impacts-of-Short-Term-Behavior-CLO.

[9] William A. Galston & Elaine Kamarck, *More Builders and Fewer Traders: A Growth Strategy for the American Economy*, Brookings Inst. (June 2015), www.brookings.edu/wp-content/uploads/2016/ [https://perma.cc/N9GL-BL4V].

[10] Lenore Palladino, Stock Buybacks: Driving a High-Profit, Low-Wage Economy 2 (Roosevelt Inst. 2018).

[11] Dominic Barton, *Capitalism for the Long Term*, Harv. Bus. Rev., Mar. 2011, at 85, 86–88 (Barton was McKinsey's managing director from 2009 to 2018).

[12] *Id.*; Dominic Barton & Mark Wiseman, *Focusing Capital on the Long Term*, Harv. Bus. Rev., Jan. 2014, at 44. *See also* Robert H. Hayes & William J. Abernathy, *Managing Our Way to Economic Decline*, Harv. Bus. Rev., July–Aug. 2007, at 67; Roger L. Martin, *Yes, Short-Termism Really Is a Problem*, Harv. Bus. Rev., Oct. 2015, https://hbr.org/2015/10/yes-short-termism-really-is-a-problem; William Lazonick, *Profits Without Prosperity*, 92 Harv. Bus. Rev., Sept. 2014, at 46–55. *See also* Alfred Rappaport, Saving Capitalism from Short-Termism (2011); Rappaport, *supra* note 2, at 65–77 (2005).

[13] The CFA Institute Centre for Financial Market Integrity and the Business Roundtable Institute for Corporate Ethics, Breaking the Short-Term Cycle 1, 2006, www.cfainstitute.org/-/media/documents/

in the *Wall Street Journal* under the headline "Short-Termism is Harming the Economy."[14]

Regulators are on board. Chairs of Wall Street's primary regulator, the Securities and Exchange Commission, both Democratic and Republican, attack trading markets as perniciously shortening corporate time horizons and thereby justify rules that insulate boards of directors from markets. SEC Chair Christopher Cox said "short-termism . . . afflicts our markets overall."[15] A Republican SEC commissioner stated that unfortunately:

> [T]here seems to be a predominance of short-term thinking [in corporate America] at the expense of long-term investing. [Stock market activists] drive a short-term pop in value: spinning off a profitable division, beginning a share buy-back program, or slashing capital expenditures or research and development expenses. Having inflated current returns by eliminating corporate investments for the future, these activists can exit their investment and move on.[16]

National political leaders like Joseph Biden, as we've seen, writing under the headline *How Short-Termism Saps the Economy*, say the same.[17] Former President Obama, as we also saw, sees stock market short-termism as a barrier to achieving Democrats' major goals, such as greater equality. Senator Sherrod Brown criticizes the "obsession with quarterly results [and] the short-term expectations from the world of finance, which too often sacrifice long-term economic growth and job creation."[18] Senator Marco Rubio laments lost investment due to stock market short-termism.[19] Democratic and Republican senatorial sponsors describe their anti-hedge-fund bill as a "bipartisan reform to protect Main St from Wall St hedge funds" and to "fight against [the economy's] increasing short-termism" emanating from predatory activists

---

article/position-paper/breaking-the-short-term-cycle.ashx; Nat'l Ass'n of Corporate Directors, Report of the 2015 NACD Blue Ribbon Commission: The Board and Long-Term Value Creation, 2015.

[14] Jamie Dimon & Warren E. Buffett, *Short-Termism Is Harming the Economy*, WALL ST. J., June 6, 2018.

[15] *Turmoil in U.S. Credit Markets: The Role of the Credit Rating Agencies*, Hearing Before the Senate Committee on Banking, Housing and Urban Affairs, 110th Cong. 24 (2008); Ben Ashwell, *Business Leaders Eye Steps toward Long-Termism*, IR MAGAZINE, Mar. 7, 2018 (Republican SEC Chair Clayton participates in investor summit on how firms can become more long-term focused).

[16] Daniel M. Gallagher, Activism, Short-Termism, and the SEC: Remarks at the 21st Annual Stanford Directors' College, June 23, 2015, www.sec.gov/news/speech/activism-short-termism-and-the-sec.html (Gallagher was an SEC Commissioner from 2011 to 2015).

[17] Joe Biden, *How Short-Termism Saps the Economy*, WALL ST. J., Sept. 28, 2016, at A13.

[18] *Examining Short-Termism in Financial Markets*, Hearing Before Senate Subcomm. on Econ. Pol'y of the Comm. on Banking, Housing, and Urban Affairs, 111th Cong. 2 (2010).

[19] Senator Marco Rubio, American Investments in the 21st Century (2019), https://www.rubio.senate.gov/public/_cache/files/9f25139a-6039-465a-9cf1-feb5567aebb7/4526E9620A9A7DB74267ABEA58810 22F.5.15.2019.-final-project-report-american-investment.pdf.

"demand[ing] short-term returns like buybacks at the expense of investments in workers, R&D and the company's long-term future."[20]

Likewise, government commissions and blue ribbon government-sponsored studies attack stock-market-driven short-termism, concluding that "it is essential that markets work in the public interest and for the long term rather than focusing on short-term returns . . . . The effects of short-termism are damaging to the economy as a whole."[21]

The nation's most important business law judges seem to be with the program. Leo Strine, Delaware's respected Supreme Court chief justice, who left the bench in 2019, powerfully excoriated financial short-termism in his off-the-bench writings for undermining US economic well-being.[22] "[D]irectors are increasingly vulnerable to pressure from activist investors . . . with short-term objectives," he said, that "may lead [them] to . . . sacrifice long-term performance for short-term shareholder wealth."[23] When these ideas are stated so often and with such conviction, it's plausible that they affect judges' decision-making on the allocation of power between shareholders, directors, and executives. (Delaware's legislature and courts are vital for US corporate law because a majority of the large US firms are incorporated in Delaware and subject to Delaware corporate law.)

As an instance of impact on policy, consider the plight of Polaroid—the iconic, long dominant instant photography company—in the Delaware corporate law courts. When shareholder activists pressured the camera and filmmaking company to adapt, management resisted, using the rhetoric of resisting short-termism and privileging the long-term.[24] The business courts supported management *and* its (purportedly) long-term practices.[25] Yet Polaroid was failing to face up to digital photography's threat to traditional film photography, and its resistant management kept their long-term strategic

---

[20] Senators Baldwin and Perdue, Brokaw Act: Bipartisan Reform to Protect Main St from Wall St Hedge Funds, www.baldwin.senate.gov/imo/media/doc/Brokaw%20Act%20OnePager.pdf (Democrat Baldwin and Republican Perdue's bill responded to Wisconsin's Wausau Paper, Inc. shutting down after a hedge fund bought into the company).

[21] *See, e.g.*, Center for American Progress, Report of the Commission on Inclusive Prosperity 14, 26, 35–36 (Lawrence H. Summers & Ed Balls, chairs, 2015).

[22] Leo E. Strine, Jr., *Securing Our Nation's Economic Future: A Sensible, Nonpartisan Agenda to Increase Long-Term Investment and Job Creation in the United States*, 71 Bus. Law. 1081 (2016). *Cf.* Steve Denning, *How Corporate America Is Cannibalizing Itself*, Forbes, Nov. 18, 2015.

[23] Leo E. Strine, Jr., *The Dangers of Denial: The Need for a Clear-Eyed Understanding of the Power and Accountability Structure Established by the Delaware General Corporation Law*, 50 Wake Forest L. Rev. 761, 790–91 (2015). *Cf.* J.B. Heaton, *The "Long Term" in Corporate Law*, 72 Bus. Law. 353–66 (2017).

[24] *Shamrock Holdings, Inc. v. Polaroid Corp.*, 559 A.2d 257, 268 (Del. Ch. 1989). Defending the long-term would not, however, said the defenders, harm short-term shareholders. *Id.* at 283.

[25] *Id.* at 260; J.B. Heaton, *The Unfulfilled Promise of Hedge Fund Activism*, 13 Va. L. & Bus. Rev. 317 (2019); J.B. Heaton, *The "Long Term" in Corporate Law*, 72 Bus. Law. 356 & n.55 (2017).

emphasis on photo-chemistry.[26] Polaroid executives believed through the 1990s that in the long run "customers would always want a hard-copy print" and not just an image on a screen.[27]

* * *

The issue is international, as well. In Britain, much attention was accorded the 2012 official Kay Report, which criticized public company short-termism and sought means to reduce it.[28] The Organization for Economic Cooperation and Development in 2011 launched a major initiative to combat corporate short-termism.[29] The European Union is, as I write, seeking to combat short-termism as a scourge of both worker well-being and climate sustainability.[30]

* * *

The stock market short-termism problem in public discourse comes in two varieties. The first is of stock market pressure forcing executives to forego long-term spending on R&D, cut back investment in machines and people, and buy back their companies' stock (and thereby lose cash needed for the future), even if more R&D, more capital investment, and fewer buybacks would be better in the long run. We can call this "Type A" short-termism—excessively favoring near-term results over longer-term results. Long-term shareholders and long-term companies suffer; short-term shareholders—traders and activists—gain. When enough companies fail in these three dimensions—investment, R&D, and buybacks—the entire economy suffers.

Short-termism in public discourse *also* encompasses corporate decisions that damage the economy via environmental degradation, which boosts

---

[26] PETER BUSE, THE CAMERA DOES THE REST: HOW POLAROID CHANGED PHOTOGRAPHY 79 (2016) (Polaroid sees the digital future but fails to adapt).

[27] Andrea Nagy Smith, What Was Polaroid Thinking?, Insights from Yale School of Mgmt., www. insights.som.yale.edu/insights/what-was-polaroid-thinking.

[28] John Kay, The Kay Review of UK Equity Markets and Long-Term Decision Making: Final Report 10–12, 14, 26, 40 (2012), www.gov.uk/government/consultations/the-kay-review-of-uk-equity-markets-and-long-term-decision-making. "Short-termism has plagued the UK economy for decades, so the Kay Review of UK Capital Markets . . . is hugely welcome . . . . John Kay's final report . . . recognizes that a sharp shock is needed to break today's short-termist mind-set." John Chapman, *Time to Tackle UK Short-termism*, FIN. TIMES, May 27, 2012, at 13 (Chapman advised UK policymakers and was secretary to the UK Innovation Advisory Board from 1989 to 1991).

[29] OECD, Financial Market Trends: Long-Term Investment and Growth (2011); OECD, Institutional Investors and Long-term Investment Project Report (2014), www.oecd.org/finance/OECD-LTI-profect. pdf.

[30] Mark J. Roe, Holger Spamann, Jesse M. Fried & Charles C.Y. Wang, *The European Commission's Sustainable Corporate Governance Report: A Critique*, 38 YALE J. ON REG. BULLETIN 133 (2021).

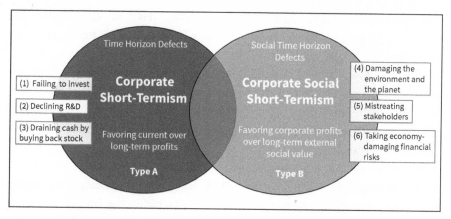

Figure 1.1. Type A and Type B Short-Termism Problems, Perceived

Figure 1.1 diagrams two classes of phenomena that are labelled as corporate short-termism. The first, Type A, has firms excessively weighting present profits over long-term returns. The second class, Type B, has the firms' focus on short-term profits creating long-term social problems, like environmental degradation and poor corporate citizenship.

profits today but degrades the economy today and tomorrow through a corporate unwillingness to protect corporate stakeholders, like employees and customers, and through a general corporate lack of public-spirited-ness. I call this the "Type B" problem (see Figure 1.1). It's not just that stock market short-term pressures hurt the company itself and its shareholders in the long run in this Type B view, but that to make a quick profit, too many corporations erode social trust, degrade the environment, and mistreat employees, customers, and communities, all of which in the long-term prove costly for the nation and the economy. In their short-sighted pursuit of this quarter's profit, say critics, the largest firms contribute mightily to a brewing climate catastrophe that will incinerate the planet later, for a few pennies of profit this quarter.

Type A short-termism degrades firms and, via that degradation, the economy. With Type B debilities, the stock market's excessive preference for short-term profits degrades long-term social value, critics say, risking the planet's long-term viability.

B. Causes: Activists and Traders

Rising shareholder activism and rapid trading, the thinking goes, are forcing executives and boards to manage more and more for immediate, short-term results.

Rising activism. Increased shareholder activism in recent years, it's thought, exacerbates short-termism. An activist buys 5% of the target firm's stock and militates for change, persuading other stockholders that a factory should be closed or its management replaced. No firm is immune, and all firms fear the activists. One of Wall Street's strongest critics of short-termism, Larry Fink, the head of the huge pension and investment firm BlackRock, said recently that "[t]he role of activists is getting larger, not smaller."[31] The activists demand results now, not next year.

Increased trading. Trading and turnover in the stock market is more rapid than ever before. How can executives think long-term when their shareholder base turns over every few months? Stock ownership in the United States has shifted from individuals who invested for the long-term, without complaint, to institutional investors like mutual funds and pension funds that want to show positive returns on their investment now, not years from now.[32]

* * *

Ownership duration has indeed shortened overall, and activism has indeed sharply increased. Figure 1.2 shows the average holding period for stocks traded on the New York Stock Exchange. In 1980, the average holding period was about three years; by the end of the century it was only a year.

Stock market trading volume is up, traders' holding periods are down, and shareholders buy and sell more quickly than ever before.[33] Program traders can move a lot of stock through the system in microseconds.[34]

Activist engagements, by which an activist buys stock in the target company and seeks operating changes or board seats, are indeed up sharply, as Figure 1-3 shows. With about 4,000 public companies in the United States, between 5 and 10% can expect to be visited by activists in any one year. The number of activist engagements went from nearly none in the early 1990s to 300 per year recently. And the nature of the activism changed: from activist pension funds seeking a shareholder resolution but without a prospect of affecting

---

[31] *See* Svea Herbst-Bayliss & Ross Kerber, *BlackRock's Fink Learns to Live with Activist Investors*, REUTERS, Nov. 13, 2017, www.reuters.com/article/us-investment-summit-fink-shareholders/blackrocks-fink-learns-to-live-with-activist-investors-idUSKBN1DD2B6.

[32] *E.g.*, Leo E. Strine, Jr., *Who Bleeds When the Wolves Bite? A Flesh-and-blood Perspective on Hedge Fund Activism and Our Strange Corporate Governance System*, 126 YALE L. J. 1870, 1871–72 (2017) ("American public corporations seem to be spending much more of their free cash flow on stock buybacks . . . and other tactics to guarantee immediate payoffs than on research and development and other forms of long-term investment.").

[33] Rappaport, *supra* note 2, at 66.

[34] Davies, Haldane, Nielsen & Pezzini, *supra* note 2, at 20.

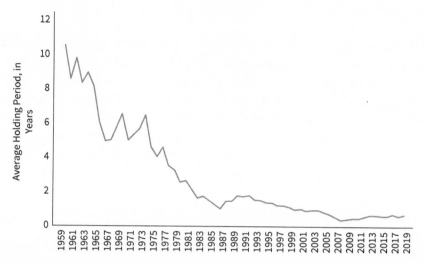

Figure 1.2. The Shortening Holding Period for Stock on the New York Stock Exchange

Source: New York Stock Exchange Databank, available through the Center for Research in Security Prices (CRSP).

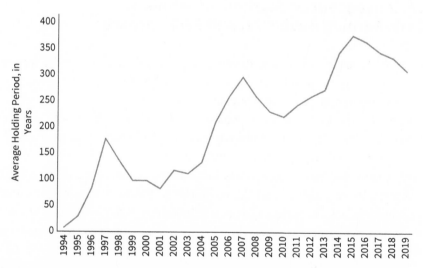

Figure 1.3. The Rising Incidence of High-Impact Shareholder Activism, 1994–2019

Source: Andrew Birstingl & Michael Coronato, 2016 Shareholder Activism Review, FactSet Research Sys. Inc., Feb. 1, 2017, https://insight.factset.com/hubfs/Resources/Research%20Desk/Market%20 Insight/FactSet%27s%202016%20Year-End%20Activism%20Review_2.1.17.pdf [https://perma.cc/ QC3F-5CQW] (covering 2009–2016 and defining "[h]igh impact activism" as campaigns in which an objective is: "board control, board representation, to maximize shareholder value, to remove officer(s)/director(s), or a public short/bear raid"). To go further back, I turned to Alon Brav, Wei Jiang & Hyunseob Kim, Hedge Fund Activism Updated, Sept. 2, 2013, at 19 https://faculty.fuqua.duke.edu/ ~brav/HFactivism_SEPTEMBER_2013.pdf [https://perma.cc/FQ94-435L] (indicating a lower number of activist engagements in 2009–2011 than FactSet reports). I also used Stuart L. Gillian & Laura T. Starks, *A Survey of Shareholder Activism: Motivation and Empirical Evidence*, 2 Contemp. Fin. Digest, 10–34 (Autumn 1998); and Stuart L. Gillian & Laura T. Starks, *Corporate Governance Proposals and Shareholder Activism: The Role of Institutional Investors*, 57 J. Fin. Econ. 275, 283 (2000).

core corporate governance in the 1980s[35] to aggressive hedge fund activists buying stock and seeking board seats and major corporate business changes.

These pressures, many say, are becoming more severe.[36] Said McKinsey's managing director, "the shadow of short-termism . . . may actually be getting worse. . . . [C]ompanies are less able to invest and build value for the long term, undermining broad economic growth . . . . The main source of the problem . . . is the continuing pressure on public companies from financial markets to maximize short-term results."[37]

* * *

The foundational predicates for the short-term theory are not contradicted by the basic data: the average duration of stock ownership is shortening, and activist engagements are increasing.

C. Consequences: Slashed Investment, Cash-Burning Buybacks, and R&D Cutbacks

Burgeoning stock trading and stronger activists induce firms, in the conventional thinking, to slash R&D, drain cash through stock buybacks, and drop investments in new property, plant, and equipment.

Capital cutbacks due to stock market short-termism. If the publicly traded firm invests in a new five- or ten-year factory, the critics' thinking runs, the stock market will punish the company, its stock price, and its executives. In this view, too many companies forgo investments that will benefit the company, its employees, and the economy in the long run, because their stockholders lack the patience to wait for investments to pay off. In 2003, 33% of the S&P 500's operating cash flow was invested in new property, plant, and

[35] Stuart L. Gillian & Laura T. Starks, *Corporate Governance Proposals and Shareholder Activism: The Role of Institutional Investors*, 57 J. FIN. ECON. 275, 277–78 (2000)

[36] *E.g.*, Chapman, *supra* note 28 ("Over the past 20 years short-termism has become worse, and has been much debated in the US."); Davies, Haldane, Nielsen & Pezzini, *supra* note 2, at 20; Biden, *supra* note 17. For McKinsey's leaders' views, see Dominic Barton, James Manyika, Timothy Koller, Robert Palter, Jonathan Godsall & Joshua Zoffer, Measuring the Economic Impact of Short-Termism, McKinsey Global Inst. Discussion paper, Feb. 2017, at 4 www.MGI-Measuring-the-economic-impact of short-term.pdf ("short-termism is increasing"); Dominic Barton, Jonathan Bailey & Joshua Zoffer, Rising to the Challenge of Short-termism, Focusing Capital on the Long-Term, 2016, at 5, www.fcltglobal.org/resource/rising-to-the-challenge-of-short-termism/.

[37] Barton & Wiseman, *Focusing Capital on the Long Term*, *supra* note 12.

equipment; by 2013, only 29% was.[38] Declining investment is a stock-market-induced problem that's getting worse.

Starved for cash: more stock buybacks lead to less cash to invest. The stock buyback is a short-termist flash point. Executives, relentlessly pressured by stockholders for cash, force their company to buy back stock, burning so much cash that the firm must skimp on paying for new R&D and on paying employees well. Investment suffers, and business contracts.[39] "[B]uybacks," we are told, "are killing the American economy."[40]

Decreasing R&D. Firms are destroying their futures by cutting R&D. Much like capital expenditures, R&D expenses reduce reported profits now, but their benefit comes from better products and profits in the future. Stockholders want cash now, so executives acquiesce. If they do not, activists will force them out. Stock markets punish firms that ramp up their R&D, states William Lazonick in a well-known *Harvard Business Review* article. "Trillions of dollars that could have been spent on innovation and job creation . . . have instead been used to buy back shares."[41]

Shunned future-oriented public firms. Investors cannot wait, so they shun long-term companies, and the stock market does not support future-oriented firms. Similarly, the corporate economy's pursuit of short-term profit means firms that respect the environment, promote greater economic and other equality, and support their communities, face so much short-term financial pressure that few can pursue positive but costly sustainable activities.

D. The Mechanisms of Stock-Market-Driven Degradation

The targets of the activists, although newsworthy and noisy, do not constitute the whole US economy. Even in years of high shareholder activism, activists

---

[38] John C. Coffee, Jr., & Darius Palia, *The Wolf at the Door: The Impact of Hedge Fund Activism on Corporate Governance*, 41 J. CORP. L. 545, 580 (2016).

[39] *See* JONATHAN HASKEL & STIAN WESTLAKE, CAPITALISM WITHOUT CAPITAL: THE RISE OF THE INTANGIBLE ECONOMY 168 (2018) ("[I]nstead of investing, there are signs companies are giving money back to shareholders"); MARIANA MAZZUCATO, THE ENTREPRENEURIAL STATE: DEBUNKING PUBLIC VS. PRIVATE SECTOR MYTHS 32–34 (2015); Coffee & Palia, *supra* note 38, at 552 ("hedge fund activism is beginning to compel corporate boards and managements to forego long-term investments (particularly in R&D) in favor of a short-term policy of maximizing shareholder payout").

[40] Nick Hanauer, *Stock Buybacks Are Killing the American Economy*, THE ATLANTIC, Feb. 8, 2015.

[41] *E.g.*, Lazonick, *supra* note 12, at 50; Rosenblum, *supra* note 1, at 708; Alana Semuels, *Can America's Companies Survive America's Most Aggressive Investors?* THE ATLANTIC, Nov. 18, 2016 ("[A]ctivist investors are . . . forcing [legacy corporations] to trim payrolls and downsize research operations—and, quite possibly, damaging the entire economy"); Robert Ayres & Michael Olenick, Secular Stagnation (Or Corporate Suicide?), July 11, 2017, at 1, https://ruayres.wordpress.com/2017/07/11/secular-stagnation-or-corporate-suicide/ ("buybacks . . . effectively reduce corporate R&D").

typically target under one out of ten of US public firms. Even if 300 of the 4,000 US public firms slash their R&D, drain their cash in buybacks, and terminate capital expenditures, that's not enough to deeply damage R&D and capital building nationwide. The activists would directly impact less than 10% of public firms, and public firms account for only half of the US economy.

But astute short-termism theorists show how the rest of the economy could be affected. Bystander public firms have incentives to do what the activists want *before* the activists target them. To preempt the activists, it's plausible that the bystanders themselves also slash R&D, buy back stock, and refuse to invest in new property, plant, and equipment.

Thus John Coffee, one of the nation's leading corporate law academics, working with economist and corporate expert Darius Palia, explains that "[f]or every firm [that activists] target[], *several more are likely to reduce R&D expenditures in order to avoid becoming a target*."[42]

Leo Strine, Delaware's long-serving corporate law judge, concurred: The problem "is not limited to firms directly targeted by activists . . . . Other companies, perhaps including those in this country's dynamic sectors, try to find ways to avoid the [hedge fund] wol[ves]."[43] Short-term theory has a logically precise mechanism by which short-term stock markets thwart overall economic well-being.

A separate, closely related, thick transmission channel goes through executive compensation and job security: executives whose compensation is tied to the value of the company's stock[44] have the incentive to boost its price. And the executives fear that a weak stock price will attract activists who will second-guess the firm's boards and executives. Stock market prices, the critics say, are too readily determined by short-term earnings reports, which executives can boost by cutting R&D, forgoing capital expenditures, and buying back more and more stock. Executives at firms not-yet-targeted by activists preemptively cut R&D, buy back their stock, and stop revitalizing their capital equipment to try to keep their stock price high and to ward off activists.

E. What Specifically Is Getting Worse?

To sum up the factual foundation for the standard stock market short-termism story: First, the stock market does not systematically support

---

[42] Coffee & Palia, *supra* note 38, at 546 (emphasis supplied).
[43] Strine, *supra* note 32, at 1938, 1947.
[44] *See, e.g.,* Center for American Progress, *supra* note 21, at 14, 26, 35–36.

long-term public firms, with frenzied trading and rampant activism making this problem worse than ever. Second, research and development spending is declining and that decline damages long-term economic performance. Third, cash is bleeding out from public corporations, mostly because of stock buybacks. Fourth, without cash, the public firm's capacity to invest weakens. Fifth, short-term-focused firms are investing less in new equipment, new factories, and employee skills. And sixth, the stock market's relentless pressure to produce short-term profits pushes most firms to ignore long-term climate change and sustainable corporate policies overall.

Any one of these debilities, if widespread, could seriously hurt the economy. Remedy must be found before it's too late. If financial markets are forcing all six problems and thereby crippling firm after firm and threatening the planet, then the economy is courting disaster.

But if these six purported facts turn out not to be primarily due to stock market short-termism—or in a few cases, just not true—then the standard short-term story must be reconsidered and possibly discarded. Short-termism might still be a local problem for some firms, here and there. But that would not put stock market short-termism on the list of the most serious US economy-wide problems.

What does the evidence show? I evaluate that next.

2

Looking for the Economy-Wide Impact

In Chapter 1, we saw how critics see the stock-market-driven short-termism problem. Shareholder pressure for immediate profit and traders moving stock too quickly degrade the economy, they say, leading to too little investment, too little R&D, too many buybacks that starve US firms of cash, and a stock market that both shuns established future-oriented firms and refuses to finance young firms with good ideas but no profits.

In this chapter, we turn from opinion and perception to evidence. We examine whether the opinion that economic decline is due to stock market short-termism is supported by economy-wide evidence. Later, in Chapters 5, 6, and 7, we evaluate the evidence of firm-level impact. To bolster the critics' economy-wide decline story with evidence, we should see (1) investment spending in the United States, where large firms depend on stock markets and activists are important, declining more rapidly than that in advanced economies that do not depend as much on stock markets, (2) rising buybacks leading to (3) cash bleeding out from the corporate sector, (4) economy-wide R&D spending lower than it should be, and (5) a stock market unwilling to support innovative, long-term, technological firms. These are the critics' central channels from stock-market-driven short-termism to economic degradation. If these channels to degradation are strong, they justify policies that seek to prevent these outcomes.

But none of these predicted economy-wide outcomes has been shown to be true. Several are either demonstrably false or implausible. Corporate R&D is not declining in the United States, corporate cash is not bleeding out, and the world's developed nations with neither US-style quarterly oriented stock markets nor aggressive activist investors are not investing more in capital equipment than is the United States. Many huge US firms are tech-oriented, R&D intensive, and eyeing the future.[1]

A. What Kind of Evidence of Consequences? Firm-by-Firm or Economy-Wide?

Academic analysis of short-termism is mostly at the firm level: are firms in one category or another—activist-influenced, quarterly-oriented, institutional-investor-owned—more short-term oriented than firms outside the category? The literature on this is both extensive and disputed.[2] We examine it in Chapters 5, 6, and 7.

But first let's look at the big picture. The short-termism critics' most worrying claim is not that some firms are afflicted by stock market short-termism, *but that the entire economy suffers*. True, it is not easy to show economy-wide effects, because we usually do not know whether alternative arrangements would have made results better. But if the short-term problems that critics have sketched are indeed severe and system-wide—and especially if they've been getting worse—then the critics should be able to show some economy-wide effects.

An economy-wide perspective is important because *even if* some large public firms failed to invest or innovate for the long-term, then other large public firms—or private firms and venture-capital-backed firms—may be the better investors or innovators. The venture capital and private equity industries profit by successfully doing what public firms fail to do. Competitive markets do not need every firm to be good at everything.

B. Capital Expenditure Cutbacks around the World

It is a widely reported business fact that in the past decades a smaller fraction of public firms' operating cash flow is being reinvested in new property, plant, and

---

[1] *See generally* Mark J. Roe, *Stock Market Short-Termism's Impact*, 134 U. Pa. L. Rev. 71 (2018), from which this chapter draws.

[2] For reviews, *see* Mark J. Roe, *Corporate Short-Termism—In the Boardroom and in the Courtroom*, 68 Bus. Law. 977, 986–87, 996–98 (2013); Andrew Bird, Aytekin Ertan, Stephen A. Karoyli & Thomas G. Ruchti, *Short-Termism Spillovers from the Financial Industry*, Rev. Fin. Stud. (forthcoming); Albert Sheen, *Do Public and Private Firms Behave Differently? An Examination of Investment in the Chemical Industry*, 55 J. Fin & Quant. Anal. 2530 (2020).

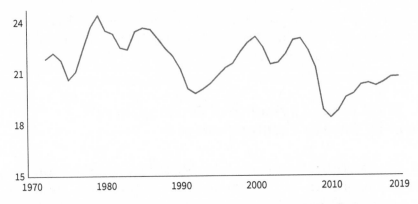

Figure 2.1. Capital Expenditure in the United States, Scaled to GDP, 1972–2019

Inquiry typically scales capital expenditure by cash flow. Capex is scaled to GDP to facilitate comparing US capital spending with the OECD's GDP-scaled data on other nations' capital expenditures in Figure 2.3.

Source: World Bank National Accounts, Gross Fixed Capital Formation, https://data.worldbank.org/indicator/NE.GDI.FTOT.ZS?end=2019&start=1960&view=char (last visited Sept. 21, 2021).

equipment,[3] demonstrating, it's said, that stock-market-driven short-termism is real and is severely degrading the economy.[4] If a firm invests its cash in a new factory, the critics' thinking runs, the stock market punishes the company, its stock price, and its executives. Figure 2.1 initially seems to confirm this view—US capital expenditure, as measured, has indeed declined over the decades.

But why is new investment dropping in recent decades? Is short-termism the best explanation for the declines and plateaus?

Figure 2.1 shows that the sharpest drop in capital spending was in 2008–2009, when there was a financial crisis, which was followed by a post-crisis recession. Investment dropped precipitously during the crisis and the recovery although steady was weak.

---

[3] Vipal Monga et al., *Activism Rises, U.S. Firms Spend More on Buybacks than Factories*, WALL ST. J., May 27, 2015, at A1 (short-term degradation).

[4] John C. Coffee & Darius Palia, *The Wolf at the Door: The Impact of Hedge Fund Activism on Corporate Governance*, 1 ANNALS OF CORP. GOV. 1, 51 & nn.137–38 (2016); Germán Gutiérrez & Thomas Philippon, *Investmentless Growth: An Empirical Investigation*, BROOKINGS PAPERS ON ECON. ACTIVITY, Fall 2017, at 89 (2017) (stock-market-driven short-termism is one of four plausible explanations for declining investment in the United States.). For influential and representative views, see William A. Galston & Elaine Kamarck, More Builders and Fewer Traders: A Growth Strategy for the American Economy (Brookings, 2015), www.brookings.edu/wp-content/uploads/2016/06/CEPMGlastonKarmarck4.pdf; Martin Lipton, *Empiricism and Experience; Activism and Short-Termism; the Real World of Business*, HARV. LAW SCHOOL FORUM ON CORP. GOV. (Oct 28, 2013), https://corpgov.law.harvard.edu/2013/10/28/empiricism-and-experience-activism-and-short-termism-the-real-world-of-business/; J.W. Mason, Understanding Short-Termism (Roosevelt Inst. Rep., 2015), http://rooseveltinstitute.org/ understanding-short-termism-questions-and-consequences/; Steven Rosenblum, *Corporations: The Short-Termism Debate*, 85 MISS. L.J. 697, 709 (2016) (Boards "want to invest for the long term . . . but they [are] constrained [to] meet[] their quarterly earnings, and that . . . is not healthy for companies in the long term").

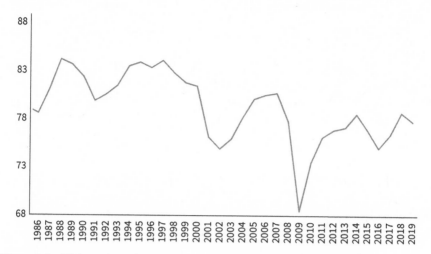

Figure 2.2. US Capacity Utilization (as a Percentage of Capacity), 1986–2019

Source: Board of Governors of the Federal Reserve System, Flow of Funds 54–55 www.federalreserve.gov/releases/g17/ipdisk/utl_sa.txt [https://perma.cc/4G2Q-WMWK] (last visited June 9, 2020).

After the 2008–2009 recession, companies did not fully use their existing capacity. They had little reason to invest in *new* equipment when *old* equipment lay fallow because of weak demand and the equipment was not yet technologically passé. Capacity utilization, which plummeted to below 70% during the crisis, was still only 75% in January 2017, down from the pre-crisis level of 81%[5] (see Figure 2.2).

As the economy improved and as capacity utilization came back, capital investment rose. The recession and the slow recovery help to explain weak capital spending over the 2010–2020 decade in the United States.

* * *

Another approach helps our understanding here. The stock market is a major channel for corporate finance in the United States but less so elsewhere. If US stock traders and activists were more important than ever in thwarting capital expenditures, then the decline in capital expenditure should have been sharper in the United States than in the rest of the developed world. But Figure 2.3 shows this is not the case. Capital expenditure is down across the

---

[5] Board of Governors of the Federal Reserve System, Flow of Funds 54–55 www.federalreserve.gov/releases/g17/ipdisk/utl_sa.txt [https://perma.cc/4G2Q-WMWK] (last visited June 9, 2020).

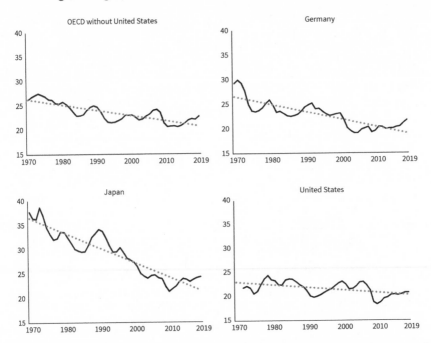

Figure 2.3. Capital Expenditure Trends in the Developed World Similar to the US Trend

The upper left graphic averages gross investment as a percentage of gross domestic product from 1970 to 2019 for all nations that were members of the OECD (the Organization for Economic Cooperation and Development) in 1990, other than the United States. (After 1990, some developing nations joined the OECD; 1990 membership is commonly used to focus on developed nations.) The US decline, pictured at the bottom right, is a version of Figure 2.1 and is not steeper than that of the rest of the developed world; in fact, the slope of the OECD decline is *twice* that of the US. Also included in Figure 2.3 are two graphics that show, for concreteness, declining investment in Germany and Japan since 1970.

Source: World Bank National Accounts, Gross Fixed Capital Formation, https://data.worldbank. org/indicator/NE.GDI.FTOT.ZS?end=2019&start=1960&view=char (last visited Sept. 21, 2021). Standard and Poor's results are similar. Standard & Poor's Ratings Services, Global Corporate Capital Expenditure Survey 2015 (Aug. 3, 2015), http://www.maalot.co.il/publications/FTS20150804101 404.pdf. The OECD compiles nation-by-nation gross investment, which includes government capital spending (and residential spending). For evaluating the potential impact of stock market short-termism, nongovernmental (and nonresidential) capital expenditure would be more appropriate.

developed world and generally declining more sharply elsewhere than in the United States.

Since national economies differ in so many ways, it's hard to control for all relevant factors. But that is not the comparison here: capital expenditures declined across the *entire* developed world. In fact, capital expenditures declined in the United States at about *half* the rate of the decline in the rest of the OECD.[6] When a trend characterizes a nation with a particularly strong

---

[6] Capital expenditures declined in Austria, Belgium, Canada, Denmark, Finland, France, Germany, Greece, Iceland, Italy, Japan, Luxembourg, the Netherlands, New Zealand, Norway, Portugal, Spain, Sweden, Switzerland, and the United Kingdom.

stock market, like the United States, as well as *all the other* developed nations, which depend less on the stock market, and it's more substantial outside the United States, then it's a jump to conclude that the US capital spending decline is primarily due to its stock market.[7]

True, the graphs' common downward slope could come from some shared feature. Activists, for example, are not absent in other nations, and stock markets play an increasing role abroad. Financialization is proceeding worldwide and perhaps is transforming all developed nations at a similar rate. Still, differences in stock market dependence, in stockholder activism, and in the depth of financialization between the United States and other developed nations are not trivial, and they persist. The critics' case for US stock market short-termism would be stronger if the capital spending decline in the United States were steeper than that in the rest of the OECD when instead it's the nations without US-style stock markets that are cutting capital spending more sharply.

More evidence might support the short-termism idea here, but the evidence we have fails to support it as the assured, or even likely, cause of declining US investment. Short-term critics have here not supported their claim.

C. Buybacks and Borrowings after the Financial Crisis

Stock buybacks have increased during the past decades, just as the short-termist theory says. Figure 2.4 confirms this nicely.

But the theory's core objection to stock buybacks is that they drain cash from public firms, thereby disabling the firms' operations. The real question is thus whether the buyback's full process is draining cash.

The answer is no, it is not.

The cross-country picture for R&D is, in contrast, mixed. Some developed nations' R&D/GDP ratio exceeds that of the United States; for most, it is lower. Several nations' R&D/GDP growth exceeds that of the United States. ORG. ECON. COOPERATION & DEV., LEVEL OF GDP PER CAPITA & PRODUCTIVITY, https://stats.oecd.org/index.aspx?DataSetCode=PDB_LV [https://perma.cc/XH9S-KWTW]. The average OECD R&D/GDP rise is less than that of the United States when the individual nations' R&D/GDP are averaged; when R&D spending and GDP are pooled, thereby more heavily weighting larger economies like Germany, the OECD rise is steeper than that of the United States.

[7] *See supra* Figure 2-3, top left graphic for the OECD's four-decade capital expenditures trend.

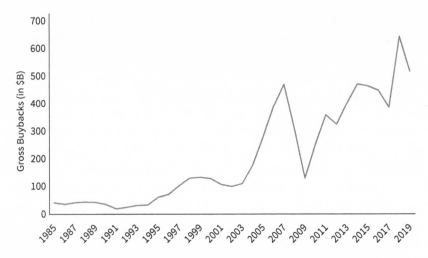

Figure 2.4. Rise in Stock Buybacks in the S&P 500 Nonfinancial Firms, 1985–2019

Source: S&P Global Market Intelligence, http://www.compustat.com [https://perma.cc/8WM8-MRHT], retrieved from Wharton Research Data Services, https://wrds-web.wharton.upenn.edu/wrds/ (last visited May 2, 2020).

After the 2008–2009 financial crisis, corporate borrowing increased greatly, as did buybacks, each at a similar pace.[8] Post-crisis interest rates were at historical lows, so many firms could borrow nearly for free, and many did. Some then bought back stock. The buyback reduced the firm's cash, but the extra borrowing increased it. Properly conceived, corporate America recapitalized its balance sheet with cheap debt.[9] A firm that buys back $100 million in stock with the cash raised from selling $100 million in debt does not have any less cash. Johnson & Johnson, the large pharmaceutical company and one of the ten largest companies by stock market capitalization in the United States, repurchased $15 billion in stock in the 2010–2019 decade but borrowed long-term even more, $19.7 billion, and explained that the two were linked: "The Company increased borrowings in . . . 2017 [by about $7 billion], capitalizing on favorable terms in the capital markets. The proceeds of the borrowings were used for general corporate purposes, including . . . the stock repurchase

[8] Adrian van Rixtel & Alan Villegas, *Equity Issuance and Share Buybacks*, BIS Quarterly Rev., Mar. 2015, at 28–29 (showing that net bond issuance proceeds of US nonfinancial corporations rise in tandem with share buybacks for the Standard & Poor's 1500); Yueran Ma, *Nonfinancial Firms as Cross-Market Arbitrageurs*, 74 J. Fin. 3041, 3045 (2019).

[9] In equilibrium theory, debt and equity have the same cost to the firm. Franco Modigliani & Merton H. Miller, *The Cost of Capital, Corporation Finance and the Theory of Investment*, 48 Am. Econ. Rev. 261–62 (1958). The Fed's suppression of interest rates to near-zero after the 2009 financial crisis upset any prior equilibrium; firms then recapitalized (and the stock market repriced equity) to reach toward a new equilibrium.

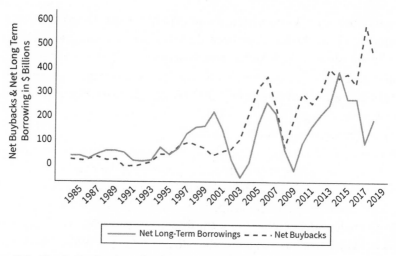

Figure 2.5. Rise in Net Stock Buybacks and Net Borrowing in the S&P 500, 1985–2019

Source: S&P Global Market Intelligence, http://www.compustat.com [https://perma.cc/8WM8-MRHT], retrieved from Wharton Research Data Services, https://wrds-web.wharton.upenn.edu/wrds/ (last visited May 2, 2020).

program."[10] The buybacks did not stop Johnson & Johnson from developing one of the three widely-used anti-Covid-19 vaccines in the United States.

Borrowing more to buy back stock, as Johnson & Johnson reports it did, scales to the entire S&P 500 in recent decades. Figure 2.5 illustrates: buybacks and borrowing rise and fall together.

Moreover, public firms also issue new stock. I adjusted the buyback measure in Figure 2.5 to net buybacks by deducting the cash corporations received for newly issued stock. That cash received was a noticeable fraction of what they paid out in buybacks.

Figure 2.5 thus shows that the overall cash inflow via new borrowings approximates the cash outflow via net buybacks in the 500 large US companies in the S&P 500. Worldwide evidence also shows that buybacks rise when interest rates are low (and decrease with they are high).[11] And on a

---

[10] Johnson & Johnson, Annual Report (Form 10-K) (Feb 21, 2018). The data on buybacks and borrowing increases come from Compustat. The buyback number is a net number, calculated from the total dollar amount of stock bought back minus the dollar value of new stock issued.

[11] Assia Elgouacem & Riccardo Zago, Share Buybacks, Monetary Policy and the Cost of Debt 22 (Banque de France working paper, July 2020), www.ssrn.com/abstract=3644859 (the authors, however, conclude that the borrow-and-buyback process reduces the effectiveness of monetary policy); *cf.* Joan Farre-Mensa, Roni Michaely & Martin Schmalz, Financing Payouts 6 (Ross Sch. of Bus., Paper No. 1263, Feb. 21, 2018), https://ssrn.com/abstract=2535675 ("42% of firms that pay out capital also initiate debt or equity issues in the same year.... Payouts financed by debt... are by far the most common"). *But cf.* Zigan Wang, Quie Ellie Yin & Luping Yu, *Real Effects of Share Repurchases Legalization on Corporate Behaviors*, 140 J. Fin. Econ. 197 (2021) (outside of the United States, although repurchases are financed by debt issuance, they are financed even more from retained earnings).

transaction-by-transaction basis, about 30% of the specific payouts on stock (primarily via buybacks) have been directly financed with new debt issued simultaneously.[12] As Federal Reserve System governor Jeremy Stein said, the post-2009 financial crisis economy had an "unusually large divergence in the costs of debt and equity—due in part to the cumulative effects of [the Federal Reserve's very large purchases of debt, which] is likely [to] make[] debt-financed repurchases of equity attractive."[13]

An aside: Adding debt while eliminating equity is not necessarily good for either the economy or the affected firms, even if their cash-on-hand stays steady. Finance thinking on debt gives it pluses and minuses. Too much debt can lead to sclerosis and bankruptcy, because debt repayment promises are rigid and required. For other firms, the fixed payments of debt discipline managers to work harder to make sure they do not default.[14] Which effect is more important is hard to know in the abstract. But regardless of whether more debt is advantageous, what happened was not *short-term* pressure draining firms of cash needed for investment. Rather it was a corporate-wide recapitalization from equity to debt.[15] Too much debt is a potential problem, but it's not a time horizon problem, and it's not stripping companies of cash.[16] As Clifford Asness, Todd Hazelkorn, and Scott Richardson conclude, the spread of the buyback should be seen as primarily "a recapitalization, shifting from equity to debt."[17]

Regardless of what the right explanation is for rising stock buybacks, the cash drainage story is incorrect. As Figures 2.6 and 2.7 show, corporate cash has been rising in recent decades.

* * *

[12] *See* Farre-Mensa et al., *supra* note 11, at 11 (demonstrating that "in the average year, 30% of aggregate total payouts are financed via simultaneous net debt issues"; payouts are primarily buybacks).

[13] Jeremy C. Stein, Governor, Fed. Res. System Address at the Boston University/Boston Federal Reserve System, Conference on Macro-Finance Linkages: Large-Scale Asset Purchases (Nov. 30, 2012), www.federalreserve.gov/newsevents/speech/stein20121130a.htm [https://perma.cc/PK3H-MRKU]; *see also* Farre-Mensa et al., *supra* note 11, at 5, 29; Valeriy Zakamulin & John A. Hunnes, *Stock Earnings and Bond Yields in the US 1871–2017: The Story of a Changing Relationship*, 79 Q. Rev. Econ. & Fin. 182 (2021).

[14] Michael C. Jensen, *Agency Costs of Free Cash Flow, Corporate Finance, and Takeovers*, 76 Am Econ. Rev. Papers & Proc. 323 (1986): Steven Kaplan, *The Effects of Management Buyouts on Operating Performance and Value*, 24 J. Fin. Econ. 217, 218, 250 (1989).

[15] *Cf.* Clifford Asness, Todd Hazelkorn & Scott Richardson, *Buyback Derangement Syndrome*, 44 J. Portfolio Mgmt. 50 (2018) ("a considerable portion of the recent share repurchase activity has simply been a recapitalization, shifting from equity to debt").

[16] So-called rational expectations economists expect that as soon as interest rates decline, the cost of equity capital must immediately decline equally, because the two are substitutes. While plausible in theory, the actual adjustment process from the text's data and graphics does not confirm it for the past decade. That firms issued new debt and bought back stock over time indicates that financial markets took time to substitute inexpensive debt for the previously more expensive equity.

[17] Asness et al. *supra* note 15.

Here, I have analyzed the buyback/borrowing trend as an economy-wide, post-crisis capital structure decision: across the corporate sector, firm after firm substituted low-interest debt for equity during the past decade. Precise work from my colleagues Jesse Fried and Charles Wang takes a different but consistent approach, analyzing another way that the conventional buyback story exaggerates how much cash is coming out.[18] They show that an accurate picture must account for stock that is indirectly issued, in ways that save the firm cash. Firms use equity—stock—to pay for business acquisitions and employee compensation. If the employees were not paid in stock (which the employees often eventually sell for cash), the firm would have had to pay more cash to the employees. The company thus is issuing stock and getting something valuable back. When the value of these indirect equity issuances is subtracted from buyback and dividend payouts, the net cash outflow diminishes greatly.

Aggregating all basic equity-based cash outflows and inflows for the 2007–2016 decade, including dividends, buybacks, and issuances, the net outflow was $3.7 trillion.[19] That's less than the $7 trillion gross payout commonly quoted for the decade, but still not a small number. Yet even this $3.7 trillion cash payout disappears, when combined with the borrowing analysis I provided above, and turns into a modest *inflow*, because low-interest long-term borrowing increased by $3.75 trillion during that decade.[20] The properly interpreted overall bottom-line, when combining the increased borrowing, the stock issuances, and the stock buybacks, is: there has been no net outflow of cash from public firms, contrary to the widespread impression.

* * *

Attention must also be paid to economic fundamentals: Money disbursed in stock buybacks does not disappear. The cash leaves the firm—perhaps one with few good investments for that cash—and reappears elsewhere. A mutual fund that owned the bought-back stock then reinvests it. If the financial market is working as it should, the mutual fund reinvests the cash in firms with good investment opportunities—perhaps putting the cash into younger firms selling their products and services into a new and expanding market.[21]

---

[18] Jesse M. Fried & Charles C.Y. Wang, *Are Buybacks Really Shortchanging Investment?* HARV. BUS. REV., Mar.–Apr. 2018, 88, 90.

[19] *Id.* at 92.

[20] *See* Appendix Figure 2.5 to visualize the rising long-term borrowing during period (the dashed line).

[21] *Cf.* Jeffrey N. Gordon, *Shareholder Activism, the Short-Termist Red-Herring, and the Need for Corporate Governance Reform*, CLS BLUE SKY BLOG (Mar. 28, 2016), http://www.clsbluesky.law.columbia.edu/2016/03/28/shareholder-activism-the-short-termist-red-herring-and-the-need-for-corporate-governance-ref orm [https://perma.cc/8Q24-K4AE] (showing that many institutional investors seeking buybacks *also* invest long-term, via venture capital or private equity channels).

A major part of the cash movement in the economy fits this pattern. About $250 billion in cash flowed annually into smaller, non-S&P 500 firms in the past decade, *exceeding* the cash outflow from the S&P 500 (see Appendix Figures 2.4 and 2.5).[22]

Consistent with this analytic, companies doing buybacks have good long-term results, undermining the idea that most buybacks are self-inflicted damage that denies firms needed cash.[23] And it's older, more profitable, and larger firms that are more likely to pay money out in dividends and stock repurchases than younger, less profitable, growing smaller firms. The composition of the United States' largest public firms changed in the twenty-first century from what it had been in the prior two to three decades: the largest ones became older, more profitable, and even larger in the first decades of the twenty-first century—exactly the kind of firms that typically and properly pay out more cash.[24]

* * *

The purportedly powerful cash starvation channel from stock market short-termism to economy-wide degradation by buybacks does not exist.[25]

D. Is Cash for Investment Disappearing?

Lastly on buybacks, there is a bottom line. Here, the purported economy-wide scourge is that short-termism saps public firms of cash, thereby crippling their capacity for R&D, capital spending, and taking care of employees. But as we've seen, buybacks are offset by new borrowing, with the combined transactions not having much effect on corporate cash levels. Short-term theorists might respond that cash could be disappearing not just via buybacks but rather through other channels—via excessive dividends or deteriorating cash flow from operations. Or via firms using any cash they earn to pay down but not replace their debt.

---

[22] *See* van Rixtel & Villegas, *supra* note 8, at 28–29; Fried & Wang, *supra* note 18. And an investor receiving cash from a public company could reinvest it in a private one. *See id.*

[23] Urs Peyer & Theo Vermaelen, *The Nature and Persistence of Buyback Anomalies*, 22 Rev. Fin. Stud. 1693 (2009).

[24] Kathleen M. Kahle & René M. Stulz, *Why Are Corporate Payouts So High in the 2000s?* J. Fin. Econ. (forthcoming, 2021). Early research indicated that "managers make repurchase decisions after [they make their] investment decisions." Alon Brav, John R. Graham, Campbell R. Harvey & Roni Michaely, *Payout Policy in the 21st Century*, 77 J. Fin. Econ. 483, 485 (2005).

[25] Perhaps short-term theory needs instead to argue that stock markets prevent firms from investing their cash hoard.

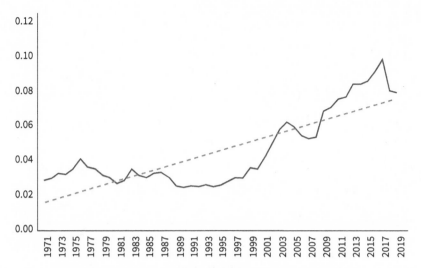

Figure 2.6. S&P 500 Cash-on-Hand Rising as Portion of GDP, 1971–2019
Source: Compustat.

But total cash in the nonfinancial S&P 500 has been rising. See Figures 2.6 and 2.7. In 2019, the S&P 500 collectively held about $75 of cash for each $1000 of GDP, more than in 2009, when they held about $50 of cash for each $1000 of GDP, which was more than in 1980, when they held about $25 for each $1000 of GDP.[26] Cash is not disappearing from the country's largest public firms.

E. Rising Corporate R&D over the Decades

For many critics, the most severe cost of stock market short-termism has been from deep cuts to corporate R&D.[27] When companies report their current profits, they deduct their R&D expenses for the current period. The payoff from the R&D comes in the future.[28] Executives who overly focus on short-term reported earnings each quarter would forgo R&D spending.

An impact may be there, but not an economy-wide cutback. The plain truth here is that R&D in the US economy has been steadily rising, not

---

[26] Even if the S&P 500 constitutes a different portion of the economy, cash-on-hand as a percentage of the S&P 500's own earnings has been steadily rising over the decades.

[27] Academically well-known, classic criticisms include Brian J. Bushee, *The Influence of Institutional Investors on Myopic R&D Investment Behavior*, 73 Acct. Rev. 305, 330 (1998); Robert H. Hayes & William J. Abernathy, *Managing Our Way to Economic Decline*, Harv. Bus. Rev., July 1980; Michael E. Porter, *Capital Disadvantage: America's Failing Capital Investment System*, Harv. Bus. Rev., Sept.–Oct. 1992, at 65, 67–68.

[28] Fin. Acct. Standards Bd., Accounting for Research and Development Costs § 12 (1974).

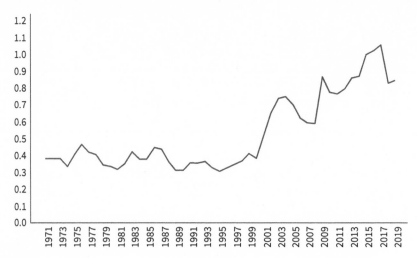

Figure 2.7. S&P 500 Cash-on-Hand Rising as a Portion of Earnings, 1971–2019
Source: Compustat.

falling—doubling since the 1970s, as Figure 2.8 demonstrates. The only place to find a major decline in US R&D is in *government* support for research.[29]

Consider another commonly used albeit crude measure of R&D output prowess—patent awards.[30] Patents increased, tripling in the past twenty-five years, even as activism rose and as stock trading quickened.

A logically appropriate response from critics would be that short-termism has long been damaging R&D. Both R&D and capital expenditures were anemic in 1979, weak in 1990, and still hold the economy back in 2020 and 2021, a critic could reply. R&D spending, held back by the stock market, should have risen even more sharply than it did.[31]

---

[29] That is, the graphics' overall increase could have been due to government spending more while activists crippled public firm R&D. But US government R&D spending is *declining*: "The National Science Foundation estimates that [total] U.S. R&D funding reached an all-time high . . . in 2015. [But o]f that total, the federally sponsored share fell to a record-low 23 percent while the business sector's share rose to a record-high 69 percent." American Institute of Physics, US R&D Spending at All-Time High, Federal Share Reaches Record Law, Nov. 8, 2016, www.aip.org/fyi/2016/us-rd-spending-all-time-high-federal-share-reaches-record-low. Backing out government spending from the article's graphics, would *increase* the slope. *Id.,* Figure 1.

[30] *See* Zvi Griliches, *Patent Statistics as Economic Indicators: A Survey,* 28 J. ECON. LITERATURE 1661, 1673–74 (1990); *cf.* Bronwyn H. Hall, Adam B. Jaffe & Manuel Trajtenberg, *Market Value and Patent Citations: A First Look,* 36 RAND J. ECON. 20, 33–35 (2005). More patents do not assure more and better R&D. The extra quantity could be small-bore. More "patent trolls" could be filing a broad spectrum of patents to squeeze payments out of users. The patent office could be awarding patents more readily than it was in the 1980s. *See* Richard A. Posner, *Why There Are Too Many Patents in America,* THE ATLANTIC (July 12, 2012).

[31] And even if R&D spending is steady, short-termism believers could investigate whether the horizon for the R&D is shortening—i.e., spending for minor improvements on current products and not on game-changing technologies. But the short-term theorists have not brought forth such evidence and, given the vibrancy of the venture capital industry, such evidence may well be hard to find.

Figure 2.8. R&D Spending in the United States Rising as a Proportion of GDP, 1977–2019

Note: R&D is scaled to GDP

Source: The R&D data is from the Department of Commerce's Bureau of Economic Analysis, a standard government source of economy-wide data. Bureau of Econ. Analysis, National Income and Product Accounts, U.S. Dep't of Commerce, Table 5.6.5, lines 2 & 6 (2017), http://www.bea.gov/itable/ [https://perma.cc/HM9A-7XM3] (last visited June 21, 2021). For the GDP data, see *id.*, Table 1.1.5, line 1.

Figure 2.9. Rising Number of Patents Awarded Annually, 1963–2019

Source: See U.S. Patent and Trademark Office, U.S. Patent Statistics Chart, 1963–2019, www.uspto.gov/web/offices/ac/ido/oeip/taf/us_stat.htm [https://perma.cc/JV09-H243] (last visited May 30, 2020).

The critics would of course have a point. The steady rise in R&D and patents does not necessarily mean all is well. The counterfactual problem is real: we don't know what the economy would look like today if the proposals of those who saw short-termism as a problem in 1970 had been implemented. Perhaps a pernicious short-term impact is buried in the data. Perhaps stock markets really do degrade R&D, cash, and investment, while other economic features buttress them. If we could knock out stock-market-driven short-termism, we'd do even better.

But before we embark on new policy ventures that could be risky, expensive, unneeded, or misguided, policymakers should see evidence that in fact we would have had even more R&D and more patenting, and that US investment in capital equipment would have been not just greater than the rest of the OECD but much greater. To support their claim that stock market short-termism is harming the economy, short-term theorists need a metric showing that—or a good reason to believe that—the corporate sector's rising R&D isn't rising as much as it should.[32] Given the widespread belief in pernicious stock market short-termism, it's surprising that the data trend lines do not support these commonly held beliefs.

* * *

The verdict thus far: stock-market-driven short-termism has not been shown to be a deep economy-wide problem.

F. The Stock Market's Support of Technology: At the Top and the Bottom

Does the stock market shun firms with weak current earnings because such firms are investing deep into the future?

Consider the nature of the business of the biggest public firms in the United States. Those ten biggest by stock market capitalization are listed here in Table 2.1.

As we saw in the Introduction, the five largest firms in the stock market—Amazon, Apple, Alphabet (Google), Facebook, and Microsoft—are all long-term operations. Each has technologies and businesses that stock markets expect will be valuable in the future. Each is investing significantly to grow.

---

[32] Steven Kaplan, *Are U.S. Companies Too Short-Term Oriented? Some Thoughts*, 18 INNOVATION POL'Y & ECON. 107, 108–109 (2018).

Table 2.1. Ten Largest US Nonfinancial Public Firms, by Stock Market Capitalization, Again

Rank	Company Name	Total stock market value (in billions of dollars)
1	Microsoft	1,200
2	Apple	1,113
3	Amazon	971
4	Alphabet (Google)	799
5	Facebook	475
6	Johnson & Johnson	346
7	Walmart	322
8	Proctor & Gamble	272
9	United Health	237
10	Intel	232

Investors are buying their growth opportunities and future earnings, not their quarterly results. The fact that these are the *most* strongly supported firms at this time fits badly with short-termist fears.

The total 2019 earnings from these companies were $159 billion.[33] Their stock price was high—30 times their current earnings—showing a stock market confident in their future.[34] "[T]hose five made up 15% of the S&P's market value, more than the entire financial, health-care or industrial sectors."[35] Perhaps five such firms are not enough either for the economy or to definitively rule out stock market short-termism, but this is not a portrait of a stock market shunning future-oriented innovation.

This stock market phenomenon is not limited to the very largest companies. It's in play before firms grow to be large. Amazon had a very high stock price long before it turned a profit, and its profits today are still a modest fraction of its stock price. Firms like Airbnb, Netflix, and Tesla had high stock market capitalizations for years before they turned a profit. Uber is another example.

---

[33] Alphabet, Inc., Annual Report (Form 10-K), at 26 (Feb. 4, 2020); Amazon.com, Inc., Annual Report (Form 10-K), at 18 (Jan. 31, 2020); Apple, Inc., Annual Report (Form 10-K), at 17 (Sept. 28, 2019); Facebook, Inc., Annual Report (Form 10-K), at 42 (Jan. 31, 2020); Microsoft Corp., Annual Report (Form 10-K), at 31 (Aug. 1, 2019). Apple and Microsoft have fiscal years that do not end on December 31. Since Covid-19 made 2020 an unusual year, I use 2019 numbers.

[34] This ratio is calculated by dividing the total market capitalization of the five companies, $4.9 trillion, by the firms' total earnings of $159 billion. A simple average of the separately calculated price-to-earnings ratios would yield a higher ratio of 70, because Amazon's price to earnings ratio is unusually high, but is diluted when earnings and price are aggregated.

[35] James Mackintosh, *Beware a Tectonic Shift in Tech Shares*, WALL ST. J., Mar. 30, 2018, at B1.

In the three years prior to its 2019 IPO, it had lost $10 billion. Yet, when it went public the stock sale was oversubscribed and priced aggressively.[36]

Moreover, there's a vibrant stock market in taking tech-oriented, research-oriented firms public. As of 2018, "[b]iotech companies have been going public at earlier stages than in the past, sometimes without having a product or drug[.]"[37] This long-termism evidence increased in 2019, as this newspaper headline indicates: "Lyft Leads Wave of Startups Debuting with Giant Losses."[38] A stock market averse to the long-term and too focused on the short-term would not fund unprofitable firms. Jay Ritter and Steven Kaplan provide data and analysis that this trend—private firms going public at an ever earlier stage—is an across-the-board phenomenon.[39] Because private companies increasingly go public with weak ongoing earnings and low revenues,[40] US stock markets are supporting R&D-oriented long-term investment and risky innovative ventures more than ever.

* * *

Two of the big five's founding shareholders have extra votes[41] that lock in their control (Google and Facebook). Similarly, some smaller firms go public with this kind of control structure. Whether these insider-favoring control structures favor the long-term or just favor insider control is debated among corporate academics. But, regardless, if the structure really dampens short-termism, then this is one way the market handles the time horizon problem. The mechanism presumably is that the insiders could resist stock market pressure if a low stock price (due to the stock market punishing long-term-oriented firms) pressed them to drop long-term projects. Some short-term critics extol the virtues of these extra votes, because they insulate the controllers from the stock market.

But these five major firms' stock prices are, and have been, high, not low, suggesting that, even if the mechanism can be anti-short-term in theory for the two that use it, it was not needed: Google and Facebook have not been

---

[36] Alexis C. Madrigal, *The Uber IPO Is a Landmark*, THE ATLANTIC, Apr. 11, 2019.

[37] Gregory Zuckerman, *Biotech Boom Ushers in $3 Million Analyst*, WALL ST. J., Aug. 30, 2018, at A1.

[38] Eliot Brown, *Lyft Leads Wave of Startups Debuting with Giants Losses*, WALL ST. J., Mar. 26, 2019, at A1.

[39] Kaplan, *supra* note 32, at 119–20, confirms more rigorously, using data from Jay R. Ritter, *IPO Data*, WARRINGTON COLLEGE OF BUS., https://site.warrington.ufl.edu/ritter/ipo-data/ [https://perma.cc/8FQN-CT7N], that IPOs overall now happen at an earlier stage in a company's profitability.

[40] Eliot Brown, *Venture Funds Bask in Blockbuster Profits*, WALL ST. J., Apr. 29, 2021.

[41] *See* Dual Class Companies List, COUNCIL OF INSTITUTIONAL INVEST., https://www.cii.org/files/JuneBoard%20Accountability/Dual%20Class%20Company%20List%202018@20Dual%20Class20List%20Upgrade.pdf [https://perma.cc/7MGH-KJ5Y].

scorned by the stock market.[42] And three of the five (Amazon, Apple, and Microsoft) do *not* protect insiders with extra votes but are thus far performing quite well for the long-term. Moreover, the big corporate R&D spenders are not the firms that use these extra votes for insiders, as Appendix Table 2.1 shows.

Nevertheless, if the extra votes really do promote the long-term (and not just lock in the founders' control, which might be the primary purpose and impact of the extra votes), it's a stock market mechanism to promote the long-term.

* * *

The overall point here is not that financial markets are perfect, or even good. Surely some firms are afflicted by short-termism. Plenty of evidence points to financial markets' other defects: persistent financial irrationality,[43] prices deviating from fundamental value for long periods,[44] major arbitrage failures with similar investments trading at different values for long periods,[45] and a financial sector plagued intermittently by massive frauds. Financial markets are plausibly too large and are seen in new analysis to be the means for cartel-like price coordination. The biotech and dot-com bubbles tell us that the stock market can grossly *over*value the long-term. These are all problems, but they are not *short*-term problems.

What counts here is that the predicted economy-wide *consequences* of a vociferously short-term stock market have not yet been well shown: (1) Capital spending is down in the United States since the financial crisis, but it's down *even more steeply* in developed economies not as dependent as the United States on the stock market. (2) Buybacks rose steeply after the 2008–2009 financial crisis, but the cash paid to buy back stock was offset by cash gained from new low-interest rate borrowings, with the two roughly equal in size. (3) Cash available for investment has increased, not decreased. (4) The

[42] Dual class firms accounted for less than one-sixth of the R&D spending of the largest US R&D spenders. *See* Appendix Table 2.1. Moreover, firms with lopsided insider votes do *not* do more R&D overall than firms with single class, one-share, one-vote structures. *See* Onur Arugaslan, Douglas O. Cook & Robert Kieschnick, *On the Decision to Go Public with Dual Class Stock*, 16 J. Corp. Fin. 170, 171 (2010). The voting structures do, however, lock in the controllers' capacity to control the company.

[43] *See* John Maynard Keynes, The General Theory of Employment, Interest, and Money 156–58 (1936) (offering up the beauty contest analogy). Keynes' evidence is as much assertion as discovery, but it is widely accepted.

[44] *See* Malcolm Baker, Robin Greenwood & Jeffrey Wurgler, *Catering through Nominal Share Prices*, 64 J. Fin. 2559, 2587 (2009).

[45] *See* Markus K. Brunnermeier & Lasse Heje Pedersen, *Predatory Trading*, 60 J. Fin. 1825, 1827-28 (2005); Owen A. Lamont & Richard H. Thaler, *The Law of One Price in Financial Markets*, 17 J. Econ. Persp. 191, 193–200 (2003); Andrei Shleifer & Robert W. Vishny, *The Limits of Arbitrage*, 52 J. Fin. 37–38 (1997).

short-termists' expected economy-wide cutback from the best level of R&D has not been shown; R&D is rising across the US corporate economy. And (5) the stock market is more willing than ever to support R&D-focused, technology-oriented, future-focused firms both at the top—the five companies most strongly supported by the stock market fit this profile—and at the bottom—more and more firms go public with weak (or no) earnings, entering a stock market focused on these firms' futures.

* * *

With each predicted economy-wide consequence undetected or contradicted, my inquiry points to the short-term problem as probably not deeply and seriously afflicting the economy as a whole. Perhaps short-termism is relevant for this or that firm, but it's not yet shown to be doing much damage. This analysis sets us up to examine conceptually in Part II *why* stock-market-driven short-termism is not the assured problem that observers quoted and cited in Part I think it is; to see in Part III why most prominent offered solutions will cost something and still not do much for whatever short-termism there is; and to consider in Part IV how politics makes short-termism a prominent issue even though the supporting evidence for its importance is so weak.

Appendix to Chapter 2

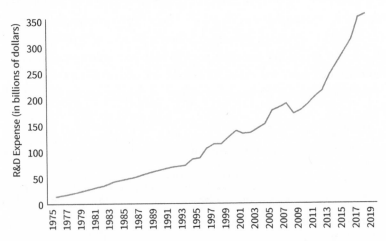

Appendix Figure 2.1. Raw R&D Spending in the Nonfinancial S&P 500, 1975–2019
Source: S&P Global Market Intelligence, http://www.compustat.com [https://perma.cc/8WM8-MRHT] (last visited May 20, 2020).

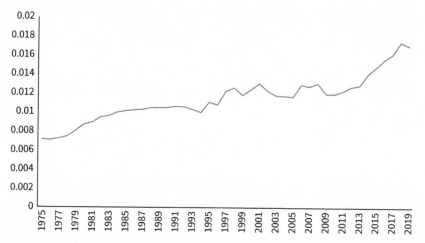

Appendix Figure 2.2. R&D Spending in the Nonfinancial S&P 500, Scaled by GDP, 1975–2019

Source: For R&D, S&P GLOBAL Market INTELLIGENCE, http://www.compustat.com [https://perma.cc/8WM8-MRHT] (last visited May 20, 2020); for GDP, U.S. DEP'T OF COMM., Table 1.1.5, https://www.bea.gov/data/economic-accounts/national [https://perma.cc/J5K7-C5MY] (last visited May 20, 2020).

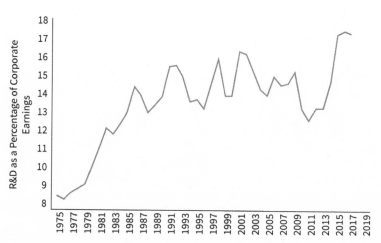

Appendix Figure 2.3. R&D Spending in the Nonfinancial S&P 500, Scaled by Corporate Earnings

Source: S&P GLOBAL MARKET INTELLIGENCE, http://www.compustat.com [https://perma.cc/8WM8-MRHT] (last visited May 20, 2020).

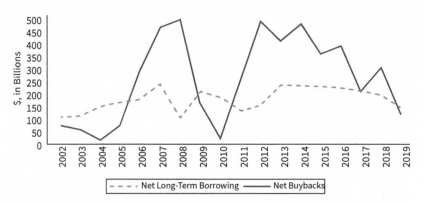

Appendix Figure 2.4. Non-S&P 500 Buybacks and Borrowings

The solid line shows the net stock issuances in nonfinancial public corporations outside the S&P 500. Companies outside the S&P 500 are overall raising money in the stock market (unlike S&P 500 companies), by issuing more new equity than they buy back, yielding a positive dollar inflow for buybacks (after accounting for stock issuances). These non-S&P 500 companies are also raising cash by borrowing. This is the dashed line. Add the two together (not graphed) for the net cash inflow to the non-S&P 500 from capital market activity.

Source: S&P Global Market Intelligence, http://www.compustat.com [https://perma.cc/8WM8-MRHT] (last visited May 20, 2020).

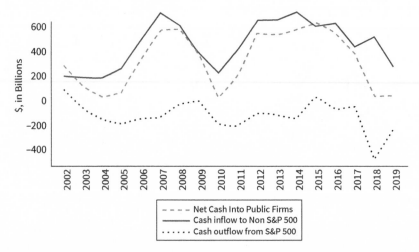

Appendix Figure 2.5. Net Cash Outflow from S&P 500 and Inflow to Non-S&P 500, Net Borrowings Minus Net Buybacks, 2002–2019

This figure compares net buybacks and borrowings for the nonfinancial S&P 500 to that of those outside the S&P 500. Gross buybacks in the S&P 500 since 2002 average one-quarter trillion dollars annually, as illustrated in Figure 2.4. But when netting borrowings against buybacks, the net cash outflow drops 60%, to $100 billion annually, shown here by the dotted line. The non-S&P 500 cash inflow is depicted by the solid line, with their total inflow exceeding the S&P 500 outflow. Overall, there is an outflow from large, mature S&P 500 firms and an inflow to smaller firms.

Source: S&P Global Market Intelligence, http://www.compustat.com [https://perma.cc/8WM8-MRHT] (last visited May 20, 2020).

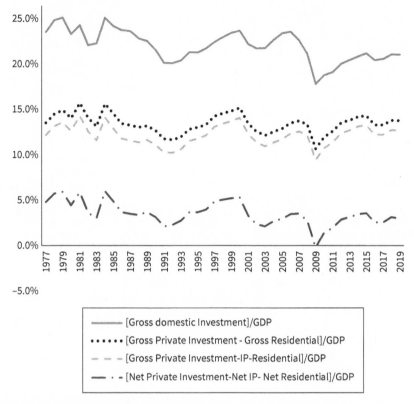

Appendix Figure 2.6. Capital Expenditure as a Percentage of GDP, without Intellectual Property and after Depreciation, 1977–2019

This figure accounts for the Department of Commerce adding film to intellectual property investment and then adding intellectual property investment to capital expenditures, thereby boosting the total in ways that have been criticized. The solid first line at the top portrays the decline in gross domestic investment. The second line, dotted, portrays a similar decline of nonresidential investment. The third, dashed, pulls out IP. And the final line pulls out government investment and nets out private investment to account for depreciation. The resulting trend still resembles the gross capital expenditure trend, in the top line of this graphic and in Figure 2.1. Further, gross capital expenditure does not capture whether the investments are in short-lived or long-lived assets. A capital expenditure decline could effectively be steeper if the capital were progressively becoming more short-lived—e.g., more computer equipment with a three-year life and less industrial machinery with a 10-year life. But deducting capital that depreciates and wears out, as in the lower dashed line, accounts for this. The deduction results in no major change in the shape of the curve. For all four measurements, the sharpest drop occurs during the 2008–2009 financial crisis.

Source: U.S. Dep't of Comm., https://www.bea.gov/data/economic-accounts/national [https://perma.cc/J5K7-C5MY] (last visited May 20, 2020). An astute criticism of the Department of Commerce capex data is that it now includes investment in intellectual property products, like film, an addition that could mask a steeper decline in traditional plant and equipment. J.W. Mason, Understanding Short-Termism (Roosevelt Inst. Rep., 2015), at 7–8, http://rooseveltinstitute.org/understanding-short-termism-questions-and-consequences/. Subtracting the category including film shows a similar, but slightly sharper, downward trend, as seen in Appendix Figure 2.6.

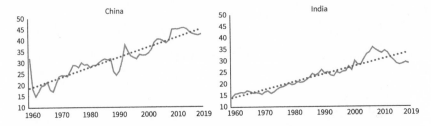

Appendix Figure 2.7. Capital Investment in China and India, 1960–2019

This figure shows the steep rise in capital investment in China and India, scaled to GDP. Contrast the rise—corresponding to rising manufacturing in Asia—with the capital spending decline in the OECD, as seen in Figure 2.3.

Source: World Bank National Accounts, Gross Fixed Capital Formation, https://data.worldbank.org/indicator/NE.GDI.FTOT.ZS?end=2019&start=1960&view=char (last visited Sept. 21, 2021) https://data.worldbank.org/indicator/NE.GDI.FTOT.ZS?end=2019&start = 1960&view=char [https://perma.cc/6XBT-UFWD] (last visited Sept. 21, 2021).

Appendix Table 2.1. Distribution of Dual Class Stock and R&D Spending in the Largest US Public Firms

A. R&D spending of dual (or more than two class) stock public companies		
2018 Rank	**Name**	**R&D Spending (in billions of $)**
2	Alphabet, Inc.	16.23
8	Ford Motor Company	8.00
9	Facebook, Inc.	7.75
30	Regeneron Pharmaceuticals, Inc.	2.08
38	VMware, Inc.	1.76
44	Expedia Group, Inc.	35.81
68	Liberty Expedia Holdings, Inc.	0.95
69	Workday, Inc.	0.91
Total R&D Spending of Dual Class Companies (in Top 100 R&D companies)		39.06

B. R&D spending of single class public companies		
2018 Rank	**Name**	**R&D Spending (in billions of $)**
1	Amazon.com, Inc.	22.62
3	Intel Corporation	13.10
4	Microsoft Corporation	12.29
5	Apple Inc.	11.58
6	Johnson & Johnson	10.55
7	Merck & Co., Inc.	10.21
10	Pfizer Inc.	7.66
11	General Motors Company	7.30
12	Oracle Corporation	6.09
13	Cisco Systems, Inc.	6.06
14	Celgene Corporation	5.92
15	International Business Machines Corporation	5.79
16	QUALCOMM Incorporated	5.47
17	Eli Lilly and Company	5.28
18	AbbVie Inc.	4.98
19	Bristol-Myers Squibb Company	4.82
20	General Electric Company	4.80
	....	
100	KLA-Tencor Corporation	0.53
Total R&D spending of single class companies		237.67
Portion of R&D spent by single class companies (238/[238+39])		0.86

In this table, dual class companies are US companies with more than one class of stock in the top 100 companies of the Stategy & Global Innovation 1000. Single class companies are the remaining companies. The largest of the top spending single class companies are listed above; the full list is in the unpublished appendix. Dual class companies account for about 14% of the R&D spending of top 100 US R&D companies. The top seven dual class companies spend much less than half as much as the top seven single class companies. The average R&D spending of these seven is, however, a multiple of that of the average of all single class companies. Dual class R&D may be a significant factor in the future, but does not seem to be now.

Sources: PWC, The Global Innovation 1000 Study (2018), https://www.strategyand.pwc.com/gx/en/insights/innovation1000.html; Council of Institutional Investors, Dual Class Companies List (Sept. 2019), https://www.cii.org/files/Board%20Accountability/Dual%20Class%20Company%20List%202018.pdf.

3

Social Costs from Stock-Market-Driven Corporate Short-Termism?

What precisely is stock market short-termism? Stock markets that overemphasize immediate results and discount long-term results too heavily are too short-term. As we saw in Chapter 1, critics say this affliction is severe and the distorted time horizon leads too many public firms to stop investing in good projects, to shut down work on viable R&D, and to use up cash by buying back stock when the firm has good ways to invest that cash.

Some readers will balk at this view. "That's Type-A short-termism, yes— it's focused on low investment, declining R&D, and stock buybacks. But that's not the only kind of short-termism. And it's not even the worst kind. Due to stock market short-term pressure, firms also degrade their workforce,[1] pollute the environment,[2] skirt sound regulation, damage stakeholders,[3] cause financial crises, and risk climate catastrophe." Recent rhetoric on corporate

---

[1] Margaret M. Blair & Lynn A. Stout, *A Team Production Theory of Corporate Law*, 85 Va. L. Rev. 247, 304–305 (1999) (director mediation needed to cure the conflict between short-termism of shareholders and the interests of employees); Jane Maley, *Sustainability: The Missing Element in Performance Management*, 6 Asia-Pacific J. Bus. Admin. 190, 190, 196 (2014) (short-term financial aims ignore the developmental needs of the employees); Katharine V. Jackson, *Towards a Stakeholder-Shareholder Theory of Corporate Governance: A Comparative Analysis*, 7 Hastings Bus. L.J. 309, 324, 349–50 (2011).

[2] Johan J. Graafland, *Price Competition, Short-termism and Environmental Performance*, 116 J. Cleaner Production 125, 130 (2016) (short-termism from fierce price competition decreases environmental performance).

[3] *See, e.g.*, Lisa M. Fairfax, *Making the Corporation Safe for Shareholder Democracy*, 69 Ohio St. L.J. 53, 57, 83 (2008); Kent Greenfield, *Reclaiming Corporate Law in a New Gilded Age*, 2 Harv. L. & Pol'y Rev. 1, 10, 12 (2008); Caroline Flammer & Pratima Bansal, *Does a Long-Term Orientation Create Value? Evidence from a Regression Discontinuity*, 38 Strategic Mgmt. J. 1817, 1829–30 (2017); David Millon, *Shareholder Social Responsibility*, 36 Seattle U.L. Rev. 911, 911–12, 939 (2013); David Millon, *Enlightened Shareholder*

social responsibility, corporate purpose, and corporate respect for ESG issues (the environment, stakeholders, and good governance) has become inextricably intertwined with stock-market-driven corporate short-termism. Short-termism is blamed for much of the purpose, social responsibility, and ESG shortfalls of large stock-market-listed companies; here, in this chapter, I untangle the two, to show that distorted time horizons have little to do with the responsibility and purpose issues.

This viewpoint linking the two is widely held; respected analysts seek to have large firms controlled by long-term shareholders who better appreciate the environment than short-term shareholders.[4] In Chapter 1, I labeled this as "Type B short-termism."

But properly understood, Type B problems are not primarily time horizon problems. They should be labelled "Type B Social Problems," with the short-term modifier struck. Such corporate misdeeds are to be condemned, but they're generally not due to truncated corporate time horizons. No one would say that a firm that leaks toxins into the aquifer year-after-year or that exploits employees decade-after-decade is sound because the misfeasance is long-term. It's the *nature* of the misfeasance that's objectionable, not its *duration*. And its long-term nature makes it more objectionable, not less.

In this chapter, I show why.

A. Employees and Stakeholders

Critics decry executives and corporations for not respecting employees, communities, the spirit of government regulation, and the environment.[5] These problems come from the stock market inducing a short-term mentality in too many corporate executives, it's thought.[6] Social values in this view—like

---

Value, Social Responsibility, and the Redefinition of Corporate Purpose Without Law, in CORPORATE GOVERNANCE AFTER THE FINANCIAL CRISIS 68, 68–72 (P.M. Vasudev & Susan Watson eds., 2012).

[4] COLIN MAYER, FIRM COMMITMENT 262 (2013). The Center for American Progress criticized short-termism and praised long-termism because it leads to "the fulfillment of environmental commitments." CENTER FOR AMERICAN PROGRESS, REPORT OF THE COMMISSION ON INCLUSIVE PROSPERITY 16 (Lawrence H. Summers & Ed Balls, chairs, 2015), www.americanprogress.org/issues/ economy/reports/2015/01/15/104266/report-of-the-commission-on-inclusive-prosperity/ (the report is a collegial undertaking, without primary authors); Senators Tammy Baldwin and Jeff Merkley www.baldwin.senate.gov/imo/media/doc/3.7.16%20-%20Brokaw%20Act%201.pdf (criticizing underinvestment in workforce and infrastructure).

[5] RALPH NADER, MARK GREEN & JOEL SELIGMAN, CONSTITUTIONALIZING THE CORPORATION: THE CASE FOR THE FEDERAL CHARTERING OF GIANT CORPORATIONS 1–25 (1976); Einer Elhauge, *Sacrificing Corporate Profits in the Public Interest*, 80 N.Y.U. L. Rev. 733, 745 (2005).

[6] European Union, Directive 2017/828 of the European Parliament and of the Council of 17 May 2017, amending Directive 2017/36/EC as regards the encouragement of long-term shareholder engagement,

environmental protection and loyalty to employees—are long-term; the public corporation is short-term.

For example, a recent British prime minister, Theresa May, contrasted the goals of "transient shareholders" with the well-being of "[w]orkers [who] have a stake, local communities [which] have a stake, and often the whole country [which] has a stake."[7] And a few years ago then-Chief Justice Strine of the Delaware Supreme Court—the prime arbiter of corporate law disputes in the United States—moved seamlessly from short-termism to stakeholders when examining the modern corporation's problems.[8] The British Prime Minister conflated stunted time horizons with distorted distributional concerns, as is common in public discourse, but the two are different. A commonly-used term—sustainability—captures this brand of short-termist idea. Sustainable activities are long-term and to be encouraged; unsustainable ones are short-term and should be discouraged.[9] Critics say that companies once saw "that investing in workers, communities and other stakeholders was key to sustainable profits."[10] But too many corporate players no longer seek such sustainability, it's said.

Global warming is in this view exacerbated by firms unwilling to go long-term.[11] "[B]usiness tends to fall victim to short-term financial markets, whereas society tends to embody longer-term challenges[.]"[12] Long-term investors will seek firms that adopt sustainable, environmentally friendly, socially stable results.[13] If stock markets and companies were more long-term focused, the environment and employees would be better treated.

Critics say that a truly long-term corporation would protect the environment and incur short-term costs that are to the environment's long-run

---

2017 O.J. (L 132) 20 May 2017, 7, 12, eur-lex.europa.eu/legal-content/EN/TXT/?uri=CELEX:32017L0828; Virginia Harper Ho, *"Enlightened Shareholder Value:" Corporate Governance Beyond the Shareholder-Stakeholder Divide*, 36 J. CORP. L. 59, 61–62 (2010).

[7] *Unilever is Safe, but We Need Better Defenses against Short-term Capitalism*, THE GUARDIAN, Mar. 19, 2017, www.theguardian.com/business/2017/mar/18/unilever-is-safe-but-we-need-better-defences-against-short-term-capitalism.

[8] Leo E. Strine, Jr., *Who Bleeds When the Wolves Bite? A Flesh-and-Blood Perspective on Hedge Fund Activism and Our Strange Corporate Governance System*, 126 YALE L.J. 1870, 1871, 1874 (2017) ("In the back and forth about short-term effects on stock price . . . the flesh-and-blood human beings our corporate governance system is supposed to serve get lost.").

[9] Natalie Slawinski & Pratima Bansal, *Short on Time: Intertemporal Tensions in Business Sustainability*, 26 ORG. SCI. 531 (2015); ALLEN L. WHITE, TRANSFORMING THE CORPORATION 2 (2006), www.corporation2050.org/pdfs/5Corporations.pdf.

[10] Paul Roberts, *Why Have U.S. Companies Become Such Skinflints?* L.A. TIMES, Aug. 27, 2014.

[11] *E.g.*, Slawinski & Bansal, *supra* note 9, at 531 ("many companies have chosen to focus on immediate profits and to delay investments in . . . emissions reductions").

[12] *Id.* at 531, 532 ("[T]he tension between short term and long term is connected intimately to the tension between business and society").

[13] The Investment Integration Project, Systems-Level Considerations and the Long-Term Investor 3 (2017), http://tiiproject.com/wp-content/uploads/2017/03/Systems_Level_Considerations_Long_Term_Investor.pdf.

benefit.[14] "The short-term payback periods of financial markets take precedent over the long-term time horizons of ecological and social systems," says one report.[15] Another critic states that a prime reason "why . . . markets [are] not currently . . . promot[ing] a sustainable economy . . . is [financial market] short-termism—for which the capital markets can be fairly criticized[.]"[16]

These environmental, climate, and stakeholder issues are serious and need attention. They can lead the economy to fall well short of providing the greatest good to the greatest number of citizens. Their worst case results are catastrophic.

But while the stock market may indeed induce the firm to act badly, the *time horizon* of either the firm or the stock market is not the core propellant; the problem is *for whom the firm works*. When an unenlightened, unregulated company works blindly for shareholders, it neglects societal values like environmental integrity *even if the company is fully working for its own long run prosperity*. These societal problems are collective action debilities and have been labelled "the tragedy of the commons," because individual users of pastures have incentives to overgraze and overuse the common pasture, thereby degrading and ruining it. Those who analyze the tragedy of the commons know it's a societal and not a corporate time horizon problem.

* * *

Consider six widely perceived failings of the large US corporation: (1) failing to invest enough, (2) declining R&D, (3) draining cash by buying back stock, (4) damaging the environment and the planet, (5) mistreating stakeholders— employees in particular—and (6) taking the big financial risks that damaged the economy in 2008–2009. The first three malfeasances could be due to stock markets having too short a time horizon. They are instances of "Type A" short-termism—and were examined in Chapter 2 for their pervasiveness. But the last three—"Type B" problems—are not primarily time horizon problems. Type B problems are real but come from the corporation offloading risks and

---

[14] *E.g.*, Slawinski & Bansal, *supra* note 9, at 545.

[15] Andrew J. Hoffman & Max H. Bazerman, *Changing Practice on Sustainability: Understanding and Overcoming the Organizational and Psychological Barriers to Action, in* ORGANIZATIONS AND THE SUSTAINABILITY MOSAIC: CRAFTING LONG-TERM ECOLOGICAL AND SOCIETAL SOLUTIONS 84, 95–96 (Sanjay Sharma, Mark Starik & Bryan Husted, eds. 2007) ("Financial markets often encourage short-term goals . . . and discount the future [so as] not [to] reflect true environmental and social risks and opportunities. . . . These pressures will lead companies to . . . diminish[] the stability of the ecosystem . . . .").

[16] Forum for the Future—Action for a Sustainable World: Sustainable Economy in 2040: A Roadmap for Capital Markets 4 (2011), https://www.aviva.com/content/dam/aviva-corporate/documents/newsr oom/pdfs/newsreleases/2013/6_2040_Vision_FftF.pdf. The report does cite market failure, but as a reason second to financial market short-termism. *Id.* at 4.

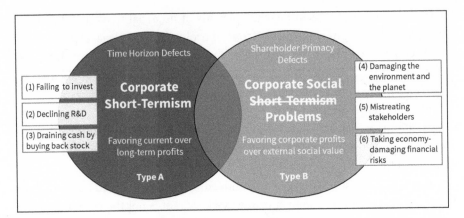

Figure 3.1. Type A and Type B Problems Again, Reconceived

In Figure 3.1, we classify six problems that critics often attribute to stock market short-termism. The first three can in principle arise from short-term corporate time distortions. But the second three are not primarily corporate time horizon failures. They are corporate externalities: the firm and its stockholders gain if their polluting when manufacturing a product lowers their costs, as long as they can push the costs of pollution off on others. Shareholders' strong influence may induce firms to pollute, but these misdeeds are remedied with tools other than lengthening the stock market's time horizon. They are problems whether they arise in the short- or the long-term.

costs to the rest of society, in both the long- and the short-run, as Figure 3.1 illustrates.

B. DuPont, Environmental Toxicity, and the Long-Term

Consider a company in a country that does not regulate environmental wrongs. The company destroys its local environment and makes considerable profit by selling its products elsewhere. The company profits but does not pay the costs. Others, external to the firm, pay. The social costs are great, but they do not result primarily from the company's time horizons. Much that is environmentally costly is miscategorized as short-termism, when it's really due to a lack of corporate conscience.

A DuPont episode illustrates this.[17] Long seen as "one of the most distinguished of . . . U.S. corporation[s]"[18] and a dedicated long-term organization

---

[17] Roy Shapira pointed this out and we develop the example elsewhere. Mark J. Roe & Roy Shapira, *The Power of the Narrative in Corporate Lawmaking*, 11 Harv. Bus. L. Rev. 233 (2021).

[18] Bill George, *The DuPont Proxy Battle is a Battle for the Soul of American Capitalism*, Huffington Post, Nov. 5, 2015, http://www.huffingtonpost.com/bill-george/the-dupont-proxy-contest_b_7256490.html.

that was lauded by corporate law judges for its long-term orientation and its respect for corporate constituencies,[19] it was embroiled in one of the major environmental debacles of our time. For six decades—a very long-term— DuPont discharged a highly toxic chemical into the environment when it made Teflon. The company knew of both the danger and the human body's inability to rid itself of the toxin. Yet it refused inexpensive abatement. Executives counted on keeping inculpating information from the public and the government. They did so for decades, as Roy Shapira and Luigi Zingales show and as the movie *Dark Waters*—named for how and where the toxins were hidden—dramatized.[20] DuPont's long-term horizon did not stop it from polluting dangerously.

True, there's typically a lag between a polluter's act and the polluter getting caught; profits are immediate and the cost of getting caught comes later, as they did for DuPont. But the time horizon consideration should not obscure the fact that the pollution was primarily an "externality:" DuPont captured the benefits while others—external to DuPont—suffered the costs. A shareholder who held DuPont's stock for the 60-year long-term made money from DuPont's 60 years of Teflon pollution, even though the company was caught.[21] DuPont did not pollute because it was pressured by short-term hedge fund activists, distracted by traders, or fixated with quarterly reporting; it polluted because its internal organizational sense of right and wrong broke down. Its long-term pollution paid off for both short-term *and* long-term shareholders.[22]

Rewarding whistleblowing and facilitating liability, even punitive liability in excess of the damage caused, are plausible cures. Better regulation to make being caught more likely is a good cure; lengthening corporate time horizons is not.

* * *

[19] Delaware's former Chief Justice Strine lauded DuPont's "track record of long-term investment and better-than-typical treatment of constituencies other than stockholders." Leo E. Strine, Jr., *Corporate Power Is Corporate Purpose I: Evidence from My Home Town*, 33 OXFORD REV. ECON. POL'Y 176 (2017). Delaware "nationalism" and pride in the local business could account for this.

[20] Roy Shapira & Luigi Zingales, Is Pollution Value-Maximizing? The DuPont Case (NBER Working Paper 23866, 2017), www.nber.org/papers/w23866; Nathaniel Rich, *The Lawyer Who Became DuPont's Worst Nightmare*, N.Y. TIMES, Jan. 6, 2016.

[21] Shapira & Zingales, *supra* note 20. (Conceivably, however, DuPont lost from reprisals and reputational degradation when caught, but prospered otherwise.)

[22] *Cf.* Pat Akey & Ian Appel, Environmental Externalities of Activism (Jan. 2020), https://ssrn.com/abstract=3508808 (hedge fund activism has a salutary effect on target firm emissions, via better management and reduced activity from a substandard organization).

My purpose here is not to prove that stock-market-driven short-term procliv-
ities have never exacerbated pollution or fraud, only that they are unlikely to
be the biggest contributors to global warming, excess methane, and spoliation
of aquifers. The social problem often emanates from a misdirected and selfish
shareholder orientation. One does not cure such problems of conscience and
cost-externalization with a longer time horizon for the stockholders. One
cures them by making the polluter pay, either right away or at least eventually. Yet too much of the rhetoric of policymaking here mistakenly aims to
lengthen time horizons.

C. Environmental Degradation and Global Warming as Corporate Selfishness

Even firms that think *solely in the long-term* can and will pollute, degrade
the environment, and warm the planet as long as they consider their selfish
benefits and not the external social costs. (And we citizens who drive our
cars and fly planes to visit relatives or do our jobs are not much different.)
Integrated oil companies are among the most long-term-oriented companies on the planet, with planning departments projecting worldwide energy
needs and oil field possibilities decades into the future. Making them think
more long-term is not a climate cure because, first, they already think long-
term, and, second, the problem is not their time horizon but that polluters
(including us, driving our cars) do not pay.

Corporate critics should stop reflexively blaming major corporate problems
on short-termism, not just because it's conceptually incorrect but because
doing so leads us to misidentify the underlying problems and to misspecify
solutions. Even if *every corporation operated for their own long-run benefit*,
bad corporate social behavior could and would persist, as long as corporations
can externalize costs. The polluting corporation is a bad citizen but not necessarily one that has a short-term outlook.

It is not surprising that those who have thought most about climate degradation typically identify a carbon tax as the best means of addressing the
problem—a tax on the volume of carbon that citizens and companies release
into the atmosphere. Carbon taxes address externalities by making people
and companies pay for the negative consequences of their actions. The payment normally should induce them to pollute less. It targets the selfishness
problem, and hence might work, and not the time horizon issue, which would
not work as it is the wrong target.

D. The Financial Crisis

A housing bubble grew during the first decade of this century until, by the decade's end, it burst and caused a worldwide financial crisis that threatened to turn into a great depression. The crisis unleashed political forces that still disturb the polity and the economy.

Analysts blamed corporate and financial short-termism as a core cause of this crisis. The government's official Financial Crisis Inquiry Commission castigated banks' short-term executive compensation systems as propelling it.[23] SEC Chair William Donaldson likewise saw "one of the root causes" of the crisis to be "[t]he excessive focus by too many corporations on achieving short-term results."[24] Timothy Geithner, who eventually became secretary of the treasury, concluded that "[t]his financial crisis had many significant causes, but . . . [i]ncentives for short-term gains [from executive compensation] overwhelmed the checks and balances meant to mitigate the risk of excess leverage."[25] Empirical studies exist on both sides: some show that the duration of executive compensation (the time until the executive received remuneration) had no impact on a financial firm's vulnerability,[26] while others detect a correlation between the two.[27]

Few analysts, even those emphasizing short-term executive compensation as a root cause, would leave out weakened financial sector capital requirements, the rise of shadow banking outside the regulated domain, and other core causes having little to do with the time horizon of stock-based executive compensation. But adding short-termism to the list of major causes is a mistake, because the systemic financial problem being analyzed is fundamentally not one of time horizons but, again, of externalities. Those who conjure up a powerful short-term driver here see executives taking risks with

---

[23] Financial Crisis Inquiry Comm'n, Financial Crisis Inquiry Report, at xix (2011). *See also* Florian Möslein & Karsten Engsig Sørensen, *Nudging for Corporate Long-termism and Sustainability?* 24 COLUM. J. EUR. L. 391, 393 (2018) ("the global financial crisis has turned public attention to issues of short-termism in the financial sector").

[24] Nicholas Rummel, *Donaldson: Short-term Earnings Led to Woes*, INVESTMENT NEWS, Sept. 18, 2008, www. investmentnews.com/article/20080918/REG/809189995/donaldson-short-term-earnings-led-to-woes.

[25] Statement by Treasury Secretary Tim Geithner on Compensation, U.S. Dep't of the Treasury, June 10, 2009, www.treasury.gov/press-center/press-releases/Pages/tg163.aspx.

[26] Andrea Beltratti & René M. Stulz, *The Credit Crisis Around the Globe: Why Did Some Banks Perform Better?* 105 J. FIN. ECON. 1, 25 (2012).

[27] Adam C. Kolasinski & Nan Yang, *Managerial Myopia and the Mortgage Meltdown*, 128 J. FIN. ECON. 466, 481–82 (2018. *Cf.* Lucian A. Bebchuk, Alma Cohen & Holger Spamann, *The Wages of Failure: Executive Compensation at Bear Stearns and Lehman, 2000–2008*, 27 YALE J. ON REG. 257, 261 (2010) (executives at two financial firms did very well financially before the crisis and came out ahead even after the losses they suffered from their firms' collapse during the crisis); Lynne Dallas, *Short-Termism, the Financial Crisis, and Corporate Governance*, 37 J. CORP. L. 265, 319, 357 (2012). *See also* Radhakrishnan Gopalan, Todd Milbourn, Fenghua Song & Anjan V. Thakor, *Duration of Executive Compensation*, 69 J. FIN. 2777, 2712 (2014).

their bank's solvency that they would have shunned if the risks were played out within the duration of the executives' compensation package. If I'm paid based only on how high *this* year's profits are, I'll take excessive risks with *next* year's profits, taking the chance that next year's profits will be obliterated in a financial crisis. This is true. And it is indeed a time horizon contribution to financial risk-taking. But overly focusing on this channel will lead policymakers to miss the high-value target.

Here's what I mean: The basic financial problem was that the costs of a bank's failure were mostly borne by others outside the bank and the executive suite. The losers were not just the risk-taking bank, its shareholders, and its executives but the government, the rest of the financial system, and, most importantly, the workers and taxpayers who suffered—all interests external to the banks.

The government loses first by backing up failing banks' deposits through the government's deposit insurance and then from bailing out sinking banks. And the economy then suffers when banks fail and are bailed out. But if the banks' risk-taking pays off, and there's no failure, the gains are garnered almost entirely by the bank's shareholders and stock-compensated executives, all of whom win big. Heads the executive wins, tails the rest of us pick up most of the loss. The executives' *time horizon* was less important than the *distorted payoffs*.

To see this more clearly: Imagine that the banks' executives were paid over the long run with company stock. If they ran their banks in a risky way that usually pays them a million dollars but inflicts a trillion-dollar loss on the economy once in a while, they would *still* be incentivized to take that bet— good for them most of the time, but very bad for the rest of us when it's a losing bet. The bankers still have incentives to take the risk, because most of the time they get the million-dollar payoff.

The critical incentive-based cure is to unlink bank executives' compensation from the banks' profits. (Conscience and public-spiritedness can help too.) Financial firms that paid their executives more in debt-like claims, such as fixed pension obligations (which did not rise if the bank did well but fell if the bank did badly) fared better during the crisis.[28] That pay package

---

[28] Sjoerd van Bekkum, *Inside Debt and Bank Risk*, 51 J. Fin. & Quant. Anal. 359, 383 (2016); Rosalind L. Bennett, Levent Güntay & Haluk Unal, *Inside Debt, Bank Default Risk, and Performance During the Crisis*, 24 J. Fin. Intermediation 487 (2015); Frederick Tung & Xue Wang, Bank CEOs, Inside Debt Compensation, and the Global Financial Crisis 1–3, 29 (Boston U. Sch. of Law working paper No. 11-49, Aug. 2013), www.ssrn.com/abstract=1570161; Frederick Tung, *Pay for Banker Performance: Structuring Executive Compensation for Risk Regulation*, 105 Nw. L. Rev. 1205 (2011). *Cf.* Bebchuk, Cohen & Spamann, *supra* note 27, at 276–77 (emphasizing excessive risk-taking incentives of financial executives' compensation).

incentivized bankers to take fewer risks. Conversely, banks with high stock-based executive compensation took more risks than was good for financial stability.[29] This is incentive alignment, not stretching the executives' time horizons. The two differ, but in too much short-termism thinking they are confused as being the same.

E. When Time Horizon Counts

In the Venn diagram presented earlier in this chapter, in Figure 3.1, there's an oval in which time horizon and social problems intersect. Some examples of this follow.

In truly short-term stock-market-based corporate action, the firm imposes the cost on others for a quick corporate benefit, but at a long-term *corporate* cost. If the long-term costs to the corporation exceed the short-term profits, then we indeed have a true *time-horizon*, short-term issue. But if the firm and its stockholders benefit in both the short- and the long-run, then we have a social but not a corporate time horizon problem—a problem for which manipulating corporate time horizons will do no good.

True, if pollution or financial risk-taking are undiscoverable for longer than the executive expects to be with the company, the self-interested executive has reason to tolerate the undetected pollution now that will diminish the company's stock price later, when the wrong is discovered and finally priced into the stock.[30] But is this problem emanating from stock market short-termism? While popular discourse ties this to executive *stock* options that are worth more now, this is largely incorrect. *Any* compensation structure that rewards the executive for current profitability, despite hidden costs, incentivizes the executive to push costs out into the future. The executive could pollute, pump up profits, and take a *cash* bonus this year, expecting to be gone from the firm when the problem is discovered and the firm finally pays up.

The pay structure is what needs fixing, not the stock market. In fact, stock-based compensation, if done well, is *better* for the long-term than a cash bonus. If the payment is in stock that the executive must keep deep into the future, then the executive cannot benefit by pushing costs into the future. The stock's value will suffer if the pollution is discovered—although only if

[29] *See* sources cited *supra* note 28; Lucian A. Bebchuk & Holger Spamann, *Regulating Bankers' Pay*, 98 GEO. L. J. 247 (2010); René M. Stulz, *Risk-Taking and Risk Management by Banks*, 27 J. APPLIED CORP. FIN. 8 (2015); Bill Francis, Aparna Gupta & Iftekhar Hasan, *Impact of Compensation Structure and Managerial Incentives on Bank Risk Taking*, 242 EUR. J. OP. RES. 651 (2015).

[30] John Armour, Jeffrey Gordon & Geeyoung Min, *Taking Compliance Seriously*, 37 YALE J. ON REG. 1 (2020).

the enforcement machinery to internalize the externality is strong. Hence, the company's shareholders—the stock market—have the incentive to keep the executive "on the hook" longer. Thus it follows that *more* stockholder power (through a say on executive pay) can be better for the environment in this delayed discovery scenario.

Consider another apparent time horizon channel: Some executives feel pressured to meet this quarter's numbers, so they put off resolving an environmental problem or postpone awarding employees a well-deserved raise. And, once they begin shortchanging employees and degrading the environment for this quarter, they get caught up in the bad behavior and fail to correct it in the next quarter. What once was a short-term action turns into a long-term one.

Such a channel fits aspects of the 2001 Enron scandal: the executives scrambled to show good quarterly results and did so fraudulently, hoping that better business in the future would hide their doctoring of the books. But that better business never came, so they found themselves pushed to falsify earnings numbers for several years, until they were caught.

The underlying problem, however, was not so much the short-termism but the fraud. Fix the fraud and the problem is reduced or gone. Moreover, the Enron scandal shows that short-termism can sometimes be healthy and reduce corporate problems. The Enron fraud was discovered partly because it had to report profits, sales, and assets quarterly. Eventually the numbers did not add up, short sellers pressured the stock price,[31] and analysts and journalists discovered the problem, blew the whistle, and stopped the problem from getting even worse.

A third possible channel could pin some negative externalities to the stock market's purportedly short-term horizon. Some companies "don't get away with it" in the long run, it's said, but the stock market does not know that in the short run. Small negatives, it's said, predict future major negative externalities but barely hurt stock price in the short run even though they lead to bigger externalities later that hurt the stock price.[32] While that once may have been so, it seems to be no longer. According to recent work, the stock market now prices these small failures better (because it has learned that they predict later bigger failures), so the stock price adjusts more quickly, making quick profits even harder to acquire.[33]

---

[31] Short sellers sell the stock for future delivery without owning the stock. They hope that the stock's price will sink before they have to deliver the stock, so that they can buy it at a low price and complete the sale profitably.

[32] Simon Glossner, ESG Incidents and Shareholder Value (Feb. 17, 2021), www.ssrn.com/abstract=3004689. For early theory on the possibility, *see* Roland Bénabou & Jean Tirole, *Individual and Corporate Social Responsibility*, 77 Economica 1 (2010).

[33] George Serafeim & Aaron Yoon, Which Corporate ESG News Does the Market React To? (Harv. Bus. Sch. Working Paper 21-115, 2021), www.ssrn.abstract=3832698; Philipp Krueger, Zacharias Sautner,

F. System-Wide Corporate Short-Termism?

The environmental problem can be confused with long-term vs. short-term issues because it *does* indeed burn up *social* resources in the short-term at the expense of *social* well-being in the long-term. If firms overconsume hydrocarbons for today's profit, contributing to long-term, civilization-threatening global warming, then *society* incurs a big cost in the long-term. But the operative mechanism is that a firm profits from hydrocarbons, while it bears only a fraction of the resulting costs.[34] The polluter does not pay enough. The corporation (like those of us who drive cars and thereby pollute) is selfish, but it's society that acts short-term, not the car driver or the corporation.

Put this problem in terms of catastrophic climate change. All corporate leaders may believe that catastrophe is probable, but each knows that a single firm's actions cannot make a difference. Each thus releases methane and burns hydrocarbons (or sells them to us, and we burn them to heat our houses and run our cars). All of us suffer later. No single firm can make a difference in avoiding catastrophe.

Even the climate-worrying CEO could contribute to the catastrophe—"I alone cannot reduce the chance of catastrophe; I can only cut my own modest pollution, which would slash my profits and still not avoid the catastrophe," he or she calculates. "If I could affect *every* firm, I could reduce the chance of catastrophic climate collapse thirty years hence. But I cannot. Only the government or some other collective action can get this done right." (Some economy-wide investors do admonish their portfolio companies to respect the environment and combat climate change.[35] Whether this rhetoric plays out positively on-the-ground is yet to be seen, but the rhetoric and, for now, the will are there. But it's an attempt at a collective action solution, not a corporate time horizon solution.)

The socially-distorted incentive of the individual free-rider is why collective organization, usually government-organized or government-mandated or (via a carbon tax) government-incentivized, is needed to remedy this so-called "tragedy of the commons." These are problems of individual firms offloading costs outside the corporation, of individuals polluting more than

Dragon Yongjun Tang & Rui Zhong, The Effects of Mandatory ESG Disclosure around the World (May 2021), www.ssrn.com/abstract=3832745.

[34] Slawinski & Bansal, *supra* note 9, at 533.
[35] Larry Fink's 2021 letter to CEOs, BlackRock, https://www.blackrock.com/us/individual/2021-larry-fink-ceo-letter?gclid=Cj0KCQjwi7yCBhDJARIsAMWFScO7HUqqKXr4aj6Q_5rw WqIbEaJkUxweEL0m QzKPod-ESa6MbWj0L-oaAncREALw_wcB&gclsrc=aw.ds (last visited Mar. 15, 2021).

they should, and of countries around the world hoping that other countries will fix the problem.[36]

G. Summary

Society here *is short-term* and foolish, while individual firms are selfish, but not short-term.

Environmental degradation, global warming, shoddy products, financial crises, mistreated employees, and severe inequality are among the most severe problems we face as a society. If we blame stock market short-termism for these societal problems—when they instead emanate primarily from corporate selfishness and a lack of political will to deal with the problems directly—then policymakers will try to cure these serious problems by lengthening the stock market's time horizon. But lengthening the stock market's time horizon will not fix these problems because they are for the most part not horizon problems. This mistaken targeting pulls policymakers away from sounder efforts, such as a carbon tax to address climate change or better regulation to keep banks well capitalized and safe. Mistakenly thinking that one can cure environmental degradation and avoid financial crises by curing stock market short-termism means that we will have more environmental degradation and risk more deeply damaging financial crises.

---

[36] MANCUR OLSON, THE LOGIC OF COLLECTIVE ACTION: PUBLIC GOODS AND THE THEORY OF GROUPS (1971); RUSSELL HARDIN, COLLECTIVE ACTION (1982); ELINOR OSTROM, GOVERNING THE COMMONS: THE EVOLUTION OF INSTITUTIONS FOR COLLECTIVE ACTION (1990).

4

The Heavy Cost of Misdiagnosis

Missing the Right Targets

Still, there surely is some corporate short-termism. As long as there is some, even if of uncertain size, critics could aim to reduce it. If it's small, we'll cure a small problem. If it's large, we'll mitigate a large one. We need not inquire deeply into whether we have an economy-wide problem and how severe it is. Big or small, let's fix it.

Such thinking is incorrect. Cures cost something, and we analyze the most prominent cures and their costs in Chapters 8 and 9. If we do not suffer from a serious problem, we should not pay much for any cures. With so much on the US economic policy agenda left unaddressed, we should not spend resources fixing small problems when big ones need attention.

And over-attention to purported stock market short-termism may divert us from the real solutions to basic problems. Two examples follow.

Rising inequality. If the corporation were not short-term oriented, then it would treat its employees better, some say. Better wages would help stabilize our uneasy polity and be fairer. But since these problems are not due to stock market short-termism, seeking to reduce short-termism will take policymakers' eyes away from better solutions to growing inequality, like a more progressive income tax.

Environmental degradation and global warming. If political activists mistakenly see time horizons as a major cause of environmental degradation and global warming, they will give up on making the difficult politics of (say) a carbon tax work. They'll instead manipulate corporate time horizons without doing much good for the environment.

There are other ways that obsessing about stock market short-termism will misdirect us. Here in this chapter I look at two, namely, industrial structure and where a US R&D shortfall lies.

A. Competition, Antitrust, and the Evolution of Industrial Organization

The organization of industry has changed greatly in recent decades, and that change could well be affecting the level and nature of corporate investment.

Consider the common claim that stock markets are killing investment in plant and equipment, thereby holding the economy back. But, according to respected analysts, competition has weakened in the United States, with some attributing the result to weakened antitrust enforcement. Other respected authorities say something similar—that business dynamism has deteriorated.[1]

Industries with weak competition invest less. They would rather raise their prices than produce more; if no competitor is pushing them, they feel less pressure to get to the next technological frontier with new equipment. Germán Gutiérrez and Thomas Philippon point to decreased US competition as holding back new investment in plant and equipment.[2] Policymakers and political leaders who blame stock market short-termism for weakening US investment could miss a more substantial cause: decreased competition.

Winner-take-all competition. Other experts reject the decline-in-competition explanation but still see large changes in industrial organization. They see the economy as evolving toward *more* competition, but with a new nature. There's more winner-take-all competition,[3] they conclude, by which

---

[1] EDMUND PHELPS, MASS FLOURISHING: HOW GRASSROOTS INNOVATION CREATED JOBS, CHALLENGE, AND CHANGE 237 (2013). *See also* Ian Hathaway & Robert E. Litan, What's Driving the Decline in the Firm Formation Rate? A Partial Explanation (Econ. Stud. Brookings, Nov. 2014), www.brookings.edu/wp-content/uploads/2016/06/driving_decline_firm_formation_rate_hathaway_litan.pdf; Ufuk Akcigit & Sina T. Ates, *Ten Facts on Declining Business Dynamism and Lessons from Endogenous Growth Theory*, 13 AM. ECON. J. 257 (2021).

[2] Germán Gutiérrez & Thomas Philippon, Declining Competition and Investment in the U.S. (working paper, Sept. 2017), https://cepr.org/active/publications/discussion_papers/dp.php?dpno=12536; THOMAS PHILIPPON, THE GREAT REVERSAL: HOW AMERICA GAVE UP ON FREE MARKETS (2019). But see, for a contrary view, James Traina, Is Aggregate Market Power Increasing? Production Trends Using Financial Statements (SSRN, Feb. 2018), www.ssrn.com/abstract=3120849. A well-debated antitrust aspect focuses on how new forms of concentrated stock ownership can undermine competition. For two prominent proponents, see Einer Elhauge, *Horizontal Shareholding*, 129 HARV. L. REV. 1267 (2017), and Martin C. Schmalz, *Common-Ownership Concentration and Corporate Conduct*, 10 ANN. REV. FIN. ECON. 413 (2018).

[3] David Autor, David Dorn, Lawrence F. Katz, Christina Patterson & John Van Reenen, *The Fall of the Labor Share and the Rise of Superstar Firms*, 135 Q.J. ECON. 846 (2020); Susanto Basu, *Are Price-Cost Markups Rising in the United States? A Discussion of the Evidence*, 33 J. ECON. PERSP. 3 (2019) ("more efficient firms . . . gain market share"); Robert E. Hall, New Evidence on Market Power, Profit, Concentration, and the Role of Mega-Firms in the US Economy (Apr. 27, 2018), https://web.stanford.edu/~rehall/Evidence%20on%20markup%202018; John Van Reenen, Increasing Differences between Firms: Market Power

companies compete ferociously but a winner emerges who dominates a relevant market for years, until replaced. The company Blockbuster distributed home entertainment to most of us for years, until Netflix replaced it with DVD mailers.

Intangibles. Much new competition, in this view, involves intangibles. Intangibles have become more important relative to hard assets, rising "tenfold from about 5% of net book assets in 1970 to about 60% in 2010."[4] That shift predicts more R&D and less spending on manufacturing assets—the very trends we saw in the data in Chapter 2. So it is not that short-termism is the cause of declining investment in capital equipment for manufacturing but that the nature of productive investment has shifted from hard assets to R&D and intangibles.

A related but more pessimistic view sees secular stagnation—which has macroeconomic characteristics and cheaper capital equipment leading to high savings and low investment—as the problem, an idea that Lawrence Summers, the Harvard economist and former secretary of the treasury, has pushed forward.[5] Equally pessimistic is Robert Gordon, also an expert on such matters: no new productivity technologies requiring massive investment in new machinery and new capital stock were strong enough in recent decades to boost capital spending.[6] Major innovation economists see scientific ideas as having become harder to find.[7] If any of these assessments are right, pursuing stock market short-termism to encourage investment would quickly reach a dead-end.

Mismeasurement. Still others say that the calculated investment decline is from mismeasurement. Investment in traditional, old-school manufacturing is measured well, while investment in networks, patent development, and organizational capacity is not. Traditional manufacturing has moved to East Asia, as Appendix Figure 2.7 shows, while new forms of enterprise dependent on intangible capital investment (brands, networks, patents, organizational capacity) have become more important in the United States, and these

---

and the Macro-Economy (Aug. 31, 2018), www.kansascityfed.org/~/media/files/publicat/sympos/2018/papersandhandouts/jh%20john%20van%20reenen%20version%2020.pdf.

[4] Antonio Falato, Dalida Kadyrzhanova & Jae W. Sim, Rising Intangible Capital, Shrinking Debt Capacity, and the US Corporate Savings Glut 8, 41 (Fed. Res. Bd. Working Paper No. 67, 2013), www.federalreserve.gov/pubs/feds/2013/201367/201367pap.pdf [https://perma.cc/XK5R-LT26]. *Cf.* Robin Döttling & Enrico C. Perotti, Secular Trends and Technological Progress 1 (June 2020), www.ssrn.com/abstract=2996998.

[5] Lawrence H. Summers, *The Age of Secular Stagnation: What It Is and What to Do About It*, FOREIGN AFFAIRS, Mar.–Apr. 2016.

[6] ROBERT J. GORDON, THE RISE AND FALL OF AMERICAN GROWTH 2, 566–68, 574–76 (2016).

[7] Nicholas Bloom, Charles I. Jones, John Van Reenen & Michael Webb, *Are Ideas Getting Harder to Find?* 110 AM. ECON. REV. 1104 (2020).

investments are undercounted. Research and development spending is more important (and rising, as we saw in Chapter 2), but traditional accounting sees R&D as an expense, when it's really an investment.

Reconfiguration. Some activities are now best not done in large firms. In the pharmaceutical industry, for example, smaller firms are thought to be more adept at the new "large molecule," biologic pharmaceutical research. This shift would show up as declining R&D in big pharma, but not declining pharma research overall. Larger firms can find it more difficult to carry out innovative research than smaller firms and more often now will partner with a smaller firm, as Ronald Gilson, Charles Sabel, and Robert Scott show.[8] The basic technology behind Pfizer's Covid-19 vaccine, the first approved in the United States, was developed by a small German research firm, BioNTech.

And significant public firm R&D spending is not well accounted for in my estimation: In some industries small firms do the new research forays. Public companies then buy (often with stock) the small firm, with the larger firms using the small firm's research to develop, manufacture, and market the product. Public firms and the stock market thereby pay, after the fact, for the small firm's R&D.[9] Hence, for such efforts, I analyze the structure as it still being the stock market that pays for the corporate R&D—even if no public corporation directly conducted that R&D.[10] This structural likelihood seems quite substantial but as far as I know has not been measured.

Neither every firm nor every productive sector must do everything well. If venture capital or private operations do some critical R&D as well as, or better than, the research departments at large firms, then that research should shift to smaller firms over time. This is the basic economics of specialization, straight from Adam Smith.[11]

* * *

Consider the right remedies if underinvestment were a major problem. Economists who look to boost business investment economy-wide typically turn to fiscal, monetary, and tax policy as the tools, not to corporate

---

[8] Ronald J. Gilson, Charles F. Sabel & Robert E. Scott, *Contracting for Innovation: Vertical Disintegration and Interfirm Collaboration*, 109 COLUM. L. REV. 431, 439–40 (2009). *See also* Walter W. Powell, Kenneth W. Koput & Laurel Smith-Doerr, *Interorganizational Collaboration and the Locus of Innovation: Networks of Learning in Biotechnology*, 41 ADMIN. SCI. Q. 116, 122–24 (1996); Weijian Shan, Gordon Walker & Bruce Kogut, *Interfirm Cooperation and Startup Innovation in the Biotechnology Industry*, 15 STRATEGIC MGMT. J. 387, 387–88 (1994).

[9] *See generally* Mark J. Roe, *Stock Market Short-Termism's Impact*, 134 U. PA. L. REV. 71, 101–02 (2018), from which this paragraph draws.

[10] *Id. Cf.* Shai Bernstein, *Does Going Public Affect Innovation?* 70 J. FIN. 1365 (2015).

[11] These paragraphs on alternative explanations draw on Roe, *supra* note 9, at 107–08.

governance and its purported short-termism.[12] The stock market is not even on the list of some experts. Yet it's high on the list of many in media and political circles. Focusing on stock market short-termism could have us aiming at the wrong target.

My purpose here is not to weigh the evidence overall for these trends and possibilities, and to then come to a definitive conclusion, but to show that changes in industrial organization could readily explain the declining investment that stock market short-termism critics attribute to short-termism. Some of these alternatives demand a policy response; some just give us a new understanding of the twenty-first century US economy. Attacking stock market short-termism as a primary cause, if it's only a minor one, misunderstands the economy and can induce us to aim at the wrong target.

B. Where is the R&D Slack in the US Economy?

Consider US R&D. Pessimists believe that stock market short-termism is stifling R&D spending, thereby severely damaging our future.[13] But US *corporate* R&D spending is *rising*, not falling, and it's rising *faster* than the US economy is growing, as we saw in Chapter 2 and Figure 2.8, which I reproduce next, as Figure 4.1. Perhaps it should be rising more and even faster, and perhaps with different arrangements it would have been higher. But, directionally, corporate R&D spending is moving up, and we have no obvious evidence that it needs to be moving up much more.

Next, consider *government* spending on R&D. For quite a long time, US industrial, military, and economic prowess partly but crucially came from astute

---

[12] N. Gregory Mankiw, Principles of Economics 560–62, 715–18, 756, 758–59 (7th ed. 2015).

[13] *See* Jamie Dimon & Warren E. Buffett, *Short-Termism Is Harming the Economy*, Wall St. J., June 6, 2018 ("Companies frequently hold back on technology spending, hiring, and research and development to meet quarterly earnings forecasts"); Erin Smith, How Short-Termism Impacts Public and Private R&D Investments, (Bipartisan Pol'y Ctr., June 7, 2016), https://bipartisanpolicy.org/blog/how-short-termism-impacts-innovation-investments/ ("[S]hort-term thinking . . . can have serious consequences for long-term competitiveness by limiting a company's access and familiarity with the cutting edge of research in their industries."); Eilene Zimmerman, *The Risks and Rewards of Short-Termism*, N.Y. Times, Nov. 4, 2015 ("[Hillary Rodham Clinton] and others have criticized practices that put a priority on share buybacks and dividend payments over sources of long-term growth like wage increases, investment in research and employee development."); Leo Strine, *Securing Our Nation's Economic Future: A Sensible, Nonpartisan Agenda to Increase Long-Term Investment and Job Creation in the United States*, 71 Bus. Law. 1081 (2016); William Lazonick, *The Curse of Stock Buybacks*, 29 Am. Prospect, No. 3, 1–10 (2018); Ashish Arora, Sharon Belenzon & Andrea Patacconi, *Killing the Golden Goose? The Decline of Science in Corporate R&D*, 39 Strategic Mgmt. J. 3 (2018) (large corporations reduced their investment in basic research between 1989 and 2006, due to "a decline in the private value of research activities, even though scientific knowledge itself remains important for corporate invention"); Brad Plumer, *The Coming R&D Crash*, Wash. Post, Feb. 26, 2013.

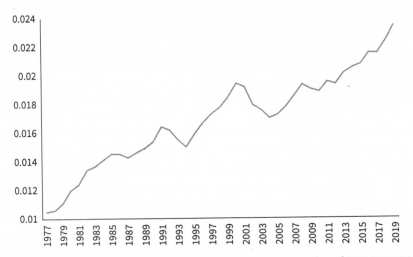

Figure 4.1. R&D Spending in the United States Rising as a Proportion of GDP, 1977–2019

Source: Bureau of Econ. Analysis, National Income and Product Accounts, U.S. Dep't of Commerce, Table 5.6.5, lines 2 & 6 (2020) (last visited Apr. 19, 2020), http://www.bea.gov/itable/ [https://perma.cc/HM9A-7XM3]. The graphic is of total US R&D. Corporate R&D spending similarly slopes upward. *See* Appendix Figure 2.1.

government R&D spending.[14] The government fostered R&D that the private sector would not pursue. The private sector does R&D that will bring profits; the government, when properly functioning, supports R&D that will benefit the nation by "provid[ing] the public good of general knowledge . . . [by] subsidiz[ing] basic research in medicine, mathematics, physics, chemistry, [and] biology."[15] When a firm cannot lock out competitors from using its R&D results (because the results cannot be patented, for example), the benefit might be wide but private profitability low—in other words, basic research is a "non-rival" good.[16] The common understanding is that:

> Profit-seeking firms . . . develop new products that they can patent and sell, but they do not spend much on basic research. Their incentive, instead, is to free ride

[14] *See* Alan Wm. Wolff & Charles W. Wessner, *Rising to the Challenge: U.S. Innovation Policy for the Global Economy, in* Comm. on Comp. Nat'l Innovation Policies: Best Practice for the 21st Century, Nat'l Res. Council 1 (Charles W. Wessner & Alan Wm. Wolff eds., 2012) ("Sustaining global leadership in the commercialization of innovation is vital to America's security, its role as a world power, and the welfare of its people. Even in a climate of severe budgetary constraint, the United States cannot afford to neglect investing in its future."); *see also* Robert D. Atkinson, Understanding the U.S. National Innovation System 4 (SSRN, 2014), https://www.ssrn.com/abstract=3079822; L. Rafael Reif, *The Dividends of Funding Basic Science,* Wall St. J., Dec. 5, 2016.

[15] *See* N. Gregory Mankiw, Principles of Microeconomics 215 (8th ed. 2018).

[16] *See id.* And if it costs nothing for another to use the good (such as for general knowledge), public provision typically makes sense.

on the general knowledge created by others. As a result, in the absence of any public policy, society would devote too few resources to creating new knowledge.[17]

Government support for R&D has major knock-on effects. Publicly funded and generally disseminated discoveries prod commercialization, by setting the innovation process in motion.[18] Some government R&D programs develop basic technology and leave it to industry to commercialize. In agriculture and public health, the government has developed new varieties of plants, the annual flu vaccine, and drugs for AIDS. These led to commercially useful products that industry took further.[19] When private firms decide whether to pursue an R&D project, they do not value spillover benefits highly enough— positive externalities in the economics vocabulary, the opposite of negative externalities like pollution considered in Chapter 3. Some companies will go ahead anyway, but they are swimming against the tide of incentives. A well-functioning government will step in. Much of the spending for Covid-19 vaccines came from the US government.

Take another example: Steve Jobs' genius was crucial to Apple's success, but he built Apple atop a foundation of government investment in the technologies that made the iPhone possible—microchips, integrated circuits, touch screens, giant magnetoresistance (which allows data to be read well from hard disk drives) were all indispensable to the iPhone and all depended on the state's visible hand and financing.[20] Foundational developments for biotechnology, genome sequencing, global positioning satellite technology, the internet, and personal computing were also government-developed.[21] All are core to the modern economy. Venture capital and corporate investment were crucial to turning ideas and possibilities into products that people use. But government-funded basic research often laid the groundwork.[22]

---

[17] *Id.*

[18] *See* N. GREGORY MANKIW, MACROECONOMICS 264 (9th ed. 2016) (one entity's research can "make[] other firms better off by giving them a base of knowledge on which to build").

[19] U.S. Congressional Budget Office, Federal Climate Change Programs: Funding History and Policy Issues 16–19 (Mar. 2010), www.cbo.gov/publication/21196. *See also* Peter Ogden, John Podesta & John Deutsch, *A New Strategy to Spur Energy Innovation*, 24 ISSUES IN SCI. & TECH. 35 (2008).

[20] MARIANA MAZZUCATO, THE ENTREPRENEURIAL STATE: DEBUNKING PUBLIC VS. PRIVATE SECTOR MYTHS 81, 88–89 (2013); JONATHAN GRUBER & SIMON JOHNSON, JUMP-STARTING AMERICA: HOW BREAKTHROUGH SCIENCE CAN REVIVE ECONOMIC GROWTH AND THE AMERICAN DREAM 6–7, 55 (2019); Peter Singer, Federally Supported Innovations: 22 Examples of Major Technology Advances that Stem from Federal Research Support 18–19 (2014), www.sciencecoalition.org/downloads/1390490336mitpetersingerfederallysupportedinnovationswhitepaperjan2014-21.pdf.

[21] *Id.* at 11–33; Mazzucato, *supra* note 20, at 89, 147.

[22] *Id.* at 147.

US government spending on basic R&D has been declining for several decades. It declined even more in the past decade, lagging behind both historic US norms *and* recent trends for China, Germany, and Japan.

Consider artificial intelligence (AI). Some AI advances can be patented, thereby excluding competitors, but others, once known, can be used by rival firms. US government spending on AI R&D has been flat in recent years and is reportedly dwarfed by China's.[23]

After the 2008–2009 financial crisis, there was a widespread political view in the United States that all government spending needed to be reduced. The 2013 budget sequestration cut government spending roughly across the board.[24] As a result, US government-sector funding for R&D fell from a peak of 0.92% of US GDP in 2009 to just 0.63% of GDP in 2017.[25] Over the same period, Japan's government-sector R&D funding declined less (0.57% to 0.48%), while China and Germany *increased* public R&D support. It's *that* spending, astutely directed, that the United States needs to repair first. Figure 4.2 tells the story.

This government spending decline is a US policy choice, and focusing R&D policy thinking on stock-market-driven short-termism makes us miss the best target. When experts, writing in one of the flagship economic journals, describe the policy toolkit for innovation, they look at "tax policies [that] favor research and development, government research grants, policies aimed [at] increasing the supply of human capital focused on innovation, intellectual property policies, and pro-competitive policies."[26] Corporate governance and

---

[23] Steve Andriole, *Artificial Intelligence, China and The U.S.—How the U.S. Is Losing the Technology War*, Forbes, Nov. 9, 2018. AI government support as a vital public good has not gone unnoticed. Executive Office of the President, National Science Technology Council, Comm. on Technology, Preparing for the Future of Artificial Intelligence 1–4, 40 (2016), https://obamawhitehouse. archives.gov/sites/default/files/whitehouse_files/microsites/ostp/NSTC/preparing_for_the_future_of _ai.pdf; World Intellectual Property Organization, Technology Trends 2019, Artificial Intelligence 16 (2019), https://www.wipo.int/edocs/pubdocs/en/wipo_pub_1055.pdf. Chris Cornillie, *Finding Artificial Intelligence Money in the Fiscal 2020 Budget*, Bloomberg Government, Mar. 28, 2019. The line between government and the private sector is not bright in China. Private and state-owned enterprises in China should both be expected to follow a government lead.

[24] Cong. Budget Office, Estimated Impact of Automatic Budget Enforcement Procedures Specified in the Budget Control Act 1 (2011), www.cbo.gov/sites/default/files/112th-congress-2011-2012/reports/09-12-BudgetControlAct_0.pdf; Damian Paletta & Janet Hook, *Cuts Roll In as Time Runs Out*, Wall St. J., Feb. 28, 2013. For an early negative view of sequestration's hit to R&D: Rafael Reif & Craig Barret, *Science Must Be Spared Washington's Axe*, Fin. Times, Feb. 25, 2013.

[25] For the fall in government R&D spending, see Figure 4.1 and the underlying OECD data. The US sequestration eroded subsequently, with some prior cuts restored. *See Understanding Sequester: An Update for 2018*, House Comm. on the Budget (Mar. 12, 2018), https://budget.house.gov/publications/report/ understanding-sequester-update-2018.

[26] Nicholas Bloom, John Van Reenen & Heidi Williams, *A Toolkit of Policies to Promote Innovation*, 33 J. Econ. Persp. 163, 163–64 (2019). The authors do not excuse management, however. "[M]any firms are well behind the technological frontier, and helping these firms catch up—for, example, by improving management practices—would [improve American productivity]." *Id.* at 164.

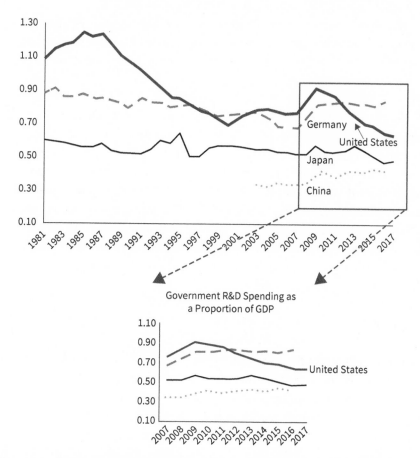

Figure 4.2. Government R&D Spending as a Proportion of GDP in China, Germany, Japan, and the United States

Source: Gross Domestic Expenditure on R-D by Sector of Performance and Source of Funds, OECD: OECD.Stat, https://stats.oecd.org/viewhtml.aspx?datasetcode=GERD_SOF&lang=en (last accessed Apr. 29, 2020); Gross Domestic Product (GDP); Gross Domestic Product (GDP), OECD: OECD. Stat, https://stats.oecd.org/Index.aspx?DataSetCode=SNA_TABLE1 (last accessed Apr. 29, 2020).

corporate time horizons are not ranked low—they do not even make the list.[27] The experts turn to the weakened government footprint in basic research:

> [A]lthough [overall] U.S. R&D intensity has been stable since the mid-1960s, the composition of R&D spending has changed dramatically, as government funding has

[27] *See also* John Van Reenen, *Can Innovation Policy Restore Inclusive Prosperity in America? in* MAINTAINING THE STRENGTH OF AMERICAN CAPITALISM 116 (Melissa S. Kearney & Amy Ganz, eds., 2019) (Aspen Institute report); Ezekiel Emanuel, Amy Gadsden & Scott Moore, *How the U.S. Surrendered to China on Scientific Research*, WALL St. J., Apr. 19, 2019; Gruber & Johnson, *supra* note 20.

declined and private-sector funding has increased to fill the void . . . . Government tends to fund higher risk, basic research that private investors are often reluctant to take on. Therefore, public R&D investment tends to produce higher value, high-spillover inventions . . . .[28]

To check these academic experts' views further, I examined the most recent two dozen articles in the relevant category in the *Journal of Economic Literature*—the flagship overview journal of the US economics profession. Only three mentioned short-termism as relevant.[29] Perhaps innovation academics missed the negative impact of the stock market and need guidance from corporate experts. But the fact that stock market short-termism is widely blamed for faltering US R&D but nevertheless is not high on innovation academics' problem list—and generally not even on the list at all—is a noticeable piece of evidence that the short-term stock market thinkers are not aiming at the high-value target.

* * *

It's been convenient for corporate elites, for corporate America, and even for policymakers to believe that the source of declining investment and falling R&D is stock market short-termism. Corporate elites can blame the stock market and justify further autonomy for executives. This is a major theme in corporate lawmaking. Public policymakers who underfunded public R&D can sidestep culpability and blame the large corporation and the stock market. This mistaken belief takes too many eyes off the likelihood that US R&D slack is not in the corporate sector and not powerfully emanating from the stock market, but is in the drop in basic government-sponsored R&D.[30]

By blaming stock-market-driven corporate short-termism for the R&D shortfall, corporate elites and their facilitators have been doing a disservice to the US economy.

---

[28] Van Reenen, *supra* note 27, at 119.

[29] The *Journal of Economic Literature* category used was "Innovation, Research and Development, Technological Change, Intellectual Property Rights, category O3, from 2001 to 2019. The two dozen articles were published in the *Journal of Economic Literature*. Summaries can be found in the unpublished Appendix.

[30] Hence, the Biden Administration's recently proposed (as I finalize this book) boost to basic research of $180 billion, as part of its big $3.5 trillion infrastructure proposal, is the best big first step for better US R&D. The White House Briefing Room, Fact Sheet: The American Jobs Plan, Mar. 31, 2021, www.whitehouse.gov/briefing-room/statements-releases/2021/03/31/fact-sheet-the-american-jobs-plan/. We shall see whether Congress enacts it.

PART II
ANALYZING THE STOCK MARKET'S IMPACT

5

Concept and Evidence for Stock-Market-Driven Short-Termism

Finding a well-lit path from the academic evidence on stock market short-termism to policy is impeded by the divided academic evidence. A simple count reveals that articles in finance journals for the past dozen years are about evenly split between those finding evidence of stock-market-induced short-termism and those not detecting any. The unpublished Appendix shows the division. This division is in itself a consideration for policymakers: why does the public debate assume a severe short-termism, despite the divided academic evidence?

Worse yet, the usual academic inquiry is well-tuned to examining a local situation, not an economy-wide one. But for policymaking the economy-wide impact counts most. If one sector fails to undertake enough long-term R&D, we want to know whether another picks up the slack. If so, and if the net short-termism result in the economy is minor, there's no compelling policy remedy required. Most research is not aiming to answer that question (and cannot readily do so). We'll see why.

In Chapter 2 we saw the economy-wide trends. In this chapter, as well as in Chapters 6 and 7, I examine the firm-level evidence for and against stock market short-termism. I do so because this evidence is not generally evaluated overall, to see whether a single story emerges. In Chapter 7, I evaluate the overall evidence in two ways that have not been done. First, I examine both sides, for and against, to see which stands up better. Second, I consider the extent to which we can extrapolate from the firm-level to find a likely economy-wide degradation. It's surprisingly harder to do so than it might seem, which may be why it's not tried.

Not every reader will want to work through the studies and evaluate the overall academic terrain with me here. Those readers could turn to the final section of Chapter 7, where I summarize the academic evidence. But the cost of jumping to the end is avoiding confronting the evidence. The widespread opinions expressed in Chapter 1 that stock market short-termism is a serious economy-wide problem would be more persuasive if the academic evidence strongly supported the popular view, which it does not.

Those who want to see the state of the academic inquiry summarized first and then analyzed, study by study, will stay with me for the next three chapters.

A. Concept

The short-termism problem is self-evident to many observers. Traders set the stock price day-to-day, executives obsess over quarterly financial results, and activists, looking for a quick short-term profit themselves, push executives to keep their short-term stock price up. Executives worry that a short-term price drop will harm their compensation—or even take away their jobs.

Short-termism has another, more subtle channel. Because investors with small positions cannot justify spending research dollars to evaluate complex, long-term, technologically sophisticated information well, they rely on simple signals to evaluate their stock's worth. Quarterly earnings loom larger than they would otherwise, because of their simplicity.[1]

This information impediment arising from dispersed stock ownership—which Jeremy Stein brought forward during the 1980s takeover era[2] and several others, including Alex Edmans and myself, extended into other areas[3]—is the most likely channel for stock-market-induced short-termism. The argument (which I modify here from Stein's original formulation) is that firms'

---

[1] *See* Jeremy C. Stein, *Takeover Threats and Managerial Myopia*, 96 J. POL. ECON. 61 (1988); Jeremy Stein, *Efficient Capital Market, Inefficient Firm: A Model of Myopic Corporate Behavior*, 104 Q.J. ECON. 655 (1989); Patrick Bolton, Jose Scheinkman & Wei Xiong, *Executive Compensation and Short-Termist Behaviour in Speculative Markets*, 73 REV. ECON. STUD. 577 (2006). The poor transmission of information could lead managers to invest too much, however. *See* Lucian Arye Bebchuk & Lars A. Stole, *Do Short-Term Objectives Lead to Under- or Overinvestment in Long-Terms Projects?* 48 J. FIN. 719 (1993); Michal Barzuza & Eric Talley, *Long-Term Bias*, 2020 COLUM. BUS. L. REV. 104 (2020). But excess investment—which could be waste—does not engage policymakers in the same way as does short-termism.

[2] Stein, *Takeover Threats, supra* note 1; Stein, *Myopic Corporate Behavior, supra* note 1.

[3] MARK J. ROE, STRONG MANAGERS, WEAK OWNERS: THE POLITICAL ROOTS OF AMERICAN CORPORATE FINANCE 240 et seq. (1994); Alex Edmans, *The Answer to Short-Termism Isn't Asking Investors to be Patient*, HARV. BUS. REV., July 18, 2017, https://hbr.org/2017/07/the-answer-to-short-termism-isnt-asking-invest ors-to-be-patient.

subtle, technological, or proprietary information does not transmit well to dispersed stock markets. Those with small positions (including mutual funds owning only a few hundred thousand shares) cannot evaluate this complex information well, so they ignore it. Management, unable to convince investors of their company's excellent long-term prospects, terminates long-term projects for less profitable short-term ones. The stock price rises but some good projects fall by the wayside.

Whether this theoretical transmission mechanism actually induces widespread, as opposed to occasional, short-termism is another matter. And whether it does so in a way that severely degrades the national economy is yet another. Hence, the reason to look at the evidence.

The next sections summarize the bottom-line firm-level evidence in favor of stock-market-driven short-termism.

B. The Evidence in Favor: Comparing Public and Private Firms

Public and private firms. Some comparisons of public and private firms suggest that the public firms, owned by the stock market, invest less than their privately-held counterparts do.[4] Key personnel often leave shortly after firms go public, whereas the same personnel stay put at similar firms that stay private.[5] This pattern suggests that the newly public firm is unable to retain key personnel for the long-term.

Stock turnover in, and analysts of, public firms. Corporate managers whose stock turns over more often are more attuned to short-term thinking, as evidenced by their persistent reference to the short-term when they communicate with investors.[6]

Similarly, public firms with a wider following of broker-based stock market analysts generate fewer high impact patents than firms with a narrower following.[7] Because securities traders hold their stock for such a short duration, it's said that they look for strong corporate results quickly, so that they can sell

---

[4] John Asker, Joan Farre-Mensa & Alexander Ljungqvist, *Corporate Investment and Stock Market Listing: A Puzzle?* 28 REV. FIN. STUD. 342 (2015). *Cf.* Albert Sheen, *Do Public and Private Firms Behave Differently? An Examination of Investment in the Chemical Industry*, 55 J. FIN. & QUANT. ANAL. 2530 (2020) ("[P]rivate firms invest ... more efficiently than public firms").

[5] Shai Bernstein, *Does Going Public Affect Innovation?* 70 J. FIN. 1365 (2015).

[6] François Brochet, Maria Loumioti & George Serafeim, *Speaking of the Short-Term: Disclosure Horizon and Managerial Myopia*, 3 REV. ACCT. STUD. 1122 (2015).

[7] *See* Brian J. Bushee, *The Influence of Institutional Investors on Myopic Investment Behavior*, 73 ACCT. REV. 305, 328–29 (tbl. 7) (1998) ("transient institutional investor behavior leads to myopic R&D investment behavior"); Jie He & Xuan Tian, *The Dark Side of Analyst Coverage: The Case of Innovation*, 109 J. FIN. ECON. 856 (2013).

profitably.[8] Too many institutional investors seek to show strong short-run results to entice new money into their funds.[9] Pension fund managers similarly seek to show good short-term results so that they can renew their management contracts and obtain new business. Activist hedge fund managers are often compensated for immediate results.[10] And their investors, ongoing and potential, examine the activists' recent results.[11]

C. The Evidence in Favor: Investor Horizons, Activists' Actions, and Corporate Horizons

Private equity funds with shorter time horizons invest in firms at a later development stage than those with longer horizons,[12] shortening their expected wait until a payoff. There is evidence that markets underestimate long-term corporate cash flows[13] and that mispriced public firms invest in line with the time horizons of their major investors.[14]

Studies show executives managing, distorting, and sometimes manipulating short-term earnings.[15] Stock market long-term flows are discounted more heavily than short-term flows, of course, since a dollar in the distant future is less valuable than a dollar today. But the discounting of the future is too severe, it's said.[16] Corporate insiders obtain higher voting rights by using dual

---

[8] Alfred Rappaport, *The Economics of Short-Term Performance Obsession*, 61 FIN. ANALYSTS J. 65, 66 (2005).

[9] Andrew M. Clearfield, *"With Friends Like These, Who Needs Enemies?" The Structure of the Investment Industry and Its Reluctance to Exercise Governance Oversight*, 13 CORP. GOVERNANCE 114, 116–118 (2005).

[10] *See* Carl Ackermann, Richard McEnally & David Ravenscraft, *The Performance of Hedge Funds: Risk, Return, and Incentives*, 54 J. FIN. 833, 834 (1999); JOHN EATWELL & MURRAY MILGATE, THE FALL AND RISE OF KEYNESIAN ECONOMICS 117–18 (2011).

[11] *E.g.*, Roger L. Martin, *Yes, Short-Termism Really Is a Problem*, HARV. BUS. REV. (Oct. 09, 2015), hbr.org/2015/10/yes-short-termism-really-is-a-problem ("Hedge fund activists loom large in the discussion of short-termism."); Yvan Allaire & Mihaela E. Firsirotu, *Hedge Funds as Activist Shareholders: Passing Phenomenon or Grave-Diggers of Public Corporations?* (Jan. 27, 2007), ssrn.com/abstract=961828; Steven A. Rosenblum, *Hedge Fund Activism, Short-Termism, and a New Paradigm of Corporate Governance*, 126 YALE L.J. FORUM 538 (2017), www.yalelawjournal.org/forum/hedge-fund-activism-short-termism-and-a-new-paradigm-of-corporate-governance; Leo E. Strine, Jr., *Who Bleeds When the Wolves Bite? A Flesh-and-Blood Perspective on Hedge Fund Activism and Our Strange Corporate Governance System*, 126 YALE L.J. 1870, 1942–43 (2017).

[12] Jean-Noel Barrot, *Investor Horizon and the Life Cycle of Innovative Firms: Evidence from Venture Capital*, 63 MGMT. SCI. 3021 (2017).

[13] Angela Black & Patricia Fraser, *Stock Market Short-Termism—An International Perspective*, 12 J. MULTINATIONAL FIN. MGMT. 135 (2002).

[14] François Derrien, Ambrus Keckés & David Thesmar, *Investor Horizons and Corporate Policies*, 48 J. FIN & QUANT. ANAL. 1755 (2013).

[15] Sugata Roychowdhury, *Earnings Management through Real Activities Manipulation*, 42 J. ACCT. & ECON. 335 (2006); Daniel A. Cohen, Aiyesha Dey & Thomas Z. Lys, *Real and Accrual-Based Earnings Management in the Pre- and Post-Sarbanes Oxley Periods*, 83 ACCT. REV. 757 (2008).

[16] David Miles, *Testing for Short-Termism in the UK Stock Market*, 103 ECON. J. 1379 (1993); David Miles, *Testing for Short-termism in the UK Stock Market: A Reply*, 105 ECON. J. 1224 (1995); Andrew G. Haldane

class stock in initial public offerings to insulate themselves from stock market pressures. They assert that they do so to better manage for the long-term.[17]

One study shows Tobin's Q (the ratio of the firm's market value to its assets' replacement cost—a standard, rough measure of the value management adds to corporate assets) increasing after a hedge fund intervention but then falling thereafter.[18] And even that initial rise, the authors added, might simply be an ordinary regression to the mean for the underperforming firms that hedge funds target.[19] Having more short-term investors in a company was associated with R&D cuts that boosted stock price in the short run; but these firms suffered a weaker stock price later.[20]

These results point to hedge fund activists as sources of short-termism.

D. The Evidence in Favor: What Executives Say They Do

That executives manage their companies to the quarterly report is a common complaint. Multiple academic studies find short-termism resulting from quarterly reports.[21]

Corporate managers regularly bemoan the pressure they feel from shareholders for strong quarterly results.[22] To evaluate potential investments, they use hurdle rates that are higher than their own cost of capital (thereby leaving money on the table by failing to invest in good

---

& Richard Davies, The Short Long, Speech at the 29th Société Universitaire Européenne de Recherches Financières Colloquium: New Paradigms in Money and Finance 1 (May 10, 2011), www.bis.org/review/r110511e.pdf (cash flows 10 years ahead are discounted at rates more appropriate at 16 years or more in reality, and those more than 30 years ahead are hardly valued at all).

[17] Dual-class stock could be an instance of economy-wide offset. If dual class stock does, as its proponents argue, insulate the dual-class firm from pernicious stock market pressures, these firms may offset the shortfalls of the firms that do not use dual-class stock, meaning the net overall economy-wide impact is modest, or nil.

[18] Martijn Cremers, Erasmo Giambona, Simone M. Sepe & Ye Wang, Hedge Fund Activism and Long-Term Firm Value (working paper, 2018), www.ssrn.com/abstract=2693231 (hedge fund campaigns degrade stakeholder relations that are important for long-term value creation and they reduce innovation).

[19] Id. at 11, 15.

[20] Martijn Cremers, Ankur Pareek & Zacharias Sautner, Short-Term Investors, Long-Term Investments, and Firm Value: Evidence from Russell 2000 Index Inclusions, 66 MGMT. SCI. 4535 (2020). Related work concludes that stock market pricing responds slowly to positive R&D spending. Allan C. Eberhart, William F. Maxwell & Akhtar R. Siddique, An Examination of Long-Term Abnormal Stock Returns and Operating Performance Following R&D Increases, 59 J. FIN. 623 (2004).

[21] See the unpublished Appendix. While the overall line-up is about evenly split, quarterly reporting is more often associated in the studies with short-termism, and shareholder activism is associated less often with short-termism.

[22] John Graham, Campbell R. Harvey & Shiva Rajgopal, The Economic Implications of Corporate Financial Reporting, 40 J. ACCT. & ECON. 3 (2005); Claire L. Marston & Barrie M. Craven, A Survey of Corporate Perceptions of Short-Termism among Analysts and Fund Managers, 4 EUR. J. FIN. 233 (1998).

longer-term projects).[23] And they bluntly state that they would give up shareholder value to report better earnings.[24] The major study of this phenomenon, from John Graham, Campbell Harvey, and Shiva Rajgopal—a star team of economists—is simple, powerful, and well-known. They surveyed chief financial officers and found that "an astonishing 78 percent [of the responding executives] *admit* that they would sacrifice . . . value to achieve a smooth earnings path."[25]

This finding has been regularly repeated with more than 2,000 citations in the academic literature[26] and has received media attention that academic papers rarely get.[27] The study is viewed positively in the academic world and as substantial proof of severe stock-market-induced short-termism in the media; as one academic citation reports: "a startling 80 percent [of executives surveyed] . . . said they would decrease value-creating spending on [R&D], advertising, maintenance, and hiring in order to meet earnings benchmarks[.]"[28]

Since the *executives themselves* say they'll sacrifice the long-term, that ought to be the opening presumption. Does it not make sense to accept the testimony

---

[23] James M. Poterba & Lawrence H. Summers, *A CEO Survey of US Companies' Time Horizons and Hurdle Rates*, 37 SLOAN MGMT. REV. 43 (1995).

[24] John Graham, Campbell R. Harvey & Shiva Rajgopal, *Value Destruction and Financial Reporting Decisions*, 62 FIN. ANALYSTS. J., Nov.–Dec. 2006, at 27.

[25] *Id.* at 47 (emphasis supplied.)

[26] A Scopus search run on March 1, 2021, showed 2,031 academic citations to the Graham et al. study—a large number and the largest of the more than 50 such short-termism studies. Scopus shows the other studies analyzed in Chapters 5, 6, and 7 also to be, for the most part, often cited.

[27] *See, e.g.*, Eilene Zimmerman, *The Risk and Rewards of Short-Termism*, N.Y. TIMES, Nov. 4, 2015, at F10 ("more than 75 percent of executives acknowledged that for a short-term lift in share price they would sacrifice long-term economic value"); Dwyer Gunn, *Is Our Focus on Quarterly Earnings Hurting the U.S. Economy?* PAC. STAND., June 12, 2018 ("In a widely cited 2005 . . . ."); Alana Samuels, *How to Stop Short-Term Thinking at America's Companies*, THE ATLANTIC, Dec. 30, 2016; Justin Lahart, *Street Sleuth: Corner Office Thinks Short-Term*, WALL ST. J., Apr. 14, 2004 ("[M]ost U.S. companies would go for the short-term target. So say the results of a survey by professors at Duke University's Fuqua School of Business and the University of Washington."); Jason Zweig, *The End of Quarterly Reporting? Not Much to Cheer About*, WALL ST. J., Aug. 17, 2018 ("In a 2003 survey . . ."); Barry Ritholtz, *CEO Pay Rewards What Was Going to Happen Anyway*, BLOOMBERG VIEW (Mar. 8, 2018, 7:00 AM), https://www.bloomberg.com/opinion/articles/2018-03-08/ceo-pay-rewards-share-price-increases-that-would-happen-anyway ("'78% of our sample admits to sacrificing long-term value to smooth earnings.'"); Joe Nocera, *A Defense of Short-Termism*, N.Y. TIMES, July 29, 2006 ("[Graham et al.] discovered that almost 80 percent . . . said they 'would decrease discretionary spending' in such critical areas as research and development, advertising and maintenance if they needed to do so to make the quarterly numbers."); Tensie Whelan, *Trump is Right: Quarterly Earnings Reports Should Go*, CNN MONEY (Aug. 23, 2018), https://money.cnn.com/2018/08/23/news/trump-quarterly-reporting/index.html ("[A] study published in The *Journal of Accounting and Economics* found that 78% of CFOs would sacrifice long-term value to make their quarterly earnings targets."); Geoff Colvin, *Amazon Earnings: Maybe Investors Aren't Obsessed with Short-Term Gains?*, FORTUNE, Oct. 23, 2015.

[28] ALFRED RAPPAPORT, SAVING CAPITALISM FROM SHORT-TERMISM 13 (2011). And *id.* at 62 ("astonishing"). At least one regression-based study points in a similar direction. Firms that just miss earnings-per-share projections buy back more shares, decrease employment somewhat, and invest less than firms that just beat earnings-per-share estimates. Heitor Almeida, Vyacheslaw Fos & Mathias Kronlund, *The Real Effects of Share Repurchases*, 119 J. FIN. ECON. 168 (2016).

of the actual players that they are all (well, 78% of them) short-termers? I long considered it to be one of the major pieces of evidence—and maybe the most major—showing substantial stock-market-driven short-termism.

E. The Evidence in Favor: Summary

The following recently-written passage summarizes prominent evidence from strong academics supporting the idea that short-termism is pernicious and excessive. I can do little better than to repeat it:

> [A]n extensive . . . literature stud[ies] the role of myopia in finance. Asker, Farre-Mensa, and Ljungqvist (2015) study the consequences of short-termism for investment decisions by investigating the difference between public and private firms. They find that private firms invest more than public firms and are more responsive to investment opportunities. Edmans, Fang, and Lewellen (2016) develop a measure of managerial short-termism based on the impending vesting of CEO equity and tie this to reductions in investment. Ladika and Sautner (2016) use the implementation of FAS 123R, which required option compensation to be expensed, to show that executives with more short-term incentives spend less on long-term investment. . . . Relative to this literature, we find that one of the key determinants of myopic behavior, the incentive to meet short-term earnings benchmarks, is transmitted from the financial sector to the corporate sector through financing relationships.[29]

* * *

Thus, serious empirical studies show that stock market short-termism affects corporate decision-making. Corporate managers say they give up real opportunities to ensure that they make their quarterly numbers. Firms that go public tend to invest less than similar firms that do not. The most natural interpretation of this evidence is that short-termism is real and widespread.

Is there strong firm-by-firm evidence to the contrary?

---

[29] Andrew Bird, Aytekin Ertan, Stephen A. Karoyli & Thomas G. Ruchti, *Short-termism Spillovers from the Financial Industry*, REV. FIN. STUD. (forthcoming). The studies summarized in the quotation are: John Asker, Joan Farre-Mensa & Alexander Ljungqvist, *Corporate Investment and Stock Market Listing: A Puzzle?* 28 REV. FIN. STUD. 342; Alex Edmans, Vivian W. Fang & Katharina A. Lewellen, *Equity Vesting and Managerial Myopia*, 30 REV. FIN. STUD. 2229 (2017); Igor Salitskiy, Compensation Duration and Risk Taking (Sept. 6, 2015), ssrn.com/abstract=2656870; Tomislav Ladika & Zacharias Sautner, *Managerial Short-Termism and Investment: Evidence from Accelerated Option Vesting*, 24 REV. FIN. 305 (2020).

6

Concept and Evidence against Stock-Market-Driven Short-Termism

Considerable firm-level evidence points to stock market short-termism being no more than minimal, in contrast to the evidence discussed in Chapter 5. As I've said, the academic work is divided.

Focus first on trading: critics think that because short-term stock price matters greatly for traders, it must matter as much to the companies' executives. But trading does not remove capital from the company; someone sells, yes, but someone else buys that stock. The investment stays inside the company. For the traders' pricing to be important, the trader's time horizon needs a transmission channel into the corporation. Otherwise the executives could just ignore traders who buy and sell stock every nanosecond. Why could executives ignore the traders? Because the traders own their stock for such a short period, they do not seek to affect corporate decision-making.[1]

Perhaps instead the channel from traders' horizons into the firm is that the trading worries executives because it affects their compensation and the immediate price of the stock. (Whether traders can depress stock price much or for long is subject to dispute.) But if that's the worry, directors could cut that purported short-termism transmission into the firm by tying compensation more to longer-term stock price (as they have tended to do in more in recent years).

Second, the fact of increased trading needs to be interpreted properly. Trading does not in itself deny capital to the firm, as just said. For every trader

---

[1] *Cf.* Mark J. Roe, Strong Managers, Weak Owners: The Political Roots of American Corporate Finance 240 et seq. (1994).

abandoning the company, there's an investor supporting it by buying its stock. The stock market's horizon is longer than that of the trader who sells. And while some traders trade more rapidly now, *other* shareholders trade less.[2] Some—especially the growing index funds that buy and hold—hardly trade at all.[3]

Third, the activists who seek to affect firms typically buy only 5–10% of a target company's stock. That's not enough to dictate to a target company. If the activist acts alone, it lacks the votes to replace the target firm's directors, who consequently could ignore the activist. Some directors do ignore activists. To be influential, the activist must persuade institutional investors to support its program. Many institutional investors, however, are long-term stockholders, like index funds that own a slice across the entire stock market index and own it for the long-term; they have little reason to support a short-term effort that degrades the company over the long-run. As Ronald Gilson and Jeffrey Gordon have shown, the activism process resembles a proposal coming from the activists that, to be influential, the institutional investors must ratify.[4] I add to their analysis that this structure is also a bulwark against excessively short-term activists. Activists who are perniciously too short-term will fail to sell their short-term program to these longer-term institutional investors, and if they fail to convince those long-term investors, who have votes, the activists cannot much influence the target firm.

Fourth, shareholder activists are said to be short-term oriented and looking for a quick sale. But, those who buy the stock from them pay a price reflecting their own estimation of the company's value. If the activist had visibly damaged the firm's long-run prospects, then the activist would be paid less for the stock.

Fifth, even relentlessly short-term focused activists who will not own their stock for long do not *want* their companies to lose out in the long-term—they

---

[2] Paul H. Edelman, Wei Jiang & Randall S. Thomas, *Will Tenure Voting Give Corporate Managers Lifetime Tenure?* 97 Tex. L. Rev. 991 (2019); Jarrad Harford, Ambrus Kecskés & Sattar Mansi, *Do Long-term Investors Improve Corporate Decision Making?* 50 J. Corp. Fin. 424, 430 (fig. 2) (2018) (volume of long-term investors steady over time); Mark J. Roe, *Corporate Short-Termism—In the Boardroom and in the Courtroom*, 68 Bus. Law. 977, 986–87, 998–1001 (2013); Martijn Cremers & Ankur Pareek, *Patient Capital Outperformance: The Investment Skill of Highly Active Share Managers Who Trade Infrequently*, 122 J. Fin. Econ. 288, 293 (2016).

[3] More specifically, much increased trading comes from a fringe of program traders who turn over their stock rapidly. But the United States' core shareholding institutions are pension funds and mutual funds, which together own about half or more of the country's public stock, and the duration of their holding stock has *increased* during the quarter-century starting in 1985.

The short-termist critics could recast their idea, however—which is why this analysis is in a footnote, not the text. The typical holding duration has not shortened, they could concede, but it is *still* too short and the *influence* of those still-too-short-term shareholders has increased.

[4] Ronald J. Gilson & Jeffrey N. Gordon, *The Agency Costs of Agency Capitalism: Activist Investors and the Revaluation of Governance Rights*, 113 Colum. L. Rev. 863, 896 (2013).

just want to win big in the short-term. Yet because companies' long-term value often follows short-term value, as Lucian Bebchuk has said, even short-term activists often will (even if only unintentionally) promote their companies' long-term success.[5]

A. The R&D Evidence

Several economists' studies are inconsistent with the widespread idea that institutional investors cause corporate short-termism in R&D. In the first major study of the issue, Brian Bushee found that "managers are less likely to cut R&D to reverse an earnings decline when institutional ownership is high, implying that institutions are sophisticated investors who typically serve a monitoring role in reducing pressures for myopic behavior."[6] "Indeed," say two prominent researchers, Sunil Wahal and John McConnell, "we document a positive relation between industry-adjusted expenditures for [property, plant, and equipment] and R&D[, on the one hand,] and the fraction of shares owned by institutional investors[, on the other]."[7] After analyzing "corporate expenditures for property, plant and equipment (PP&E) and research and development (R&D) for over 2500 US firms[,]" they conclude that "[w]e find no support for the contention that institutional investors cause corporate managers to behave myopically."[8]

Other prominent researchers conclude that "[c]ontrary to the view that institutional ownership induces a short-term focus in managers, we find that their presence boosts innovation . . . ."[9] Particularly when managers are *less* entrenched and less isolated from shareholders, investors induce the firm to innovate more effectively.[10] These findings thus imply the opposite of the short-termism analysts' common policy prescription of giving executives and boards more discretion to act independently of shareholders. Executives with more discretion invest less and do less R&D. Alon Brav, Wei Jiang, Song Ma,

---

[5] Lucian Bebchuk, *The Myth that Insulating Boards Serves Long-Term Value*, 113 COLUM. L. REV. 1637, 1663–64 (2013).

[6] Brian J. Bushee, *The Influence of Institutional Investors on Myopic R&D Investment Behavior*, 73 ACCT. REV. 305, 305 (1998).

[7] Sunil Wahal & John J. McConnell, *Do Institutional Investors Exacerbate Managerial Myopia?* 6 J. CORP. FIN. 307, 307 (2000).

[8] *Id.*

[9] Philippe Aghion, John Van Reenen & Luigi Zingales, *Innovation and Institutional Ownership*, 103 AM. ECON. REV. 277, 302 (2013). For similar results, of greater institutional investor involvement inducing higher managerial efficiency, *see* Ghasan A. Baghdadi et al., *Skill or Effort?: Institutional Ownership and Managerial Efficiency*, 91 J. BANK & FIN. 19 (2018).

[10] *Id.*

and Xuan Tian show that hedge fund activism improves R&D results in the five years after the activist engagement.[11] Institutional ownership is associated with higher R&D intensity[12] and firms that become *more* insulated from financial markets *reduce* long-term R&D investments.[13]

Takeover protection and insulation from aggressive shareholders are prominent policy prescriptions here. If the insulation prescription were correct, then isolating boards and management from takeovers, as occurred in the 1980s and 1990s, would have induced higher R&D. Although two studies fit this view,[14] at least as many studies find no such R&D increases following takeover protection.[15] Recent studies find that patents and innovation *decrease* "for firms incorporated in states that pass antitakeover laws relative to firms incorporated in states that do not."[16]

---

[11] Alon Brav, Wei Jiang, Song Ma & Xuan Tian, *How Does Hedge Fund Activism Reshape Corporate Innovation?* 130 J. Fin. Econ. 237 (2018) (R&D expense down, R&D results up); Tingfeng Tang, *Hedge Fund Activision and Corporate Innovation*, 85 Econ. Modelling 335 (2020).

[12] Gary S. Hansen & Charles W. Hill, *Are Institutional Investors Myopic? A Time-Series Study of Four Technology-Driven Industries*, 12 Strategic Mgmt. J. 1 (1991). To the same effect: Barry D. Baysinger, Rita D. Kosnick & Thomas A. Turk, *Effects of Board and Ownership Structure on Corporate R&D Strategy*, 34 Acad. Mgmt. J. 205, 205–14 (1991); Peggy M. Lee & Hugh M. O'Neill, *Ownership Structures and R&D Investments of U.S. and Japanese Firms: Agency and Stewardship Perspectives.* 46 Acad. Mgmt. J. 212, 212–25 (2003); Jennifer Francis & Abbie Smith, *Agency Costs and Innovation: Some Empirical Evidence*, 19 J. Acct. & Econ. 383, 383–409 (1995); Li Li Eng & Margaret Shackell, *The Implications of Long-Term Performance Plans and Institutional Ownership for Firms' Research and Development (R&D) Investments*, 6 J. Acct., Audit. & Fin. 117 (2001).

[13] "[Our] results contradict the managerial myopia hypothesis: firms significantly decrease R&D intensity relative to industry R&D intensity following an antitakeover amendment." Lisa K. Meulbroek, Mark L. Mitchell, J. Harold Mulherin, Jeffry M. Netter & Annette B. Poulsen, *Shark Repellents and Managerial Myopia: An Empirical Test*, 98 J. Pol. Econ. 1108, 1115 (1990). Several studies in this and note 12 are from about three decades ago. What once was not detrimental could now be.

[14] William N. Pugh, Daniel E. Page & John S. Jahera, Jr., *Antitakeover Charter Amendments: Effects on Corporate Decisions*, 15 J. Fin. Res. 57 (1992); Ali R. Malekzadeh, Victoria B. McWilliams & Nilanjan Sen, Antitakeover Amendments, Ownership Structure, and Managerial Decisions: Effects on R&D Expenditure (working paper, St. Cloud State University, 2005). *Cf.* Andrei Shleifer & Lawrence H. Summers, *Breach of Trust in Hostile Takeovers*, *in* Corporate Takeovers: Causes and Consequences 33 (Alan J. Auerbach ed., 1988) (lower managerial incentives to invest in innovation, managerial effort, and firm-wide human capital when shareholders have strong takeover power).

[15] Ravi Jain & Sonia Wasan, *Adoption of Antitakeover Legislation and R&D Expenditure*, 6 Investment Mgmt. & Fin. Innovations 63 (2009); Paul Mallette, *Antitakeover Charter Amendments: Impact on Determinants of Future Competitive Position*, 17 J. Mgt. 769 (1991); Mark S. Johnson & Ramesh P. Rao, *The Impact of Antitakeover Amendments on Corporate Financial Performance*, 32 Fin. Rev. 659 (1997).

[16] Julian Atanassov, *Do Hostile Takeovers Stifle Innovation? Evidence from Antitakeover Legislation and Corporate Patenting*, 68 J. Fin. 1097 (2013); Meulbroek et al., *supra* note 13, at 1108; James M. Mahoney, Chamu Sundaramurthy & Joseph T. Mahoney, *The Effects of Corporate Antitakeover Provisions on Long-Term Investment: Empirical Evidence*, 18 Managerial Decision Econ. 349 (1997) ("This paper's empirical results indicate that the average effect of antitakeover provisions on subsequent long-term investment is negative."). Associations between antitakeover laws and R&D associations are commonly reported. However, the corporate lawyer in me wants to discard them. Since the early 1990s (although not necessarily before), target firm boards can put in place the most potent antitakeover mechanisms themselves and need no further state corporate law authorization to do so. On the problems of using state takeover laws as the independent variable, see John C. Coates IV, *Takeover Defenses in the Shadow of the Pill: A Critique of the Scientific Evidence*, 79 Tex. L. Rev. 271 (2000); Emiliano M. Catan & Marcel Kahan, *The Law and Finance of Antitakeover Statutes*, 68 Stan. L. Rev. 655 (2016). *See also* Holger Spamann, On Inference When Using

Moreover, increased institutional investor ownership is associated with *greater* innovation, as measured by patent intensity, and more innovative "home runs." Investors who trade pressure executives to innovate even if the innovation fails to produce an immediate accounting profit.[17] More institutional investor stockholding is associated with more R&D[18] and "[i]nstitutional [investor] activism increased R&D inputs over both the short and long terms."[19] *More* analysts for a company—meaning more intense stock market scrutiny and presumably more pressure to meet or beat short-term projections—lead to *more* investment and higher R&D spending.[20] That's not what short-term theory would predict.

Lastly, R&D spending is an investment in the company's future. Recent results indicate that public firms invest *more* overall in R&D than corresponding private firms (contrary to evidence reported in the previous chapter).[21]

B. The Hedge Fund Activism Evidence

Activist hedge fund engagements are followed by *higher* long-term stock prices for the activists' targets, the bulk of the activism studies find. Targets

---

State Corporate Laws for Identification (Jan. 2020), www.ssrn.com/abstract=3499101; Andrew Baker, David F. Larcker & Charles C.Y. Wang, How Much Should We Trust Staggered Difference-In-Differences Estimates (Mar. 2021), www.ssrn.com/abstract=3794018.

[17] Aghion, Van Reenen & Zingales, *supra* note 9, at 277, 278.

[18] *Id.* at 278–79, which summarizes:

> [There are few studies of] the role played by institutional investors in the R&D process of publicly traded firms. The small existing empirical evidence suggests the impact of institutional investors is positive. For example, [one study] find[s] a positive correlation between ownership concentration (which includes institutions) and R&D expenditures, and [a second] finds a positive correlation of institutions with R&D. In a similar vein, [a third] finds that companies with greater institutional ownership are less likely to cut R&D following poor earnings performance.

[19] David Parthiban, Michael A. Hitt & Javier Gimeno, *The Influence of Activism by Institutional Investors on R&D*, 44 ACAD. MGMT. J. 144 (2001). Similarly, see Eng & Shackell, *supra* note 12, at 117–39 ("holdings by institutional investors are positively and significantly associated with R&D intensity"); Ricky W. Scott, *Do Institutional Investors Influence R&D Investment Policy in Firms with High Information Asymmetry?* 7 INT'L BUS. RES. 22 (2014) ("Institutional investors encourage higher R&D investment primarily in firms with high information asymmetry indicating they have an advantage in discerning the value of R&D investments in such firms.").

[20] François Derrien & Ambrus Kecskés, *The Real Effects of Financial Shocks: Evidence from Exogenous Changes in Analyst Coverage*, 68 J. FIN. 1407, 1408, 1424 (tbl. III, panel B) (2013) (poor information flow due to weak analyst coverage leads to a rise in the cost of capital, making investment more expensive). For the same result on property, plant and equipment increasing (but with no finding on R&D), see John A. Doukas, Chansog Kim & Christos Panzalis, *Do Analysts Influence Corporate Financing and Investment?* 37 FIN. MGMT. 303 (2008). The findings are not unanimous, however, see Jie He & Xuan Tian, *The Dark Side of Analyst Coverage: The Case of Innovation*, 109 J. FIN. ECON. 856 (2013).

[21] Naomi Feldman, Laura Kawano, Elena Patel, Nirumpama Rao, Michael Stevens & Jesse Edgerton, *Investment Differences Between Public and Private Firms: Evidence from U.S. Tax Returns*, 196 J. PUB. ECON. 1 (art. 104370, 2021).

lagged behind their peers before the activists acted and lagged less or caught up afterward.[22] The resulting hedge fund profits do not seem to be short-term artifacts: the target firms are altered for the better for shareholders.[23] Moreover, the targets' competitive rivals strengthen their production and sharpen their pricing. This impact on the targets' rivals fits best with the inference that the hedge funds make their targets more effective competitors for the short- and long-run.[24] Activism's invigorating of competition is good for the US economy, in both the short- and long-run.

C. Stock Market Valuations: Apple and Amazon

Consider again the nature of the business of the biggest public firms in the United States. The five US companies *most strongly supported* by the stock market in 2020 were Amazon, Apple, Alphabet (Google), Facebook, and Microsoft—all quintessential long-term companies, as I said in the Introduction. Their current earnings cannot justify their persistently high stock price; only a belief that they will grow over the long-term can. Each has technologies and products that stock markets expect will be more valuable in the future.

Amazon's CEO has been aggressive on the issue:

In 1997, the year Amazon.com went public, its chief executive, Jeff Bezos, issued a manifesto: "It's all about the long term," he said. He warned shareholders "we may make decisions and weigh tradeoffs differently than some companies" and urged them to make sure that a long-term approach "is consistent with your investment policy." Amazon's management and employees "are working to build something important, something that matters to our customers, something that we can tell our grandchildren about," he added.[25]

---

[22] Matthew R. Denes, Jonathan M. Karpoff & Victoria B. McWilliams, *Thirty Years of Shareholder Activism: A Survey of Empirical Research*, 44 J. CORP. FIN. 405 (2017) ("We summarize . . . 73 studies [and conclude that activism with] significant stockholdings[] is associated with improvements in share values and firm operations . . . [and] has become more value increasing over time."); Lucian A. Bebchuk, Alon Brav & Wei Jiang, *The Long-Term Effects of Hedge Fund Activism*, 115 COLUM. L. REV. 1085, 1085 (2015); Alon Brav, Wei Jiang, Frank Partnoy & Randall S. Thomas, *Hedge Fund Activism, Corporate Governance, and Firm Performance*, 53 J. FIN. 1729, 1729 (2008).

[23] Jonathan B. Cohn, Stuart L. Gillan & Jay C. Hartzell, *On Enhancing Shareholder Control: A Dodd-Frank Assessment of Proxy Access*, 71 J. FIN. 1623 (2016). This study shows enhanced shareholder control benefiting stock prices.

[24] Hadiye Aslan & Praveen Kumar, *The Product Market Effects of Hedge Fund Activism*, 119 J. FIN. ECON. 226 (2016).

[25] James B. Stewart, *Amazon Says Long Term and Means It*, N.Y. TIMES, Dec. 17, 2011, at B1. *Cf.* Amir Bhide, *Efficient Markets, Deficient Governance*, HARV. BUS. REV., Nov.–Dec. 1994, at 128, 135.

D. IPOs and Stock Market Long-Termism

The nature of the IPO market of recent decades also suggests a long-term oriented stock market. Stock markets have been readier than ever before to support the initial public offering of not-yet-profitable firms.[26] Although fewer firms were going public in recent years (until 2020 when the pace picked up), more of those that did were unprofitable. Companies like Airbnb, DoorDash, Snowflake, Nikola, and ZoomInfo have recently successfully sold stock into public stock markets.[27] Financial markets were betting on the long run. Amazon, Facebook, and Google were not exceptions; they were the most successful. A hopelessly short-term stock market would not finance these firms or buy their stocks to the degree that it has.

---

[26] Jay Ritter, Initial Public Offerings: Updated Statistics tbls. 4b, 9, 12 & 12a (2017), https://site.warrington.ufl.edu/ritter/files/2017/03/IPOs2016Statistics_Mar29_2017.pdf; Eugene Fama & Kenneth R. French, *New Lists: Fundamentals and Survival Rates*, 73 J. Fin. Econ. 229, 245 (2004) (showing similar trend for 1973 to 2001). This possibility, and the related IPO evidence, is brought forward in Steven Kaplan, *Are U.S. Companies Too Short-Term Oriented? Some Thoughts*, 18 Innovation Pol'y & Econ. 107 (2018).

[27] Anne Sraders, *The IPO Market in 2020 Was "Record-breaking"—and 2021 Is Looking Just as Busy, Says NYS President*, Fortune, Dec. 1, 2020; James Titcomb, *Tech IPO Bonanza as $100bn of December Listings Set to Cap Record Breaking Year*, The Telegraph, Dec. 1, 2020.

7

Evaluating the Firm-Level Short-Termism Evidence

About five dozen studies in recent decades examine short-termism. Half find stock market short-termism, half do not.[1] In this chapter, I evaluate major studies on each side, several of which I discussed in Chapters 5 and 6.

Academic work targets evidence on whether or not a particular situation— e.g., missing earnings projections, exercising stock options, responding to activists—induces short-term actions. The research generally does not globally assess whether any detected local short-termism also means that the economy is overall too short-term. Hence, I ask two questions: Do the studies tell us that we have an economy-wide problem? And is one or the other side's evidence weaker (or stronger) than usually thought? On the latter question, I conclude yes: the studies failing to find significant stock-market-driven corporate short-termism are weightier.

A. Three Studies Finding Stock-Market-Driven Corporate Short-Termism

One study finding stock-market-driven corporate short-termism is particularly powerful.[2] John Graham, Campbell R. Harvey, and Shiva Rajgopal—all

---

[1] A table summarizing and categorizing the papers is in the unpublished Appendix.
[2] John Graham, Campbell R. Harvey & Shiva Rajgopal, *The Economic Implications of Corporate Financial Reporting*, 40 J. Acct. & Econ. 3 (2005); John Graham, Campbell R. Harvey & Shiva Rajgopal, *Value Destruction and Financial Reporting Decisions*, 62 Fin. Anal. J., Nov.–Dec. 2006, at 27.

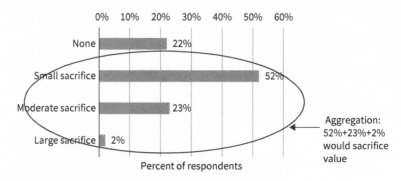

Figure 7.1. The Sacrifice: Nearly 80% Would Sacrifice Value

Source: John Graham, Campbell R. Harvey & Shiva Rajgopal, *The Economic Implications of Corporate Financial Reporting*, 40 J. Acct. & Econ. 3, 49 (2005).

leading financial researchers—surveyed executives, who reported that they would take actions to maintain stable reported short-term earnings even if doing so damaged the firm. The evidence, the researchers report, is "astonishing." After all, I'd add, the executives *themselves* admit they are operating in the short-run at longer-run cost. Why not take their confession at face value?

This study is widely referenced both in the media[3] and in academic research, with more than 2,000 academic citations.[4] Their core evidence is summarized in Figure 7.1. Executives were asked whether they would sacrifice value to avoid stock-performance-damaging earnings volatility. Nearly 80% said they would do so in order to stabilize reported earnings.

Academics (including me) have found a second study[5] particularly persuasive. John Asker, Joan Farre-Mensa, and Alexander Ljungqvist compare similar public and private firms and find that the public firms invest less than their private counterparts. Similar research strategies have returned analogous results.[6]

---

[3] *See, e.g.,* Eilene Zimmerman, *The Risk and Rewards of Short-Termism*, N.Y. Times, Nov. 4, 2015, at F10; Dwyer Gunn, *Is Our Focus on Quarterly Earnings Hurting the U.S. Economy?* Pacific Stand., June 12, 2018 ("In a widely cited 2005 paper that surveyed over 400 leaders . . . .").

[4] *See, e.g.,* Gustavo Manso, *Motivating Innovation*, 66 J. Fin. 1823, 1827 (2011); Sugata Roychowdhury, *Earnings Management through Real Activities Manipulation*, 42 J. Acct. & Econ. 335, 337–38 (2006) (managers manipulate earnings reports by temporarily increasing sales with aggressive price discounts and reducing discretionary expenditures); S. P. Kothari, Susan Shu & Peter D. Wysocki, *Do Managers Withhold Bad News?* 47 J. Acct. Res. 241, 243 (2009); Mariassunta Giannetti & Xiaoyun Yu, *Adapting to Radical Change: The Benefits of Short-Horizon Investors*, 67 Mgmt. Sci. 4032 (2021). The other studies, pro and con, that I highlight in this chapter are also generally well-cited.

[5] John Asker, Joan Farre-Mensa & Alexander Ljungqvist, *Corporate Investment and Stock Market Listing: A Puzzle?* 28 Rev. Fin. Stud. 342 (2015).

[6] Albert Sheen, *Do Public and Private Firms Behave Differently? An Examination of Investment in the Chemical Industry*, 55 J. Fin. & Quant. Anal. 2530 (2020) ("[P]rivate firms are more likely than public firms to increase capacity prior to a positive demand shock . . . [but] less likely to increase capacity before

A third study has been well-circulated among corporate academics. Martijn Cremers, Erasmo Giambona, Simone M. Sepe, and Ye Wang compare the stock price performance of activist-targeted firms to that of similar untargeted companies. "[T]arget stocks outperform control stocks [in the short-run], but underperform control stocks in the subsequent five years[.]"[7]

These three studies build a strong case for widespread stock market, activist-driven, quarterly-focused short-termism.

B. Three Studies Failing to Find Stock-Market-Driven Short-Termism

Persuasive studies also support the opposite conclusion.

Three sets of studies looked for evidence of financial market short-termism in the usually suspected places and could not find it. In the first, three leading economists—Philippe Aghion, John Van Reenen, and Luigi Zingales—examined whether the entry of institutional investors to a company's stockholder base led to the company decreasing its R&D.[8] It did not. Yet, if the stock market is inducing short-termism, a strong Wall Street presence should be associated with, and cause, cuts in R&D. Moreover, the study found that, contrary to common thinking, CEOs in firms with higher institutional ownership were *less* likely to be sacked after a profit setback than those in firms with lower institutional ownership. Institutional owners could better distinguish profit downturns due to bad luck from those due to managerial error; noninstitutional investors have less capacity to make such distinctions.[9]

---

a negative demand shock."); Shai Bernstein, *Does Going Public Affect Innovation?*, 70 J. Fin. 1365 (2015). Bernstein found key innovation personnel leaving the public firm shortly after the offering, which suggests an inability of the newly public firm to manage and create for the long-term. However, the public firms spent on R&D differently, principally by buying the research or buying companies that did the research the public firm needed.

[7] K.J. Martijn Cremers, Erasmo Giambona, Simone M. Sepe & Ye Wang, Hedge Fund Activism and Long-Term Firm Value 23 (working paper, 2018), www.ssrn.com/abstract=2693231. *Cf.* Martijn Cremers, Lubomir P. Litov & Simone M. Sepe, *Staggered Boards and Long-Term Firm Value, Revisited*, 126 J. Fin. Econ. 422 (2017).

[8] Philippe Aghion, John Van Reenen & Luigi Zingales, *Innovation and Institutional Ownership*, 103 Am. Econ. Rev. 277 (2013). For studies with similar conclusions, see Sunil Wahal & John J. McConnell, *Do Institutional Investors Exacerbate Managerial Myopia?* 6 J. Corp. Fin. 307, 307 (2000); Alon Brav, Wei Jiang, Song Ma & Xuan Tian, *How Does Hedge Fund Activism Reshape Corporate Innovation?* 130 J. Fin. Econ. 237 (2018) (firms that activists target cut R&D spending, but their R&D becomes more effective); Alon Brav, Wei Jiang, Frank Partnoy & Randall S. Thomas, *Hedge Fund Activism, Corporate Governance, and Firm Performance*, 53 J. Fin. 1729 (2008).

[9] *Cf.* Mark J. Roe, Strong Managers, Weak Owners: The Political Roots of American Corporate Finance 240 et seq. (1994); Alex Edmans, *Blockholder Trading, Market Efficiency, and Managerial Myopia*, 64 J. Fin. 2481 (2009).

In a second study, short-term investors facilitated adaptability. Short-term corporate decisions are not necessarily mistakes, of course. Adaptability when needed is valuable. In this study short-term investors were associated with better adaptation to a sharply changing economic environment.[10] Mariassunta Giannetti and Xiaoyun Yu describe how an economic shock, in their case a large tariff imposed on the firms' products, affected firm behavior. Firms with a short-term stockholder base reacted strongly and more quickly.[11]

In a third set of studies, one research team found that activist shareholder engagements led to better long-term outcomes for the targeted firms.[12] Lucian Bebchuk, Alon Brav, and Wei Jiang, expanding on an earlier foundational study by Brav, Jiang, Frank Partnoy, and Randall Thomas, examined firms that activist investors target, looking for long-term declines in performance. They found none. The targets lagged in their industry before the activists intervened but lagged less afterward. If activist investors were short-term, one would expect their targets to suffer in the long-term, but the researchers did not find this to be so. Earlier and later studies by some of the same authors yielded similar results.[13]

Competitive reaction in the targeted firms' markets points to the activists as improving their targets' performance. If activist interventions sacrificed the target firms' long-term prospects in order to obtain more short-term profit, then rival firms would benefit over the long run. But rivals of the activist's target sharpen their competitive game,[14] which implies that hedge funds make their targets stronger competitors.

Evidence on stock analysts' reactions also points to activists as not diminishing long-term performance. Analysts tend *not* to recommend the target firms' stocks *before* the activists intervene but do recommend them *after* the interventions. If activist interventions caused a long-term hit to the stock, then Wall Street stock analysts are persistently failing to learn from their mistakes. Such a failure to learn—and for their clients to stick with them despite these failures—is possible but would be surprising. And institutional

---

[10] Giannetti & Yu, *supra* note 4.

[11] Unlike the other articles highlighted in this chapter, this study is not widely cited, although I find its focus on short-term adaptability to be important. An alternative focus would be on the frequency of financial reporting—"quarterly capitalism." I discuss this further in Chapter 9 when evaluating remedies, one of which is to decrease financial reporting frequency.

[12] Lucian A. Bebchuk, Alon Brav & Wei Jiang, *The Long-Term Effects of Hedge Fund Activism*, 115 COLUM. L. REV. 1085 (2015).

[13] Brav, Jiang, Ma & Tian, *supra* note 8; Alon Brav, Wei Jiang, Frank Partnoy & Randall S. Thomas, *Hedge Fund Activism, Corporate Governance, and Firm Performance*, 43 J. FIN. 1729 (2008).

[14] Hadiye Aslan & Praveen Kumar, *The Product Market Effects of Hedge Fund Activism*, 119 J. FIN. ECON. 226 (2016). This dynamic fits with firms that do worse, by kicking away a good long-term opportunity, inducing competitors to pick up that opportunity.

investors buy stock of the targets *after* the activists intervene; again, if activists were unhealthy for the targets, then institutional investors are being system-atically fooled.[15]

* * *

Taken together, these studies weaken the likelihood that stock-market-driven short-termism is powerful and harming the US economy. Strong researchers look for short-termism where it should be found but do not find it. We thus have strong work by highly qualified researchers that reach opposite conclusions.

Which evidence is weightier?

C. The Six Studies, For and Against, Analyzed

The evidence for: what the executives say. Nearly 80% of US executives admit to their short-term orientation in the justly famous study. The authors charac-terize the finding as "astonishing," which it certainly seems to be.

Is this the best way to interpret the survey responses—as an astonishing example of short-termism? A closer examination of the study results leads us to interpret them as less astonishing than the 80% headline suggests. First, the survey's response rate was less than 15%.[16] Those who responded were not *randomly* chosen, possibly leading to a standard problem of selection bias. That is, it's plausible that executives feeling salient short-term pressure were more motivated to respond than those feeling no quarterly pressure. Many of the former could well have responded, while many of the latter could have tossed the survey papers into the wastebasket. The risk of a distorted selection effect is real, as the authors prominently warn.[17] But the authors' caution is

---

[15] Alon Brav, Wei Jiang, Frank Partnoy & Randall S. Thomas, *Hedge Fund Activism, Corporate Governance, and Firm Performance*, 53 J. Fin. 1729, 1731–32, 1753, 1772–73 (2008). *See also* Edward P. Swanson & Glen M. Young, Are Activist Investors Good or Bad for Business? Evidence from Capital Market Prices, Informed Traders, and Firm Fundamentals (unpublished manuscript, 2017); Glenn M. Young, Causes and Consequences of Shareholder Activism (2017) (Ph.D. dissertation, Texas A&M University), http://hdl.han dle.net/1969.1/165715. More generally, firms that analysts follow widely invest *more* in property, plant and equipment than weakly followed firms, and they spend more on R&D, suggesting that stock analyst scru-tiny was not inducing short-termism. François Derrien & Ambrus Kecskés, *The Real Effects of Financial Shocks: Evidence from Exogenous Changes in Analyst Coverage*, 68 J. Fin. 1407, 1408 (2013) (poor informa-tion flow due to weak analyst coverage raises capital costs, making investment more expensive).

[16] Graham, Harvey & Rajgopal, *Value Destruction, supra* note 2, at 27 (3,174 surveyed, 401 responded).

[17] Graham, Harvey & Rajgopal, *Economic Implications, supra* note 2, at 9, 10 n.5. The authors, aware of the problem, point out that they did not see a disproportionate response from those with an axe to grind be-cause early responders (who presumably were more motivated and with an axe to grind) reported no more short-termism than late responders. *Id.*

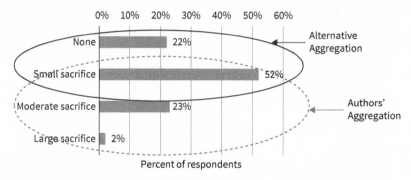

Figure 7.2. Reassessing the Sacrifice: 74% Refuse More than a Small Sacrifice

Source: For the distribution: John Graham, Campbell R. Harvey & Shiva Rajgopal, *The Economic Implications of Corporate Financial Reporting*, 40 J. Acct. & Econ. 49 (2005). The authors' aggregation is the dashed oval: 78% of the respondents would sacrifice value. The solid oval is an alternative aggregation: 74% of the respondents say that they'd make no more than a small sacrifice, or none at all.

dropped in follow-on media and policy analysis.[18]

The study's second impediment is more profound yet unexamined. Properly interpreting the severity of the local short-termism is crucial for informing policy. For policy purposes, the study could have been interpreted to indicate that we have no more than a *small* problem according to *three-fourths* of the executives responding! That, in my view, is the better interpretation of the study's famous core finding.

How could that be? The authors aggregated responses from corporate chief financial officers who said that they would make only a *small* sacrifice with those saying they would make a moderate or large sacrifice. That aggregation is correct, but is only one of several equally correct aggregations. Only a quarter of the respondents indicated that they would make more than a small sacrifice. And only 2% said they would make a large sacrifice.

That reframed result is just not so bad.

For policy purposes, the study could be interpreted—and I assert should be interpreted—to mean that the short-termism problem is small. With our economy and polity facing so many problems, policymakers should infer from this evidence that this kind of short-termism problem is not one to prioritize, as Figure 7.2 illustrates.

This more innocuous interpretation fits with an earlier and simpler yes-no survey on the issue that James Poterba and Lawrence Summers conducted.

---

[18] Ryan Beck & Amit Seru, *Short-Term Thinking is Poisoning American Business*, N.Y. Times, Dec. 21, 2019; Roger L. Martin, *Yes, Short-Termism Really is a Problem*, Harv. Bus. Rev., Oct. 9, 2015; William A. Galston, *Clinton Gets It Right on Short-termism*, Wall St. J., July 29, 2015.

Their responding executives said that they would *not* sacrifice value for short-term accounting results.[19]

Hence, the study's result is not the short-term steamroller it is often reported to be. The study evidences short-termism, yes, but, properly interpreted, it reveals short-termism to be only a minor problem. Yes, 78% said they'd sacrifice *some* value, but *only 2%* said their sacrifice would be large, and *74%* said they would sacrifice *no more than a small amount.* Properly interpreted, the study is just not saying that we have a large short-termism problem.

Moreover, the CFOs' testimony shows what the responding CFOs *believe.* But their beliefs may be incorrect[20] and their actions could be just what the company needs for the long run. Until pressured in the short run, some senior executives could avoid facing up to hard decisions to stabilize their company's long-run business. For example, another study finds *long-term* rewards for executives who meet or beat short-term earnings forecasts, indicating that the seemingly short-run action is a long-run positive.[21] And executive behavioral findings offer reason to question the link between executives' beliefs and their actions: successful executives are typically optimistic.[22] That optimism makes many executives reluctant to end weak projects. Overoptimistic executives in the famous survey could have believed that they were sacrificing profits when they were really ending bad investments. Terminating negative projects and moving to good ones is typically in the long-run interest of the firm.

Consider further why self-image and self-esteem could lead executives to overemphasize quarterly and stock market pressure. Executives do not relish laying off employees. And, even if not personally bothered by doing so, they should expect negative media coverage for themselves and their firm after layoffs.[23] Blaming financial markets and quarterly pressure can help with their own peace of mind. It allows the executives to cast themselves—for their own sense of self-worth and their own respect inside the company— as reluctant

---

[19] James M. Poterba & Lawrence H. Summers, *A CEO Survey of US Companies' Time Horizons and Hurdle Rates*, 37 Sloan Mgmt. Rev. 43, 48–49 (1995) (81% "of the respondents said that they had never passed up" a profitable investment "because the stock market might penalize the decision").

[20] Again, the authors make this clear, but subsequent renditions often do not.

[21] Eli Bartov, Dan Givoly & Carla Hayn, *The Rewards to Meeting or Beating Earnings Expectations*, 33 J. Acct. & Econ. 173 (2002).

[22] *Cf.* J.B. Heaton, *Managerial Optimism and Corporate Finance*, 31 Fin. Mgmt. 33 (2002).

[23] *See* Paul R. La Monica, *You're Fired. Stock Rises. Wall Street Loves Layoffs*, CNN Money: The Buzz (Oct. 1, 2013, 1:23 PM), http://buzz.money.cnn.com/2013/10/01/layoffs-stocks ("Wall Street encourages companies to keep slashing costs because investors like the higher earnings that come along with fewer workers"); Suzanne McGee, *Layoffs Make CEOs Look Like Heroes—That's Why Corporate America Is Sick*, The Guardian: US Money Blog (Jul. 24, 2014, 10:30 AM), www.theguardian.com/money/us-money-blog/2014/jul/24/corporate-america-sick-layoffs-ceos ("They're . . . opting to try to earn more money with fewer staff").

agents of nefarious forces ("the stock market made me do it") and not as the layoffs' primary instigators.[24]

Moreover, the frequent repetition of the study's dramatic bottom-line—that 78% would sacrifice value—suffers from the conceptual problem that I set forth earlier. Local firm-level short-termism could be offset elsewhere in the economy—with many competitive players having the incentives to do so. When told that 78% of the surveyed senior executives would sacrifice long-term profit, the policymaker and opinion-leader might mistakenly conclude that the authors definitively demonstrated a system-wide, difficult-to-offset problem. After all, 78% is a big number, large enough to cover nearly the entire public market. But the authors did not conclude that 78% of public firms *were* excessively short-term. They found that 78% believed they *would* sacrifice real value, presumably by underinvesting, *if* necessary to meet quarterly earnings projections. But not all firms give out earnings targets and most that do so do *not* miss them. Hence, the policy inferences from the study are far less powerful than a dramatic headline that 78% of public firms sacrifice value every quarter.

The evidence for short-termism: what public firms do. Recall next the Asker et al. study's principal finding: public firms invest less than similar private ones. This well-conducted study provides some of the strongest evidence that public firms are afflicted by short-termism. But is this study as powerful for policymaking as many academics, including me, have thought?

First, remember that our ultimate question here is whether there is a damaging *economy-wide* impact. The authors do not assess this question. Proposition (A)—that public firms invest less than private firms—differs from Proposition (B)—that lower public firm investment is holding the economy back.

A major reason why (A) differs from (B) is embedded in the core of the Asker et al. study: yes, the public firm invests less, but then *the matched private firm invests more.* The study does not establish whether the correct baseline is the investment level of the private or the public firm, or somewhere in the middle. For the Asker et al. study to be interpreted as indicating an economy-wide problem, we need to know whether the public or private firm is closer to the optimal investment level.

Second, policymakers should be cautious in taking the finding—that public firms systematically invest less than private firms—as assured. An earlier

---

[24] *See supra* Chapter 5. Moreover, several studies failed to find that accounting reports facilitate short-termism. David Marginson, Laurie McAulay, Melvin Rousch & Tony Van Zijl, *Performance Measures and Short-Termism: An Exploratory Study,* 40 ACCT. & BUS. RES. 353 (2010); David Marginson, 'Accounting Controls Cause Short-Termism': (Empirical) Fact or (Conceptual) Fiction? 16 IRISH ACCT. REV. 39 (2009).

study, with pre-2003 data, indicated that R&D spending changed in nature when a firm went public but R&D did not decline.[25] And a recent study, using a matching methodology like that of the Asker et al. study but with US corporate tax returns as the data source, found that public firms did not invest less.[26]

That later study is a substantial contradicting finding, pointing to the stock market as a source of longer-term funding, contrary to the implications of the Asker et al. study. This new study finds that "R&D investments . . . are approximately 50% higher for public firms relative to a set of observationally-similar private firms." (R&D is a kind of investment in the firm's future. Asker et al. focus on physical investments, not R&D, mostly because of their data sources.) This new result is consistent with the view that firms *often go public precisely to get better financing* to invest and expand, especially for long-term investment and for R&D that would be too risky for weakly-diversified private shareholders, and the public firms often do so with funding that is sometimes simply unavailable to the private firm.[27] This result suggests that policymakers should be cautious before jumping from the Asker et al. study to an anti-stock-market short-termism policy initiative.[28]

A third, conceptual aspect of the study impedes us from drawing a conclusion from the findings about the economy-wide impact of companies being public instead of private.[29] Successful firms that sell their stock often do so to raise money to invest and grow further.[30] If they grow rapidly and become very large, *they leave Asker et al.'s comparison set*, because the study compares *similarly sized* public and private firms. The comparison set retains *slowly moving public firms*, not the rapidly growing ones that invest most. Figure 7.3 illustrates; the study compares good, strong private firms to not-so-good, weak public ones.

---

[25] *See* Bernstein, *supra* note 6.

[26] Naomi Feldman, Laura Kawano, Elena Patel, Nirumpama Rao, Michael Stevens & Jesse Edgerton, *Investment Differences Between Public and Private Firms: Evidence from U.S. Tax Returns*, 196 J. Pub. Econ. 1 (art. 104370, 2021).

[27] *Id.* But while consistent, the study is observational and cannot exclude a selection effect—i.e., that firms that expect to invest intensely and do much R&D go public and firms that do not stay private. The study includes investment in R&D, which the Asker et al. study was unable to include.

[28] Financial flows are changing. Very large private companies—Uber comes to mind—can raise funds similarly to public firms. Whether this is substituting for the IPO'd firm financing channel or adding to it remains to be seen.

[29] It's a problem that the authors, leading finance economists, anticipate.

[30] Richard A. Brealey, Stewart C. Myers & Franklin Allen, Principles of Corporate Finance 396–97, 412–13 (13th ed., 2019) (raising additional cash, having a market for shares, and broadening the base of ownership are top reasons for firms to go public). For a recent real-world example, *see, e.g.,* Corrie Driebusch & Maureen Farrell, *Lyft is Planning to List Shares on Nasdaq*, Wall St. J., Feb. 20, 2019. Asker et al. anticipate an approximation of the problem ("our results may not generalize beyond smaller public firms"). They reject that possibility. Asker, Farre-Mensa & Ljungqvist, *supra* note 5, at 345.

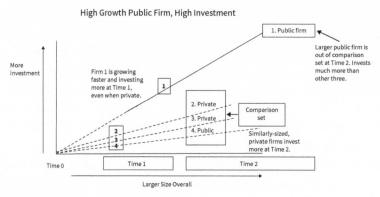

Figure 7.3. High Investment, High-R&D Firm Excluded from Public-Private Comparison Set

At Time 0, four retailers start up. By Time 1, all are still private, but Firm 1 is already investing more and is larger than the other three. At Time 2, Firms 1 and 4 are public. The fast-growing, high-investing Firm 1, which is public, invests much more than the other three, but it is already outside the comparison set, because it is no longer comparably-sized. Inside the similarly-sized matched set, the private firms invest somewhat more than the remaining similarly-sized public firm. The full set of private firms is compared to the more slowly growing public firm, not to the full set of public firms.

Consider four hypothetical internet retailers that set up their initial businesses in their owners' garages. All start small and in a few years two go public. One of these two then grows faster and is bolder and stronger. Within a year, that one has a major information-technology distribution operation that the others cannot match; that retailer becomes much larger than the other three, and its sales grow faster than the others. Call that company, say, Amazon. A few years later, this fast-growth company (Amazon) is tremendous in size, growth, and investment. A private retailer that was once the same size, however, is sluggish and has not grown.

The problem in moving from this study's results to a strong policymaking effort follows directly: when the study examines the relative investment intensity of similar public and private firms, it matches similar public and private firms so that the compared firms are similar. Huge firms differ from mid-sized firms, so the huge firm in the sample (Amazon) is excluded from the comparison set because there is no longer any comparably-sized private firm. The consequence is that the full set of private firms is compared only to more slowly growing public laggards.[31]

---

[31] The Feldman et al. (2021) study, *supra* note 26, which found public firms investing more in R&D and about as much physical capital, also matches similarly-sized firms. Hence, the true public-private difference may be even greater than it found, unless firms slack off from R&D and investment as they grow.

This conceptual fissure counsels caution in drawing strong policy conclusions from the study.

If no such public-firm growth stars existed, then this problem would be merely conceptual. However, Vojislav Maksimovic, Gordon Phillips, and Liu Yang recently found evidence of something similar. Some private firms grow rapidly from the get-go, then continue to grow rapidly in the years after they go public.[32] They too disappear from the public-private comparison, disrupting the comparison's importance for policymaking. Some firms, they found, were on a strongly upward trajectory from their founding and quickly disappear from the comparison set.

The evidence for short-termism: do hedge fund targets underperform nontargets? The Cremers et al. methodology matches firms targeted by hedge funds with similar firms that were not targeted and then compares their long-term results.[33] The targeted firms' stocks do worse over the longer run. Hedge fund activism thus damages targeted firms, they conclude.[34] And even if activists do well over the longer run, they might just be good at picking winners that were bound to turn around anyway, not by helping them to recover.

Matching studies are inherently difficult because it is hard for researchers to determine what dimensions need matching (industry? speed of decline? nature of ownership structure? size of firm? managerial features? capital structure of the firms?). For example, hedge funds may target the most stubborn firms that are not adjusting on their own. Those firms' transitions could be more difficult, costlier, and less likely to yield as much value as the firms whose managers are already adapting, and which activists leave alone. This makes the matching uneven. Still, the study adds weight to the short-termism-is-real side of the scale.[35]

* * *

[32] Vojislav Maksimovic, Gordon M. Phillips & Liu Yang, Do Public Firms Respond to Investment Opportunities More than Private Firms? The Impact of Initial Firm Quality (Mar. 1, 2020), http://ssrn.com/abstract=3093125.

[33] Cremers, Giambona, Sepe & Wang, *Hedge Fund Activism, supra* note 7.

[34] *Id.* at 21.

[35] The Bebchuk, Brav, and Jiang group, which had come up with competing and different conclusions, was unable to replicate an earlier version of the newer 2018 Cremers et al. study. Presumably the 2018 study handles the discrepancies.

The replication effort is described in Lucian Bebchuk, Alon Brav, Wei Jiang & Thomas Keusch, The Long-Term Effect of Hedge Fund Activism (Dec. 10, 2015), https://corpgov.law.harvard.edu/2015/12/10/the-long-term-effects-of-hedge-fund-activism-a-reply-to-cremers-giambona-sepe-and-wang.   Few studies here have been subjected to a replication effort.

The studies looking for, but failing to find, stock-market-driven short-termism have their own limits.

The evidence against short-termism: institutional investors and portfolio firms spending more on R&D. Institutional investor ownership correlates positively with R&D spending, Aghion, Van Reenen, and Zingales show, contradicting the idea that institutional investors induce more short-termism. The authors describe a hurdle their study faced, namely whether the institutions buy stock because they anticipate that a firm will spend more on R&D and then do well, or because more institutional ownership induces the firms to undertake more R&D. In other words, are the institutions just good stock pickers or are they making good things happen? By looking at firms just after they are included in an index, the authors assess whether institutions instigate more R&D spending. Indexes, such as the S&P 500—Standard & Poor's index of 500 prominent companies—provide common templates for institutional investors. When a company is included in an index more institutions usually automatically buy the stock. The authors classify index inclusion as exogenous to the firm's quality—i.e., institutions are not buying stock because they think the firm is doing good R&D.

But something else could be responsible for institutional investor ownership correlating with greater R&D spending. Growing companies could be more likely to make it into the index and growth could in itself attract more institutional investors to become stockholders. Growth could lead *simultaneously* to (1) inclusion in the index, (2) more institutional investor ownership, and (3) more R&D, without (1) or (2) causing (3). Rather, growth could directly cause each of the three. Underlying growth could be the omitted, but determinative, cause. And other researchers, using a similar methodology based on index inclusion got differing results.[36]

The evidence against: short-termism as adaptability. Mariassunta Giannetti and Xiaoyun Yu describe how an economic shock led firms with a short-term stockholder base to quickly take ameliorative steps.

They find short-termism, though it's good short-termism. But the implications of the quicker reaction speed are mixed. The authors study reactions to tariffs, not to more important long-term technological and global change. It is entirely possible that firms react differently to the latter. The study could mean that short-term stockholders induce adaptability when it is needed and steadfastness when steadfastness is needed. That's good. But the study could also mean that short-term investors induce short-term

[36] Martijn Cremers, Ankur Pareek & Zacharias Sautner, *Short-Term Investors, Long-Term Investments, and Firm Value: Evidence from Russell 2000 Index Inclusions*, 66 Mgmt. Sci. 4535 (2020).

reactions across the board, both when needed and when detrimental. That is not so good.

Considering adaptability raises an interpretive issue for the short-termism-is-a-problem studies. Quick action that looks like short-termism could be desirable—a positive adaptation to a changing environment, not a negative one. Recall the Wausau paper mill shutdown from the Introduction; had the company been more adaptable as digital technologies eroded their traditional paper market, they would have shifted earlier—in the short-run—to household paper products, where a good market persisted.

The evidence against short-termism: activist hedge funds' value, in the long- and the short-term. The original Brav, Jiang, Partnoy, and Thomas study, and the Bebchuk, Brav, and Jiang study both show that hedge fund interventions led to good results in both the short and long run. They match the activists' targets' results to industry average results, showing that the targets outperform the industry over the long run. The studies point to activism as promoting long-term shareholder value. They yield a strong result overall, associating activism with long-term value and evidencing that the first causes some of the second.

However, other explanations have been offered for the association. In general, if the targets differ in some important characteristic from the rest of the industry, then the causal link weakens. The activists, for example, might just be better stock pickers, but have no operational impact on their targets.

The studies' strength is reduced by a typical data problem: Businesses do not sit still for academics to measure impact. Over time, many firms vanish or morph such that the vanishing or morphing firms' final results could not be ascertained. This is normal—firms sell off assets, disappear, acquire others, and transform themselves. Disappearances could either strengthen or weaken the authors' conclusion. If firms disappeared because they were bought and merged at a premium price, that would be good for targeted firms and would strengthen the result. But if the firms disappeared because they went bankrupt or closed, that would weaken the result. In the absence of definite information or sampling, one could assume that these missing observations include some of each and so do not change the general trend. But this dropout factor introduces uncertainty.

However, this line of research is stronger, because an overlapping set of researchers traced the productivity of factories owned by hedge funds' targets (including factories owned by target firms that disappeared or delisted from the stock exchange—such as factories sold to new owners). They found that the productivity of the targets' factories improved more than that of factories owned by similar firms that the hedge funds did not target.[37] This information fills in more of the usual gaps than other academic work on short-termism.

Still, some important results from the Bebchuk, Brav, and Jiang study are small in magnitude—e.g., the target firm's return on assets was only marginally higher five years after hedge fund activism.[38] And other research shows shifts in value following activist efforts from bondholders to shareholders.[39] Such shifts are good for stockholders, but not a plus for the economy. Whether the shift from stakeholders to stockholders is large or small is yet to be determined.[40] But, again, shifting value is not in itself a plus for the economy overall. Lastly, the study weights each firm's percentage results equally. A good return at a small firm counts as much as a good percentage return at a giant firm. But much of the positive return seems to have come from smaller firms.[41]

Three final limits here impede us from drawing strong policy implications: First, the study is a type of matching study, subject to reservations already stated—matching is precarious. Second, the result—like others in this research genre—is an aggregate one. Aggregate data could mask a situation in which, say, 60% of the interventions promote the long-term while 40% are too short-term. But if a policy instrument could improve just the 40% that fosters short-termism, then we would have a useful anti-short-termism mechanism.

Third, this genre of study looks at the impact of hedge fund intervention and not at the overall impact of the stock market on public firm time horizons. Hedge funds could well be long-term, but traders, stock analysts, quarterly reporting, and the stock market in general need not be. Stock markets could in principle still damage the long-term through these other channels. Or hedge funds could be positive and long-term on average, but we do not know whether executives' fear of activists and belief that they're short-term push managers at untargeted firms to be more effective over the long-term, or less so.

Lastly, there's evidence that analysts recommend targets after the activist enters and that institutional investors buy when the activist enters. True,

---

[37] Alon Brav, Wei Jiang & Hyunseob Kim, *The Real Effects of Hedge Fund Activism: Productivity, Asset Allocation, and Labor Outcomes*, 28 REV. FIN. STUD. 2723 (2015).

[38] Bebchuk, Brav & Jiang, *supra* note 12, at 1105 (tbl. 3): Five years after the hedge fund action, the median return on assets of the targets was only 0.2% higher than the industry average.

[39] April Klein & Emanuel Zur, *The Impact of Hedge Fund Activism on the Target Firm's Existing Bondholders*, 24 REV. FIN. STUD. 1735 (2011); Surendranath Jory, Thanh Ngo & Jurica Susnjara, *The Effect of Shareholder Activism on Bondholders and Stockholders*, 66 Q. REV. ECON. & FIN. 328 (2017).

[40] *Cf.* Mark J. Roe, *Corporate Purpose and Corporate Competition*, 99 WASH. U. L. REV. 203 (2021) (if rents rise in the economy, then the role of hedge funds could increasingly be to retain rents for shareholders, as opposed to primarily reversing managerial error).

[41] Ed deHaan, David Larcker & Charles McClure, *Long-Term Economic Consequences of Hedge Fund Activist Interventions*, 24 REV. ACCT. STUD. 536 (2019).

analysts and institutions often have incentives to assess long-term prospects accurately. They bet their money, or recommend that others bet their money, on the activists getting good results. However, because the institutions have short-term preferences on their own for immediate results (to raise new money, to provide good results before a salary review), the power of this evidence weakens.

* * *

All studies have limitations, but the short-termism-is-a-problem studies have larger weaknesses and are overshadowed by the strengths of studies to the contrary. Regardless, one cannot take from the academic work that there is a strong consensus—or even a weak one—that short-termism is the deep problem that the policy sphere says it is.

D. Why Economy-Wide Problems Cannot Be Extrapolated from Firm-By-Firm Studies: The Economy as Ecosystem

Some readers may disagree with how I evaluated the firm-level studies and might conclude that the short-termism-is-a-problem studies are more persuasive. Some readers may conclude that one feature (say, activism) is not damaging but another feature (say, quarterly reporting) is.

But such readers and policymakers should not stop there and conclude that short-termism is a major actionable problem. Doing so faces another hurdle—and it's a high one—which I describe next: before one concludes that there's an economy-wide problem, the reader needs to think about the US economy as an ecosystem.

The local and the general, distinguished. Even definitive *firm-level* studies cannot reliably demonstrate powerful *economy-wide* harm. True, for some business issues—say, child labor—the moral dimension means extrapolation is not important. Every instance of such a moral failing demands to be avoided. But for short-termism, the moral quality is modest or nonexistent; the primary concern is whether stock markets damage the overall economy. If nearly all firm-level studies found rampant short-termism, that could support a policymaking inference of a systemic time horizon problem. But the studies are divided, with about half saying, yes, there's short-termism and half saying no. And the half that find a problem do not by themselves scale to indicate an economy-wide problem.

It's not that researchers tried to scale from the local to the economy-wide and failed to do so; it's that the typical research methodologies are not attuned to successfully doing so.

Why is that?

Local research. To use research tools effectively, economists generally must focus on a local issue: Do firms with activist engagements evince more short-term behavior than firms that do not? Do firms whose executives exercise stock options act more short-term that quarter than otherwise? Do firms that announce quarterly earnings targets invest less than firms that are silent? But local findings need not scale to an economy-wide finding.

Michael Mauboussin and Dan Callahan use a strong metaphor on how understanding a financial system is like understanding an ant colony:

> Say you want to analyze an ant colony, a system made up of thousands of individual ants. You can study the behavior of the individual ants . . . . Alternatively, you can examine the colony . . . .
>
> An ant colony is a "complex adaptive system" that emerges as the result of the interaction of the individual ants. Complex adaptive systems generally have properties and features that are difficult to predict by examining the individual agents. . . . [I]t is very difficult to understand a system by examining only its parts. If you want to understand the [ant] colony, study the colony. If you want to understand the ants, study the ants.[42]

If we want to understand whether we have an economy-wide debility, the local problems are relevant but not dispositive.[43]

Substitutes. Again, other firms can counterbalance a deficient time horizon found in some firms. In fact, a local short-term problem in a stock-market-financed firm creates incentives and opportunities for *other* firms—both public firm competitors, private firms, private equity buyouts of public firms, and venture capital firms—to pick up the slack.[44] If they do pick up enough of

---

[42] Michael J. Mauboussin & Dan Callahan, *A Long Look at Short-Termism: Questioning the Premise*, 27 J. App. Corp. Fin. 70, 71 (2015).

[43] Policymakers should want to know whether for this problem, if there is one, "the market will take care of it," to use an economic cliché. For most serious corporate problems, the market, in my view, will not take care of it; for this one, it could, rendering the serious question to be not whether it doesn't at all, but how much it takes care of it.

[44] For this reason, I did not analyze in the text an unpublished study that could become important. Stephen Terry estimates volatility in firms just missing or barely making their own earnings forecasts. Their R&D growth falls. The R&D cutbacks in public firms are then extrapolated to assume *similar* cutbacks in private firms. Stephen J. Terry, The Macro Impact of Short-Termism 27 (Boston U. working paper, June 2017), http://people.bu.edu/stephent/files/MIFET_LATEST_DRAFT.pdf. But most analysts see private firms as reducing the economy-wide costs of public firm shortfalls. Since private firms account for half of the US economy and one-third of our R&D expenditures, the more normal aggregation would mitigate public firm costs.

the slack, then the purported problem diminishes. Indeed, sometimes even the short-term firm that's overly focused on quarterly results can *itself* pick up the slack, at another time.

The last sentence may seem paradoxical, but unpacking it reveals the limits to extrapolating from the local to the general. Consider two excellent studies of executives' equity compensation. Alex Edmans, Vivian Fang, and Katharina Lewellen showed that when the vesting of executives' options and other stock compensation rises in a quarter, the growth rates of their companies' R&D declines.[45] And Tomislav Ladika and Zacharias Sautner validated this finding with a parallel one: When firms eliminate the option vesting period (that is, when the firms eliminate the time delay—often years—before executives can exercise the options granted them), R&D and capital spending decline.[46]

These are important findings, especially for firms seeking to fine-tune how to set up stock options. But the findings do not demand that there be a severe economy-wide problem—and the research teams, composed of first-tier finance economists, do not claim that they do. The firm that goes shorter-term when there's a burst of option-vesting presumably is then longer-term when the executives do not have a vesting burst. Overall, the firm may well invest enough, with options disrupting the timing of the investment. And when some firms have a vesting burst, others do not and can pick up the slack. Delay and repositioning the R&D are costly to the economy, yes, but they are not the heavier costs of the R&D just not getting done. Normal market processes would then make economy-wide R&D good, even if it is weak for a time at some firms when they have heavy options vesting.

Barriers to entry in antitrust. Consider a business regulation parallel: barriers to entry are a mainstay of antitrust thinking, especially for mergers.[47]

Mergers among competitors could decrease competition and allow the merged firms to raise their product's or service's price. But, as the government's merger-challenge guidelines state: "A merger is not likely to enhance market power if entry . . . is so easy that the merged firm . . . could not profitably raise price or otherwise reduce competition."[48]

---

[45] Alex Edmans, Vivian W. Fang & Katharina A. Lewellen, *Equity Vesting and Investment*, 30 REV. FIN. STUD. 2229 (2017). *Cf.* Benjamin Bennett, J. Carr Bettis, Radhakrishnan Gopalan & Todd Milbourn, *Compensation Goals and Firm Performance*, 124 J. FIN. ECON. 307 (2017) (firms that slightly exceed earnings per share estimates do less R&D than those that just miss the goal).

[46] Tomislav Ladika & Zacharias Sautner, *Managerial Short-Termism and Investment: Evidence from Accelerated Option Vesting*, 24 REV. FIN. 305 (2020).

[47] JOE S. BAIN, BARRIERS TO NEW COMPETITION (1956). *See also* RICHARD A. POSNER, ANTITRUST LAW: AN ECONOMIC PERSPECTIVE 59 (1976); GEORGE J. STIGLER, THE ORGANIZATION OF INDUSTRY 67 (1968).

[48] U.S. Dep't of Justice & Fed. Trade Comm'n, Horizontal Merger Guidelines 28 (rev. Aug 19, 2010). For a judicial example, see Rebel Oil v. Atlantic Richfield Co., 51 F.3d 1421 (9th Cir. 1995).

Such thinking is typically absent in corporate policymaking. For analyzing economy-wide short-termism, its absence is a mistake. (The social science construct here is that the direct effects of the merger are a partial equilibrium, in that the merger's first impact is to lessen competition. But, critics of stopping there point out, the general equilibrium need not lessen competition because the merger's impact, by lessening competition, will also increase the profitability of the industry and thereby attract new competitive entry. The question is how much and how fast.[49])

Imperfect substitutes. This concept of counterbalance making up for a local weakness does not mean that the market will take care of any problem here fully, with certainty, and without cost. For example, even though venture capital and private equity often have horizons of 5–10 years, both typically raise money regularly (and return old investments to investors). Their need to raise new funds (and report results)[50] can push them to sell good firms too soon so as to successfully book a good profit to show potential new investors.

Worse, some projects are too big for either private firms or venture capital firms to handle at all.[51] Funds available for private equity to invest have grown severalfold during the past few decades—and amount to about 10% of the value of public markets. But while private equity now has the capacity to take private very big firms, they still cannot take the very biggest off of public markets.[52] The point is that there's a substitute, albeit an imperfect one.

The ecosystem thinking is not that alternative arrangements will always be perfect substitutes, but that if there are time horizon costs from trading and activism, those costs to the economy overall are reduced because some of that slack can be picked up elsewhere. The business world is not, and does not have to be, perfect.

Fallacies of composition. Another way to see why general, economy-wide results can be weaker, or stronger, or the opposite of local and firm-level results is to consider three closely-related sets of propositions. The two in each pair seem identical when read quickly, but are not. Start with Set A:

---

[49] The usual thinking in this area is that most "partial" results have such a small knock-on impact that it can safely be ignored. For many corporate issues, I believe this assumption correct. But for short-termism, as for antitrust merger analysis, it is not safe to assume so. The appendix to this section expands on this.

[50] Amil Dasgupta & Mike C. Burkart, *Competition for Flow and Short-Termism in Activism*, 10 Rev. Corp. Fin. Stud. 44 (2021).

[51] Josh Lerner & Ramana Nanda, *Venture Capital's Role in Financing Innovation: What We Know and How Much We Still Need to Learn*, 34 J. Econ. Persp. 237 (2020).

[52] Prequin Report, North America-Focused Private Equity Assets Under Management (June 27, 2017) (report provided privately to the author); Eli Talmor, *Private Equity: Rethinking the Neoclassical Axioms of Capital Markets*, 21 J. Alternative Inv. 10 (2018); John C. Coates IV, *Thirty Years of Evolution in the Roles of Institutional Investors in Corporate Governance*, in Research Handbook on Shareholder Power 79, 90 (2016).

1. When a company buys back its stock, it then invests less in capital equipment.
2. When stock buybacks increase in the economy, that causes economy-wide investment in capital equipment to decline.

Or, Set B:

1. Stock market activists force cash out of their target firms.
2. Stock market activists force cash out of their targets and thereby starve the corporate sector of the cash it needs.

Or, Set C:

1. Increasing quarterly orientation, increased trading, and rising activism induce targeted public firms to do less R&D.
2. Increasing quarterly orientation, increased trading, and rising activism induce the US economy to do less R&D than it should.

Whether or not each of the first propositions is true (and they are disputed), the second propositions are, in order, probably false (A), demonstrably false (B), and not shown to be true (C). We saw this in Chapters 1 and 2. Analysis and policy thinking need to avoid a fallacy of composition.

* * *

Lastly, we need to be mindful of a "package deal" aspect of the large public firm. To get the vital capital raising and scale benefits of the large firm, we need to put up with intermittently excessive short-termism in some firms and intermittently excessive long-termism in other firms—when executives stick to a technology or product with which they are familiar even though it's in decline. This is no different than homeowners and office managers putting up with waste heat from lightbulbs—we need the light, so we accept some waste heat. Some excessive short-termism (like some excessive long-termism) is embedded in the public firm. Truly precise policy instruments would be needed to extract the bad aspects from what is overall a beneficial package of stock market funding for the public firm. Even if some effort to reduce the negatives turns out to be worthwhile, policymakers need to be careful about going too far and thereby damaging the public firm.

* * *

A plausible bottom-line synthesis of all this echoes the conclusion I advanced when interpreting the Graham-Harvey-Rajgopal finding. Overall, the evidence is that there is some corporate short-termism, but it is, as most of the executives reported, small.

Appendix to Part D

The ecosystem concept put forward in Part D is important for stock market short-termism policy because our vital concern is whether we have a serious economy-wide problem. The chapter's distinction between the local and the general conveys the point.

In social sciences, these local versus general distinctions are understood as important and, while they have not been widely applied to the short-termism issue, they could and should be. In this short appendix to Part D, I outline the relevant referents: (1) via a more formal statement of the issue, (2) via a reference to statistics concepts of validity, and (3) via economic distinctions between partial and general equilibria.

1. *Stated formally*: existing high-quality stock market short-termism research examines whether in a Population of firms, P_1, a treatment, X_1, such as option vesting for executives or voluntary quarterly projections, induces effect Y_1, namely less investment and lower R&D by the P_1 firms. This is local evidence of a detrimental effect, which should perk up policymaking interest. But, for policymaking purposes, we want to know whether X_1 induces Y_0, namely decreased investment in the *overall* economy. At first it seems a plausible consequence.

But Y_1 need not generalize beyond P_1 to Y_0. That's because Y_1 (lower investment when a firm might miss a financial projection, or decreased investment of firms when options vest) in Population P_1 becomes a treatment—X_2—for firms in Population P_2. X_2 (namely decreased investment by the P_1 firms) should induce the P_2 firms to invest more and do more R&D—because Y_1 hands them a competitive profit-making opportunity. Y_1's effect on P_2 *boosts* Y_0—overall investment in the economy.

Hence, the full impact of X_1 on Y_0 (economy-wide investment) is Y_1 (the effect in Population 1, which should be negative) + Y_2 (the effect in Population 2, which should be positive). If $Y_1 = Y_2$, in absolute value, there's no policy issue, because there's no net impact on Y_0. If $Y_1 > Y_2$, in absolute value, but the magnitude is not much, then there's only a minor policy issue. If the short-termism problem in Population A is big enough to be an economy-wide problem demanding policy action and that Y_1 is large, then there's reason to think it plausible that it would be big enough to affect the incentives of Population B and thereby make Y_2 large as well.

Policymakers should want to see evidence (or a good theoretical basis for expecting) that the magnitude of $Y_1 > Y_2$ is substantial enough to warrant policy effort. Theory and incentives would indicate reason, but not certainty, for the difference not to be substantial. The evidentiary record is silent.

2. Construct validity and external validity. The validity of a study's results can be questioned or affirmed for multiple reasons. Over the years the statistics profession has developed categories of validity, with the two most relevant for us being construct validity and external validity. The boundary between the two is not definitive and disagreements exist as to how to separate the two.[53] But for our purposes, demarcating the boundary is unnecessary, as long as we see the underlying policy issue.

External validity—which assesses whether the effect occurs outside the sample studies—in a loose sense is in play. But, the issue is better seen as a matter of construct validity. For example, in financial quarters when options vest, the sample investigated shows companies investing less. The result is (probably) valid externally, in the sense that out-of-sample vesting, and perhaps similar out-of-sample compensation aspects, probably also lead to lowered investment. But the validity issue *for policymaking* is whether we should infer an economy-wide problem. For example, while studies show R&D *decreases* in important circumstances, we know that the local effect cannot be the economy-wide effect, because R&D has been *rising* in the economy during the relevant period (making the question not whether there is a decline, but whether it's been rising enough). Somewhere in the economy there is increasing R&D that reverses the effect of the studies showing that a particular treatment reduces investment or R&D). That is, there's construct validity to a study showing that a treatment leads to less R&D in the directly affected firms, but *not* to extrapolating from that result that there's less R&D in the economy overall.

3. Partial and general equilibrium. For economists studying the impact of a tax or a regulation or a shock to, say, a particular industry, the typical analytic form is to study the impact on the targeted industry, and to assume that all outside arrangements stay nearly constant, unchanged. For many analyses, the approximation is good enough, such that useful information can be gleaned from the partial equilibrium analysis. Such studies are "partial" because the researcher does not consider all the knock-on effects.[54]

---

[53] WILLIAM R. SHADISH, THOMAS D. COOK & DONALD T. CAMPBELL, EXPERIMENTAL AND QUASI-EXPERIMENTAL DESIGNS FOR GENERALIZED CAUSAL INFERENCE 64–102 (2002)).

[54] James J. Heckman, Lance Lochner & Christopher Taber, *General-Equilibrium Treatment Effects: A Study of Tuition Policy*, 88 AM. ECON. REV. 381, 385 (1998). *Cf.* David F. Bradford, *Factor Prices May Be*

Generally speaking, this is also a fair beginning assumption for corporate lawmaking. But for stock market short-termism, it is not. If the stock market really makes a class of firms more short-term than profit maximization warrants, then more profit opportunities arise for the other firms. The returns to long-termism will increase for the rest of the economy, creating money-making openings for (1) public firms immune to a debilitating short-termism (think: Amazon, Google, Microsoft, Johnson & Johnson), (2) private firms safe from these stock market influences, and (3) venture capitalists looking for research opportunities. There will be an offset. How much of an offset is the issue for policymaking.[55]

Constant but Factor Returns Are Not, 1 ECON. LETTERS 199 (1978) (similar analytic: a local tax has economy-wide impact).

[55] Tests are possible: i.e., if a short-termism treatment led to local short-termism, investigators could see whether competitors compensated. This kind of effort has not regularly been made for short-termism. But until tested, policymakers could and should go with the presumptions of how the incentives would affect competitors and other sectors. If the unmitigated local loss to the economy overall would be great, it should create a nice profit opportunity, making the question how much the local problem gets mitigated.

PART III

THE PROPOSED SOLUTIONS' LIMITED EFFICACY—AND THEIR COSTS

8

Cures and Their Limits

Insulating Executives from Financial Markets

For a problem that is yet to be shown to be serious, proposed solutions abound. Fear of short-termism propels ideas for tax reforms, for ending quarterly reporting, and for giving executives more autonomy. In this chapter we consider cures focusing on executives; in the next we consider cures focusing on financial markets.

A. Greater Discretion for Boards and Executives

The major corporate law cure for stock-market-driven short-termism, regularly espoused by executives and their representatives, is to accord executives and boards more autonomy from stock markets. Autonomous boards and executives would operate for the long run, it's said, and, hence, they should be freed from the yoke of financial markets.[1] How to achieve this goal? Fewer corporate elections of directors, more rules that stymie shareholder activists, and more control for boards and executives over the shareholding voting apparatus that elects directors and approves major transactions.

Insulation proposals usually come from boards, executives, and their representatives,[2] but sometimes also from the corporation's progressive critics. One

---

[1] *See* Lawrence Mitchell, *The Legitimate Rights of Public Shareholders*, 66 WASH & LEE L. REV. 1635, 1667–75 (2009).

[2] Martin Lipton & Steven A. Rosenblum, *A New System of Corporate Governance: The Quinquennial Election of Directors*, 58 U. CHI. L. REV. 187 (1991) (proposing that directors be elected for five-year terms).

example: Senator Warren's proposed Accountable Capitalism Act would drive a wedge between boards and stock markets, justified in no small measure by stock market short-termism. Progressives are not directly seeking to bolster executives over shareholders (although that's a likely effect), but to bolster employees and other stakeholders.

Another progressive example: the proposed Brokaw Act, which we saw in the Introduction, sought to deter short-termism with corporate governance roadblocks that would disrupt activists. A law firm's analysis:

> [R]ather than directly seeking to curb short-term activity sometimes promoted by activist investors (such as buybacks, dividends, and high debt-leveraging), the legislation attempts to make it more difficult for an investor to become an activist in the first place. That is, *the proposal makes it more difficult for a person to accumulate a significant enough stake in a company to impact its governance.*
>
> . . . [T]he Securities and Exchange Commission (the "SEC") would . . . [be instructed to] promulgate new rules . . . [to] decrease, from ten to two days, the time investors have to disclose [that they've bought stock]. . . . [This would make it more expensive for activists, because as soon as they announced they've bought stock, the stock price would rise for the rest of their purchases.]
>
> . . . [S]hould the legislation pass, management and corporate defenders would be advantaged . . . .[3]

Another example, a non-progressive one: the SEC sharply cut back proposed rules that would have made it easier for shareholders to get their own director nominees onto target firm boards of directors.[4] Critics of the original proposal said short-termism justified a cutback. For background: The corporation itself pays the legal and other expenses when sitting directors nominate themselves for reelection. But shareholders who nominate their own slate of directors traditionally must pay their own way, which was often expensive enough to deter them from running their own directors. The SEC's original proposal would have made it easy for shareholders to piggyback their own nominees onto the corporation-paid ballot; the SEC's final approved proposal, less so.

---

[3] Jenner & Block, The Brokaw Act's Regulation of Activist Investing: Can it Curb Short-Termism? (June 28, 2016), www.lexology.com/library/detail.aspx?g=16415189-b49d-4901-aa58-09a35b5b5701 (emphasis added). The law firm memo notes the potential cost:

> Some commentators suggest that the Brokaw Act's effort to protect employees and larger communities only benefits entrenched management—a constituency that also may engage in short-term activity. Just as activist investors can promote short-termism, they argue, so too can they serve as a check on short-term behaviors by corporate management.

[4] Facilitating Shareholder Director Nominations Final Rule, 75 Fed. Reg. 56,668 (Sept. 16, 2010); Mark J. Roe, *The Corporate Shareholder's Vote and Its Political Economy, in Delaware and in Washington*, 2 Harv. Bus. L. Rev. 1 (2012).

Good reasons for much managerial autonomy. There are good reasons for high day-to-day executive autonomy from shareholders. Boards and executives cannot coherently run their companies if they are second-guessed on every decision, every day.[5] Shareholders are not generally well-informed on company strategy, will disagree with one another, and could disrupt the boardroom if given too much authority. These bases for board and executive autonomy are sound: the corporate question has long been how much accountability versus how much autonomy.

Stock-market-driven short-termism is not one of those reasons. Stock market short-termism has been used to justify more executive autonomy from shareholders, particularly by managerial-oriented analysts.[6] But the thinking on stock market short-termism should not alter the balance between necessary autonomy and sound accountability. The next paragraphs show why.

First, the available evidence does not show the economy to be suffering from severe stock market short-termism, as we've seen. Second, more insider discretion could enhance short-termism, not reduce it, because executives and boards can be the source of corporate short-termism. It's basic human nature for the CEO to want good results during his or her tenure. With the average CEO's tenure at about six years,[7] many CEOs must think their time left as CEO is short. As a matter of personal pride, some seek good results during those few years left and are less concerned with what follows.[8] Profits may not be their only or even primary goal; their legacy could motivate them more. Or avoiding disruption during their remaining tenure could motivate them more. There's consistent evidence: CEOs increase R&D spending during their first year as CEO but reduce it in their final years.[9] Older CEOs diversify more, diminishing firm focus.[10] Older CEOs put their firms on a low-risk path when

---

[5] Stephen M. Bainbridge, *Director Primacy: The Means and Ends of Corporate Governance*, 97 Nw. U. L. Rev. 547 (2003).

[6] *See, e.g.*, Dominic Barton, Jonathan Bailey & Joshua Zoffer, Rising to the Challenge of Short-Termism 12 (Focusing Capital on the Long-Term, 2016), www.fcltglobal.org/docs/default-source/default-document-library/fclt-global-rising-to-the-challenge.pdf?sfvrsn=0 ("The key to breaking the negative feedback loop driving corporate short-termism lies in empowering executives and directors . . . .") (executives at McKinsey, a leading management consultant firm, wrote the report).

[7] Steven N. Kaplan & Bernadette A. Minton, *How Has CEO Turnover Changed?* 12 Int'l Rev. Fin. 57, 58 (2012) (seven years in the 1992 to 2007 period; six from 2000 to 2007). According to the Spencer Stuart study, 6.6 years. *See* Joann S. Lublin, *CEO Tenure, Stock Gains Often Go Hand-in-Hand*, Wall St. J., July 6, 2010.

[8] The problem is more complex, and causation need not be one-way. Financial markets could press firms to produce results, which in turn could press boards to fire CEOs more frequently, which in turn could press CEOs to emphasize immediate firm performance. But the fact that older CEOs are more susceptible to under-investment suggests that at least some of the cause emanates from the CEO, in that older CEOs are more likely to expect their current position to be the one from which they retire.

[9] Patricia M. Dechow & Richard G. Sloan, *Executive Incentives and the Horizon Problem: An Empirical Investigation*, 14 J. Acct. & Econ. 51, 52 (1991).

[10] Matthew A. Serfling, *CEO Age and the Riskiness of Corporate Policies*, 25 J. Corp. Fin. 251, 252 (2014).

their firms become more insulated from shareholder influence. Younger CEOs do the opposite.[11] Entrenched, older CEOs invest less than younger ones,[12] meaning more autonomy from financial markets leads to *more* short-termism through this channel, *not* less.

Overall, the *internal* organizational structure of the large firm and its executives' motivations are sources of short-term impulses. More autonomy would heighten these difficulties. Before acting, we ought first to have reason to believe that these managerial short-term pressures are small and the stock market's negative time-horizon influence big.

Third, giving boards and executives too much discretion is in itself dangerous. In prior decades, when many thought that this discretion was too wide, firms became empires, acquiring one another for little reason beyond enhancing the power and prestige of the acquiring firm's executives.

Yet this view—insulate boards from short-term stock markets to unleash them to strive for the long-term—is quite strong among policymakers. It is particularly powerful among corporate luminaries in Delaware, the state that makes much of the on-the-ground corporate law governing the allocation of power between corporate America's executives, boards, and shareholders.

Executive empowerment. One of the most corrosive political issues of our day has been the rise of elites and their populist antagonists. Many voters resent the wealthy and powerful. Corporate lawmakers who accord more autonomy to already powerful executives and directors elevate these corporate elites further, facilitating more power and higher compensation in ways that cannot be good for today's polity. If a mistaken belief in short-termism contributes to rules that further empower corporate elites, then that mistaken belief contributes to one of our core political and social problems.

To this author, it seems odd that a plank in some progressives' program is to reduce the influence of the stock market and of activists inside the large corporation. Reducing the stock market's influence is, from a progressive perspective, understandable, if stock markets press on employees. But the consequence of most such reductions is to empower executives, whom progressives would not normally support. The impact weakens one progressive antagonist—Wall Street—but boosts another, namely the corporate elite.

---

[11] Jon A. Garfinkel, Jaewoo Kim & Kyeong Hun Lee, The Interactive Influence of External and Internal Governance on Risk Taking and Outcomes: The Importance of CEO Career Concerns (2013), www.ssrn.com/abstract=2171005.

[12] Yakov Amihud & Baruch Lev, *Risk Reduction as a Managerial Motive for Conglomerate Mergers*, 12 Bell J. Econ. 605, 609–10 (1981); Andrei Shleifer & Robert W. Vishny, *Management Entrenchment: The Case of Manager-Specific Investments*, 25 J. Fin. Econ. 123, 125 (1989); ; Anil K. Makhija, *Career Concerns and the Busy Life of the Young CEO*, 47 Corp. Fin. 88, 105 (2017).

The boost comes directly, in obvious ways, and also indirectly. A deep conviction that short-termism is pernicious and rampant gives executives a coherent world view. They need not view themselves as selfish when seeking more power to ignore shareholders and activists and to diminish shareholders' authority so as to stop short-termism. It is not self-aggrandizement; they are doing the right thing for the economy and society. Banishing self-doubt and bolstering self-justification are themselves sources of executive power.

* * *

The point here is not that short-termism emanating from executives' career concerns and preferences is a central, economy-wide debility. After all, we saw in Chapters 2 and 7 that short-termism has not been shown to be a major economy-wide problem, and much evidence suggests the contrary—that it is not severe. The point here is that insulating executives could plausibly exacerbate whatever short-termism problem we have, and not ameliorate it.

Proposals for greater board and executive autonomy deserve to have their overall merits considered—will greater autonomy improve business, economic performance, and fairness? But such proposals should gain no strength from a belief—mistaken—that greater autonomy will reduce stock-market-induced short-termism. Better to put our limited resources for reform elsewhere.

And keep in mind that most greater-autonomy ideas would benefit business players—often boards, executives, and those employees who gain from slowing change. As such, we should not dismiss the possibility that some proponents are driven—consciously or subconsciously—to favor reforms that benefit themselves and their allies.

B. The Role of the Corporate Law Courts

While Congress sets the overall rules, the corporate law courts and the securities regulator are where much of the day-to-day US corporate law is made—and I address this book's analysis in large part to them.

Corporate lawmakers who fear stock market short-termism are more likely to favor laws according autonomy and power to directors and executives, in the expectation that directors and executives are likely to steer their companies for long-term success if short-term investors do not interfere.[13]

---

[13] *E.g.*, Jack B. Jacobs, *"Patient Capital": Can Delaware Corporate Law Help Revive It?* 68 Wash & Lee L. Rev. 1645, 1657 (2011); Leo E. Strine, Jr., *Who Bleeds When the Wolves Bite? A Flesh-and-Blood*

Executives and directors have used the short-term cudgel to amass more corporate decision-making power and to convince corporate lawmakers to diminish shareholders' power. Corporate and securities laws, for example, can make it easy or hard for shareholders to control board of director elections. Corporate and securities laws can make it easy or hard for executives and directors to push their own nominees and for outside shareholders to push for their own directors. For the most part these laws empower the executives and directors while impeding the outsiders.

Boards and executives often invoke stock-market-induced short-termism when seeking to persuade the Securities and Exchange Commission to empower boards and executives further and weaken shareholders. The corporate lawmaking trend—more autonomy for boards—fits well with the judges' off-the-bench views of short-termism. They see short-termism as real and important and, when they rule, they tend to accord more autonomy to boards and executives.

Overemphasizing a modest problem leads lawmakers to distort how they structure authority in the public corporation.

* * *

Consider the corporate law courts.

The importance of Delaware for corporate lawmaking. First, some background: A majority of US public corporations are incorporated in the small state of Delaware. Accordingly, Delaware judges and lawmakers make much of the day-to-day governing law of corporate America; they balance the relative power of shareholders and executives inside the corporation.

Fear of stock market short-termism has been regularly invoked in Delaware to justify broad executive autonomy. Tellingly, prominent lawyers for executives push the short-termist idea most aggressively, as if they were lobbying the courts to adopt a short-termist worldview of pernicious short-term trading and activism—one that is most favorable to their clients.

Leo Strine, former Delaware supreme court chief justice, who left the bench in 2019, regularly bemoaned stock market short-termism as damaging the United States.[14] "[D]irectors are increasingly vulnerable to pressure from

---

Perspective on Hedge Fund Activism and Our Strange Corporate Governance System, 126 YALE L.J. 1870, 1872–73 (2017).

[14] Leo E. Strine, Jr., *Securing Our Nation's Economic Future: A Sensible, Nonpartisan Agenda to Increase Long-Term Investment and Job Creation in the United States*, 71 BUS. LAW. 1081 (2016). *Cf.* Steve Denning, *How Corporate America Is Cannibalizing Itself*, FORBES, Nov. 18, 2015.

activist investors ... with short-term objectives," he has said, "lead[ing them] to ... sacrifice long-term performance for short-term shareholder wealth."[15]

True, one wonders how much of the actual on-the-ground corporate law result—more autonomy for executives, more power to boards of directors, and less power for shareholders—is due to judges believing that short-termism is rampant and pernicious. The judges often say, and surely sincerely believe, that their views on short-termism and their judicial decisions on corporate law run through separate channels. But it's human nature for one to affect the other. A longstanding school of jurisprudence has such baseline views conditioning judicial decisions. If judges think that shareholders are dysfunctionally too short-term, they are more likely to rule that boards and executives, not shareholders, should have the last word.

The setting. For example, one key corporate legal duty is that of corporate directors' loyalty to the corporation and its shareholders. When boards and executives turn down an outsider's offer to buy the company or when they thwart a shareholder activist, they are in dereliction of their duties if their true motivation is to preserve their own positions and autonomy, at the company's expense.

A key justification for allowing boards and executives wide discretion in handling such takeovers and activists is shareholder short-termism. (In a takeover, an outsider offers to buy the company's stock from a target firm's current stockholders. If most stockholders sell, the outsider then owns the company and can elect new directors. But corporate law now empowers the target firm's board to refuse the offer and never allow the choice to reach the company's stockholders in usable form.)

The target firm's board, in this view, thwarts a short-term offer for the long-term well-being of shareholders. Managerial representatives and lawyers—Martin Lipton being the most persistent and effective—have aggressively pushed this genre of argument.[16] Or, stated more neutrally, executives and shareholders disagree as to where the path to long-term value lies. Judges' belief that the executives are more likely to be correct seems to influence their corporate law decisions toward more executive autonomy.

Short-term action in the corporate law courts. Litigants press Delaware's corporate law courts to give boards more autonomy because shareholders

---

[15] Leo E. Strine, Jr., *The Dangers of Denial: The Need for a Clear-Eyed Understanding of the Power and Accountability Structure Established by the Delaware General Corporation Law*, 50 WAKE FOREST L. REV. 761, 790–91 (2015). *Cf.* James B. Heaton, *The "Long Term" in Corporate Law*, 72 BUS. LAW. 353 (2017).

[16] See Martin Lipton, *Takeover Bids in the Target's Boardroom*, 35 BUS. LAW. 101 (1979); Martin Lipton, *Corporate Governance in the Age of Finance Corporatism*, 136 U. PA. L. REV. 1 (1987).

are short-term focused. The *Airgas* 2011 case exemplifies this.[17] The targeted board asserted that the short-termism of too many stockholders justified its stymieing of those seeking to buy the target company. Said Chancellor Chandler: Their argument is "based on the particular composition of Airgas's stockholders (*namely, its large 'short-term' base*). In essence, Airgas's argument is that 'the substantial ownership of Airgas stock by these *short-term, deal-driven investors* poses a threat to the company . . . . [The defendants assert that the board should have more discretion to stymie the offer because of the] risk . . . that a majority of Airgas's [excessively short-term focused] stockholders . . . will tender into Air Products' offer despite its inadequate price tag, leaving the [longer-term] minority 'coerced' into taking $70 as well."

The Delaware Chancellor rejected this argument at first, thinking in short-/long-run terms: "[T]he [short-term] arbs bought their shares from long-term stockholders who viewed the increased market price generated by Air Products' offer as a good time to sell."[18]

But the Chancellor then seemingly reversed his initial and correct rejection of the time horizons argument, when quoting the defendants' assertion as a question: Were enough stockholders "so 'focused on the short-term' that they would 'take a smaller harvest in the swelter of August over a larger one in [an] Indian Summer?'" Yes, the judge answered. The investors would sell even if the price offered failed to reflect the company's long-term value.[19] The rhetoric of pernicious short-termism was in play in *Airgas*.[20]

Or consider Polaroid's plight in the Delaware courts, which we saw earlier in Chapter 1. When shareholder activists pressured the camera and film maker, management resisted, and justified their resistance as thwarting short-termism for a more profitable long-term.[21] The courts supported management *and* its long-term rhetoric.[22] Yet Polaroid was failing to face up to the threat to traditional film photography posed by digital photography, and its

---

[17] Air Products & Chemicals, Inc. v. Airgas, Inc., 16 A.3d 48, 108–09 (Del. Ch. 2011) (emphasis supplied), discussed in Mark J. Roe, *Corporate Short-Termism—In the Boardroom and in the Courtroom*, 68 BUS. LAW. 977 (2013).

[18] "Arbs," short for arbitrageurs, buy or sell stock when a transaction is sought, based on the arbitrageurs' assessment of whether the transaction will succeed or fail, and at what price. *Airgas, supra* note 17.

[19] *Id.* at 111–12.

[20] A subtlety: Delaware lawmakers have long deferred to boards in corporate decision-making. The court could well have been deferring to the boards' view that it had to protect the firm from short-term shareholders and in principle would have deferred to the board even if it said it preferred the short-term. Still, the court took the board's negative view of short-term shareholders at face value.

[21] *Shamrock Holdings, Inc. v. Polaroid Corp.*, 559 A.2d 257, 268 (Del. Ch. 1989). Defending the long-term would not, however, said the defenders, harm short-term shareholders. *Id.* at 283.

[22] *Id.* at 260; J.B. Heaton, *The Unfulfilled Promise of Hedge Fund Activism*, 13 VA. L. & BUS. REV. 317, 356 & n.55 (2019).

resistant management persisted with their defective long-term strategic emphasis on photochemistry.[23] The company soon went bankrupt.

Delaware decided the iconic *Time Warner* takeover case roughly contemporaneously with *Polaroid*. The rhetoric of investor short-termism supported the decision—interpreted by some as giving boards carte blanche to "just say no" to a takeover offer. It's the board's duty, said the court, to "select[] a time frame for achievement of corporate goals. That duty may not be delegated to the stockholders. . . . Directors are not obliged to abandon a deliberately conceived corporate plan for a short-term shareholder profit. . . ." Delaware's broad mandate to boards "includes [the power to choose the corporation's] time frame [for action]." The court approvingly recited the Time board's view that institutional investors failed to appreciate the long-term benefits of preserving Time's distinctive culture.[24]

This view persists in the corporate law courts: "[S]tockholders of corporations, especially given the[ir] short-term nature[,]" the court said in 2011, "put strong pressures on corporate management to produce immediate profits."[25] Some "investors may espouse short-term investment strategies and [seek] to benefit economically from those strategies, thereby creating a divergent interest in pursuing short-term performance at the expense of long-term wealth." Activist hedge funds were, said the court, impatient shareholders looking for short run gains.[26]

Overall, the Delaware judiciary accords boards of directors wide discretion. Looking over the sweep of decades of Delaware's corporate law jurisprudence, that is the core operative principle for corporate jurisprudence: the board is the central decision-making institution in the corporation. Even without time horizon controversies, board discretion was, and one suspects would be, core to Delaware corporate law.

But that does not make views on short-termism irrelevant. The judges' (apparent) buy-in to the short-term view buttresses their deference to boards. It makes courts less likely to wander from a board-centric principle to, say, a balancing test. It gives the judges more confidence that board centrality is right, if they see boards as more long-term than activists or stock markets.[27] True,

---

[23] Peter Buse, The Camera Does the Rest: How Polaroid Changed Photography 79 (2016) (Polaroid sees the digital future but fails to adapt); Andrea Nagy Smith, What Was Polaroid Thinking? (Insights from Yale School of Mgmt.), www.insights.som.yale.edu/insights/what-was-polaroid-thinking (Polaroid executives believe through the 1990s that in the long-run "customers would always want a hardcopy print" and not just an image on a screen).

[24] Paramount Communications, Inc. v. Time, Inc. 571 A.2d 1140, 1148–50, 1154 (Del. 1989).

[25] In re Massey Energy Co. Derivative & Class Action Litig. 2011 Del Ch. LEXIS 83 (Ch. Strine).

[26] In re PLX Tech. Inc. Stockholders Litig., No. CV 9880-VCL, 2018 WL 5018535, at *41 (Del. Ch. Oct. 16, 2018), aff'd, 211 A.3d 137 (Del. 2019).

[27] Some of these thoughts and cases are also used in Mark J. Roe & Roy Shapira, *The Power of the Narrative in Corporate Lawmaking*, 11 Harv. Bus. L. Rev. 233 (2021).

empowering the board probably came first, because the judges thought board autonomy makes for stronger companies or because boards and executives are quite influential in Delaware lawmaking.[28] But whether board empowerment is good policy or just Delaware's favoritism, the short-term narrative lowers its visibility. ("We're promoting good long-term economic policy, not favoring executives.") The fact that influential law firms and lawyers who promote board centrality in Delaware prominently push the stock market short-termism justification suggests to me that they think it persuasive, effective, and useful in assuring that the corporate courts continue to favor boards over shareholders when the two are at odds.

Courts as makers of economic policy? But *is* judicial action on short-termism appropriate—either way? Some judges imply it is not: Justice Jacobs—long an influential and now retired Delaware judge—called short-termism "a *national* problem that needs to be fixed,"[29] not a narrow corporate law problem.

Justice Jacobs' surmise was correct. Courts are the wrong institution for such economic policymaking: they lack the staff and the range of policy tools—and perhaps for this reason it only sometimes figures explicitly in their on-the-bench statements. If the corporate planning horizon is indeed too short and leads to less investment, too little R&D, and cash drained in buybacks, policymakers should consider tax credits for investment, government spending on R&D, and tighter regulation of stock buybacks through securities law, not basic corporate law doctrines. Policymakers with a professional staff are better placed than judges to decide whether or not stock market short-termism is a major cause of these economic setbacks and, if it is, they are the right ones to consider whether transaction taxes and capital gains tax adjustments are the right remedies. The corporate law courts lack the power to use these policy tools.

Such economic policymaking also fits badly with core corporate law doctrines. Judges do not second-guess the corporation's business decisions, because judges are poorly positioned to evaluate business decisions. They are lawyers in judicial robes, not business people. This so-called "business judgment rule" is central to corporate law. The corporate judiciary ought to be *more* reluctant to assess whether the corporate economy is too short-term, too long-term, or just right. Even a state legislature, with its parochial concerns—such as raising tax revenue or promoting the well-being of local businesses, employees, and executives—is ill-placed to make such judgments, except

---

[28] Whether Delaware lawmakers are overly influenced by boards and executives has been a major debate among corporate law academics for decades.

[29] Jacobs, *supra* note 13, at 1657 (emphasis supplied).

possibly for firms operating primarily within the state's own borders. To allow short-termism issues into the courtroom is to facilitate business and economic engineering that the best business judges rightly decline to undertake even on the much-reduced scale of a single firm's mistaken business decision.

If there's pernicious economy-wide short-termism that needs fixing, it's best evaluated in Congress or by an administrative agency. Legislatures and administrators (and their academic and political advisors) are hardly mistake-proof. But they have, and the courts lack, the tools to dig into the issue.

C. The Role of the Securities and Exchange Commission

The Securities and Exchange Commission (SEC) makes many of the rules that govern the trading of stock, the voting of stock, and the allocation of authority inside the large corporation, and this book's message is addressed as well to the commissioners and their staffs. Short-termism has been on the SEC's agenda, and the prior president pushed it farther up the agenda. The SEC has the staff and skills to evaluate big picture policy.

Those seeking to influence the SEC regularly assert that stock market short-termism must be diminished and long-termism bolstered, and that their policy preferences will do so. For instance, the Business Roundtable (the association of large public firm executives) lobbied the SEC for executive autonomy from activists because, said the Roundtable, activists "demand changes that may not be in the long-term interests of . . . stockholders[.][30]

When the SEC opens up rulemaking efforts on the allocation of authority between shareholders and executives, the public submissions to the SEC, often from executives, boards, and their allies, regularly invoke stock market short-termism rationales.[31] How much those perspectives affect the regulator's ultimate decision is difficult to gauge; but it is telling that those who seek to persuade the SEC highlight the short-termism argument, telling the regulators that this or that rule—often insulating management from the stock market—will help combat it.

One recent example: when Silicon Valley interests sought SEC approval of a new corporate structure enhancing the voting rights of insider stockholders,

---

[30] Letter from Business Roundtable to SEC, Nov. 9, 2018, at 23, www.sec.gov/comments/4-725/4725-4635930-176425.pdf. *See also* Request for Comment on Earning Releases and Quarterly Reports, SEC Release No. 33-10588, 34-84842 (2018), www.sec.gov/rules/other/2018/33-10588.pdf.

[31] See the unpublished Appendix's catalog of instances of short-termism being raised in SEC submissions, usually seeking greater executive autonomy.

they promoted the effort as creating a *Long-Term* Stock Exchange.[32] The structure for the most part would benefit company founders, whose control would be solidified, as we shall see in Chapter 9. Whether this control would foster the beneficial long-term is uncertain.[33] The static control could induce longer-term sclerosis (and therefore be detrimental to the long run) if the extra votes for the founder facilitated control even after the founder had become ineffective. But long-term labeling is a sales point in its favor.

D. Compensate Executives for the Long-Term

Why not pay executives more for long-term company performance?[34] Josh Lerner and Julie Wulf show that long-term-weighted compensation to firms' R&D chiefs produced more and better patents.[35] Others show that managers with exercisable stock options are less likely to make long-term investments than managers with stock options that cannot be exercised soon.[36] Executives' compensation horizons count.

Shareholders vote on executive pay proposals in public firms and they reject some pay proposals. By comparing the after-vote performance of firms in which a long-term pay proposal barely passed with those in which a long-term pay proposal barely failed, Caroline Flammer and Pratima Bansal bring forward evidence that the time horizon of compensation affects performance. Firms whose shareholders approved the long-term pay package got better long-term performance; firms whose shareholders disapproved it got stronger short-term results.[37]

Boards and executives could design longer-term compensation.[38] They could tie stock option grants not to current prices but to long-term stock

---

[32] SEC, LTSE [Long Term Stock Exchange] Listings on IEX, Release No. 34-82948, 83 FED. REG. 14074 (Apr. 2, 2018).

[33] Mark J. Roe & Federico Cenzi Venezze, *Will Loyalty Shares Do Much for Corporate Short-Termism?* 76 BUS. LAW. 467 (2021).

[34] Lynne L. Dallas, *Short-Termism, the Financial Crisis and Corporate Governance*, 37 J. CORP. L. 265, 357 (2012).

[35] Josh Lerner & Julie Wulf, *Innovation and Incentives: Evidence from Corporate R&D*, 89 REV. ECON. & STAT. 634 (2007). *See also* Pierre Azoulay, Joshua S. Graff Zivin & Gustavo Manso, *Incentives and Creativity: Evidence from the Academic Life Sciences*, 42 RAND J. ECON. 527 (2011).

[36] Tomislav Ladika & Zacharias Sautner, *Managerial Short-Termism and Investment: Evidence from Accelerated Option Vesting*, 24 REV. FIN. 305 (2020); Alex Edmans, Vivian W. Fang & Katharina A. Lewellen, *Equity Vesting and Investment*, 30 REV. FIN. STUD. 2229 (2017); David Souder & J. Myles Shaver, *Constraints and Incentives for Making Long Horizon Corporate Investments*, 31 STRATEGIC MGMT. J. 1316 (2010).

[37] Caroline Flammer & Pratima Bansal, *Does a Long-Term Orientation Create Value? Evidence from a Regression Discontinuity*, 38 STRATEGIC MGMT. J. 1827 (2017).

[38] Brian D. Cadman, Tjomme O. Rusticus & Jayanthi Sunder, *Stock Option Grant Vesting Terms: Economic and Financial Reporting Determinants*, 18 REV. ACCT. STUD. 1159, 1159 (2013) ("vesting schedules are longer in growth firms where lengthening the executive's investment horizon is more important and . . . firms with more powerful CEOs and weaker governance grant options with shorter vesting periods").

performance or another, better measure of corporate long-term strength. Some boards do, more could, and more are doing so in recent years. If there's a short-termism problem to ameliorate, they could do more. Pay could be held in escrow for a longer period—and forfeited if performance lags. Or pay could be pulled back, even after an executive leaves the company, if performance falls by some large measure.

So why has executive compensation historically been tightly tied to short-term stock price?

Consider the possibility that it's not the stock market but the internal organizational structure of the large firm that linked pay to current results. Executives sought, and their boards of directors too often have given them, pay tied to immediate profits and sales, not long-term value. Boards might not have pushed hard enough for the long-term, at least historically. There's evidence that the shorter-than-optimal vesting periods come at the behest of the CEO,[39] that investors want pay to be more long-term than directors and executives want it to be,[40] and that when the salary, bonus, restricted stock, and option components of CEO and senior executive pay are weighted for their time-to-receipt, their duration has historically not been particularly long.[41] In fact, it's been slightly *shorter* than the average duration of many institutional investors' stockholding.[42] The shortening impetus seems to come from inside the firm: "firms with more powerful CEOs and weaker governance grant options with shorter vesting periods."[43]

---

[39] *Id.* at 1179; Jianxin D. Chi & Shane A. Johnson, The Value of Vesting Restrictions on Managerial Stock and Option Holdings 5 (Mar. 9, 2009), www.ssrn.com/abstract=1136298.

[40] Alex Edmans, Tom Gosling & Dirk Jenter, CEO Compensation: Evidence from the Field (European Corp. Gov. Inst. Finance Working Paper No. 771, July 8, 2021), www.ssrn.com/abstract-3877391.

[41] Radhakrishnan Gopalan, Todd Milbourn, Fenghua Song & Anjan V. Thakor, *Duration of Executive Compensation*, 69 J. FIN. 2777, 2781 (2014): "[T]he average CEO pay duration [is] 1.44 years.... This duration does appear short when compared to the average tenure of a CEO in a firm (six years) or to the average duration of a firm's projects.... The ... short average pay duration is [because] 30% of CEO pay consists of salary and bonus, which vest immediately, while the noncash components typically vest within five years." *Id.* at 2781. Pay duration for executives below the CEO level was shorter. *Id.* at 2779.

[42] See Mark J. Roe, *Corporate Short-Termism—In the Boardroom and in the Courtroom*, 68 BUS. LAW. 977, 980, 993, 997–98 (2013). *Compare* Gopalan et al., *supra* note 41, *with* Martijn Cremers, Ankur Pareek & Zacharias Sautner, Stock Duration and Misvaluation, at 3 (working paper, Jan. 2013) (stockholding duration of more than 1.5 years in 2010), *and* Martijn Cremers & Ankur Pareek, *Patient Capital Outperformance: The Investment Skill of High Active Share Managers Who Trade Infrequently*, 122 J. FIN. ECON. 288, 293 & App. A1 (2016) (median mutual fund duration at 1.7 years by 2013). Others find a similar, but slightly shorter holding duration for institutional investors. Tanja Artiga Gonzalez, Iman van Lelyveld & Katarína Lučivjanská, *Pension Fund Equity Performance: Patience, Activity or Both?* 115 J. BANKING FIN. 1, 5 (2020) (pension fund duration just under a year); Ann M. Tucker, *The Long and the Short: Portfolio Turnover Ratios and Mutual Fund Investment Time Horizons*, 43 J. CORP. L. 582, 583 (2018) (average duration of about 1.25 to 1.41 years: "the assumption that mutual fund investor time horizons have been shortening during the past decade [is] incorrect").

[43] Cadman et al., *supra* note 38, at 1159. *Cf.* Andrew Schotter & Keith Weigelt, *Behavioral Consequences of Corporate Incentives and Long-Term Bonuses: An Experimental Study*, 38 MGMT. SCI. 1280 (1992) (long-term compensation necessary for long-term executive actions).

The facts just provided in the previous paragraph should be interpreted: The short-term theory—particularly when it calls for *more* executive autonomy from stock markets—is that executives *want* to manage for the longer-term, but are stymied by the short-term stock market. But if that is correct, then their firms' internal organizational dynamics should lean *against* the stock market's short-term pressure, leading to executive compensation duration *exceeding* stockholders' holding duration. But the *opposite* is true. It is shorter.

* * *

Overall, those seeking to fix the stock market's purported short-termism by insulating boards further from stock markets need to consider whether that would do much good and whether it could exacerbate short-termism if executives and boards are a major source of it. While wide executive and board autonomy is inevitable, where to draw the autonomy vs. accountability line should not be influenced by short-termism considerations, based on the evidence we now have. But in the name of fighting economy-wide short-termism we see a push for more autonomy and less accountability, often from those with an interest in the results, namely the executives and their allies, but peculiarly enough also from progressives and those who would not ordinarily promote the interests of corporate elites.

Bottom line: corporate policymakers should not allow short-termism considerations to enter their balancing of the costs and benefits of autonomy vs. accountability.

9

Cures and Their Limits

Taxing and Regulating Financial Markets

Since the popular view on short-termism is that it originates in financial markets, prominent proposals to fight it seek to affect financial markets, by ending stock buybacks, eliminating quarterly reporting, taxing short-term trading gains heavily, and giving more voting power to long-term stockholders. But none is likely to affect time horizons much and some would have other costs. Although several would possibly have desirable benefits, fighting short-termism is not among them.

One well-developed academic idea is that long-term information flows better to larger blockholders than to small ones. The most plausible conceptual source of stock market short-termism comes from information distortion (as I outlined in Chapter 4): small stockholders cannot efficiently acquire and evaluate complex information, so many rely on simple informational signals like quarterly earnings. Shareholders with bigger blocks of stock can evaluate complex technological information better, by spreading their evaluation costs over a larger investment.

But those fighting short-termism do not promote a policy of enhancing such blockholders. One can understand a self-interested reason for this silence from many influential real-world players. Bigger blockholders would impinge on boards' and executives' autonomy and potentially tighten workplace slack.

A. End Stock Buybacks

Stock buybacks, which we examined in Chapter 2, are big and controversial. News reports regularly see them as crippling firms and reducing investment.[1] "Companies in Japan, the United States and Europe are . . . doling out the money to shareholders rather than investing in new buildings, equipment or innovative products," states the *New York Times*.[2] Larry Fink, head of BlackRock, writes that buybacks "deliver immediate returns to shareholders" while their companies "underinvest[] in innovation, skilled workforces or essential capital expenditures." Prominent pronouncements declare buybacks to be killing the US economy.[3]

But as we saw in Chapter 2, US business is not liquidating itself. The net cash outflow from the S&P 500 was not, if properly analyzed, the huge buyback number but a much smaller one, because larger firms in the United States borrowed about as much as they bought back in stock. Increasing corporate debt is probably unwise, but cash is not disappearing.

Even if policymakers remain unconvinced by the evidence presented in Chapter 2 that, properly analyzed, buybacks are not overall draining firms of cash, banning or impeding them would not do much for the anti-short-termism program. What would big companies do if buybacks were banned or reduced? Critics hope that impeding buybacks will lead the affected firms to invest more in the firm's core business. But it would just as, or more likely, lead them to invest in poor projects that satisfy executives and employees, without helping the economy overall. In the 1970s and 1980s, big companies with excess cash bought other companies, first buying companies in their own lines of business, thereby potentially harming competition, and then buying companies in unrelated businesses, thereby building conglomerates that executives managed poorly overall.[4]

---

[1] Steve Denning, *How Corporate America Is Cannibalizing Itself*, FORBES, Nov. 18, 2015; Edward Luce, *US Share Buybacks Loot the Future*, FIN. TIMES, Apr. 26, 2015; Gretchen Morgenson, *In Yahoo, Another Example of the Buyback Mirage*, N.Y. TIMES, Mar. 25, 2016. *See also* John C. Coffee, Jr. & Darius Palia, *The Wolf at the Door: The Impact of Hedge Fund Activism on Corporate Governance*, 1 ANNALS OF CORP. GOV. 1, 9 (2016).

[2] Jack Ewing, *Robocalypse Now? Central Bankers Argue Whether Automation Will Kill Jobs*, N.Y. TIMES, June 28, 2017.

[3] William Lazonick, *Profits Without Prosperity*, 92 HARV. BUS. REV., Sept. 2014, at 46. See also William Lazonick et al., US Pharma's Financialized Business Model (Inst. for New Econ. Thinking Working Paper No. 60, July 13, 2017), www.ineteconomics.org/uploads/papers/WP_60-Lazonick-et-al-US-Pharma-Business-Model.pdf (pharma industry buybacks, says the author, mean less pharmaceutical innovation); Gretchen Morgenson, *Big Pharma Spends on Share Buybacks, but R&D? Not So Much*, N.Y. TIMES, July 14, 2017.

[4] Michael C. Jensen, *Agency Costs of Free Cash Flow, Corporate Finance, and Takeovers*, 76 AM. ECON. REV. 323 (1986).

Those acquisitions weakened the US economy. The conglomerates facilitated executive power and pay, but economic resources were wasted that should have gone to employing working people in better, longer-lasting jobs. The worst of the conglomerates were thereafter broken up by takeovers and activist investors.[5] If we plan to force more companies to retain more cash by cutting buybacks, we should be wary of similar negative results—somewhat degraded competition and more corporate empire-building.

This is not to say that buybacks are always beneficial, or even benign. While most push out cash that the firm cannot use effectively, some make executives' own stock and options more valuable. Buybacks can help insiders own a bigger percentage of their firm after the buyback takes outsiders' stock out of play.[6] Such transactions are not acutely beneficial and could be discouraged, but these are not short-termism, cash-draining issues.

Even if buybacks were banned,[7] companies with excess cash have other ways to return it to owners: dividends, of course, but also by paying down debt and not borrowing anew. (True, buybacks do not create shareholder expectations that they will be regularized, as dividends do. And buybacks are tax-favored over dividends, because they allow low-taxed stockholders to sell while high-taxed stockholders do not; for dividends, every stockholder receives the cash and has taxable income.) Not much would be lost if dividends became the primary channel by which firms with excess cash moved it elsewhere in the economy. And for some companies, less debt and more equity would be a better capital structure. But critics of buybacks should not think that by channeling the cash exit from buybacks to dividends (or debt paydowns) that they will meaningfully change corporate time horizons.

* * *

Moreover, much anti-buyback short-termism talk is misguided. Old guard companies with excess capacity should *not* keep excess cash but should recycle that cash back to investors to put it where it's more needed.[8] The interest group explanation is important here; those damaged by cash moving from declining businesses—namely, the old guard's management, board, and

---

[5] Nickolay Gantchev, Merih Sevilir & Anil Shivdasani, *Activism and Empire Building*, 138 J. Fin. Econ. 526 (2020); Michael C. Jensen, *Takeovers: Their Causes and Consequences*, 2 J. Econ. Persp. 21, 34 (1988).

[6] *Cf.* Jesse M. Fried, *Insider Trading via the Corporation*, 162 U. Pa. L. Rev. 801, 817 (2014).

[7] Or taxed. In late 2021, a serious proposal arose in Congress for a 2% tax on a wide class of buybacks.

[8] This section on buybacks draws from Mark J. Roe, *Share Buybacks Are Not the Problem*, Fin. Times, Sept. 6, 2015.

sometimes employees—have self-interested reasons to slow down that cash outflow. The rest of us do not.[9]

B. Eliminate Quarterly Reports

Quarterly reports to shareholders are said to push management to forgo attractive long-term projects. Executives scramble to meet the expectations of investors and traders for earnings that rise smoothly from quarter to quarter. Quarterly reporting of financial results—which the Securities and Exchange Commission requires for public companies—is regularly criticized as fostering a short three-month time horizon for US management.[10] "Quarterly capitalism" is the pejorative here for short-termism.[11]

Public firms smooth their earnings over time, to eliminate quarterly bumps up and down,[12] and their doing so, some (disputable) evidence indicates, diminishes long-term investment in property, plant, and equipment, not to mention research and development.[13] Many executives say they would give up some value to smooth and meet earnings targets, as we saw in Chapters 5 and 7. The emphasis on quarterly results makes it harder for a company's long-term picture to emerge vividly for investors.[14] Thus, they say, financial reporting should be longer-term—say, every six months.

The United Kingdom ended mandatory quarterly reports in 2014. The European Union's Commission went to semi-annual reporting, concluding that "quarterly financial information is not necessary for investor protection."[15] The handful of studies on the change's impact on time horizons reach

---

[9] A complex political picture could render this buyback aspect ambiguous. If disgruntled employees at such firms contribute greatly to political upheaval *and* the only (or best) way to calm the political waters is to keep cash locked up in those companies (and if banning buybacks would really do so), then the rest of us do have an interest in banning those buybacks. *See* Mark J. Roe, *Backlash*, 98 Colum. L. Rev. 217 (1998). Chapters 12 and 13 consider this kind of concern.

That is, cutting the buyback avenue cutoff for excess cash, if the other outlets are not good enough, will lead some companies to keep cash inside their firms, reinvesting it even when expecting only a weak return. Perhaps that's what some antibuyback proponents prefer. The trapped cash would benefit those associated with a firm that has diminished opportunities—its executives and employees, for example. Such a result is a kind of long-termism—locking the cash up so that firms stick with investments beyond their sell-by expiration date—but it's not an attractive one.

[10] *E.g.*, Dominic Barton, *Capitalism for the Long Term*, 89 Harv. Bus. Rev., Mar. 2011, at 84, 85; Andrew Ross Sorkin, *Some Heresy on Wall Street: Look Past the Quarter*, N.Y. Times, Feb. 1, 2016 (reporting views of Lawrence Fink, BlackRock's CEO).

[11] *See* Barton, *supra* note 10, at 85, who opines that we now live the era of quarterly capitalism.

[12] John R. Graham, Campbell R. Harvey & Shiva Rajgopal, *Value Destruction and Financial Reporting Decisions*, 62 Fin. Anal. J. 27, 33–34 (2006).

[13] *Id.* at 31–32.

[14] *See* Sorkin, *supra* note 10.

[15] Directive 2013/50/EU, 2013 O.J. (L 294) 1, 1 ("The obligations to publish interim management statements or quarterly financial reports . . . encourage short-term performance and discourage long-term investment"). *But see* Robert Pozen, *In Defence of Corporate Quarterly Reports*, Fin. Times, Oct. 9, 2016.

differing results,[16] with one failing to find that the shift increased investment. Nevertheless, despite the lack of strong evidence, some executives and their representatives in the United States are eager to follow the Europeans on this. Martin Lipton, a prominent US corporate lawyer who often represents boards and management, proposed, with noticeable media attention, that boards be allowed to end quarterly reporting and choose to report semiannually.[17] The proposal resonates in Washington circles: then-presidential candidate Hillary Clinton criticized "quarterly capitalism," and so did Daniel Gallagher, a Republican SEC commissioner.[18] Donald Trump, after meeting with prominent executives, asked the SEC to re-examine its quarterly reporting requirement, which it did.

But ending quarterly reports will not have the desired impact: it is a small and bent arrow unworthy of its target. It requires one to believe that if public firms reported results every six months instead of every three months, then they would make more five-year investments in plant and equipment, and throttle up R&D.[19] The multi-year investment goal is a mismatch with the multi-month change.

Six months is not the long-term.

* * *

While good things are unlikely to come from eliminating quarterly reports, bad things could. If the firm's financial profile goes dark for a few more months, its stock's trading price will drift farther from its fundamental value because the market knows less. What consequence will that informational drift have? If firms now distort their behavior and investments because they want to show good quarterly earnings, they would still distort them, but every

---

[16] *Compare* Suresh Nallareddy, Robert Pozen & Shivaram Rajgopal, *Consequences of More Frequent Reporting: The UK Experience*, 6 J.L. Fin & Acct. 51, 55, 80–81 (2021) (requiring quarterly reporting in the United Kingdom did not change investment levels) *with* Jurgen Ernstberger, Benedikt Link, Michael Stich & Oliver Vogler, *The Real Effects of Mandatory Quarterly Reporting*, 92 Acct. Rev. 33 (2017) (mandatory quarterly reporting in the European Union correlates with R&D cuts), *and* Arthur G. Kraft, Rahul Vashishtha & Mohan Venkatachalam, *Frequent Financial Reporting and Managerial Myopia*, 93 Acct. Rev. 249 (2018). *See also* Yongtae Kim, Lixin Su & Xindong Zhu, *Does the Cessation of Quarterly Earnings Guidance Reduce Investors' Short-Termism?* 22 Rev. Acct. Stud. 715 (2017) (companies that eliminate quarterly guidance—projections of their financial results, not the quarterly statement itself—attract longer term investors).

[17] David Benoit, *Time to End Quarterly Reports, Law Firm Says*, Wall St. J., Aug. 19, 2015.

[18] *Hillary Clinton Transcript: Building the 'Growth and Fairness Economy'*, Wall St. J. Blog, July 13, 2015, https://blogs.wsj.com/washwire/2015/07/13/hillary-clinton-transcript-building-the-growth-and-fairn ess-economy/; Daniel M. Gallagher, Commissioner, Sec. Exchange Comm'n, Activism, Short-Termism, and the SEC: Remarks at the 21st Annual Stanford Directors' College (June 23, 2015), https://www.sec.gov/ news/speech/activism-short-termism-and-the-sec.html.

[19] Robert Pozen & Mark J. Roe, *Six Months Isn't Long Term*, Wall St. J., Aug. 20, 2018.

six months instead of every three months. Stock prices could readily drift further from actual value over six months than over three, so one should expect more deeply distorted stock pricing.[20] And with market price drifting further away from fundamental value, the temptation and opportunity for executive insider trading would rise.

Stock analysts value quarterly earnings reports because they want up-to-date information on the company, as Robert Pozen and I indicated elsewhere.[21] Even John Kay—the principal author of a widely-disseminated British government report promoting Britain's elimination of mandatory quarterly reporting—recognized that most US investors disliked the United Kingdom's move from quarterly to semiannual reporting and worried "that this kind of deregulation could make companies more opaque." Investors in firms subject to semiannual reporting extrapolated quarterly information from similar quarterly sources, like US companies in the same industry.[22] Worse yet, reducing reporting frequency makes investors worry more, potentially increasing stock price volatility and capital costs: when investors lack quarterly information, they overreact to alternative news sources.[23]

Some proposals would let each company's shareholders decide on reporting frequency. Investor choice often has much to say for itself. But letting each company's shareholders decide on reporting frequency could undermine the efficiency of US capital markets. If American Airlines reports semiannually, but Delta does not, then stock analysts cannot as readily compare firms within the airline industry.[24]

And as I said earlier, a more plausible channel for some public companies' short-termism is that those owning a small percentage of a firm's stock lack the incentive to evaluate subtle, technological, and soft information. The smaller stockholders—and stock analysts in a hurry—rationally highlight easy-to-evaluate information, like quarterly results. If we shift to semiannual reporting, we should expect them to focus on the semiannual reports and other easy-to-evaluate information. They still will be poorly informed and no more

[20] A lucky confluence could make six-month reporting help. If temporary bad results would have upset the expected quarterly numbers but are reversed before the semiannual report is due, management would not have been motivated to distort at the quarter because the quarterly numbers would not be reported. And, since the temporary difficulty reversed before the semiannual report was due, they had little motivation to distort for the semiannual report. How often there's a temporary problem that gets reversed in six months (but not seven months, or longer) would have be gauged.

[21] Robert Pozen & Mark J. Roe, *Those Short-Sighted Attacks on Quarterly Earnings*, Wall St. J., Oct. 7, 2015.

[22] Emmanuel T. de George & Salman Arif, The Dark Side of Low Financial Reporting Frequency: Investors' Reliance on Alternative Sources of Earnings News and Excessive Information 27 (Kelley School of Bus. Res. Paper No. 17-7, Aug. 16, 2018), www.ssrn.com/abstract=2900988.

[23] *See* Pozen & Roe, *supra* note 21.

[24] *See id.*, from which this section draws.

longer-term than they were before.[25] One of the most academically-supported short-termism channels is noisy information that shareholders cannot evaluate well; yet, ironically, one of the most politically popular treatments is to reduce information flow by ending quarterly reporting requirements.

C. Tax Short-Term Capital Gains Heavily

Profits on stock sales are taxed; if this tax is high enough, stockholders will hesitate to sell.[26] Especially if the tax hits short-term traders but not longer-term investors, the thinking runs, stockholders will hold onto their stock for long enough to save on their tax bill.

The profit on sales of stock held for more than one year has long been taxed favorably. In the 2016 presidential campaign, proposals arose to tax these capital gains at higher rates until the stock was held for two years. Profit on stock held for longer than two years would be taxed at a rate declining each added year it was held until, for stock held long enough, the profit would be taxed at only 20%.[27] This would discourage trading and encourage long-term holding.

But would it discourage short-termism? If stockholders expect lower taxes from holding stock longer, the argument went, they will more willingly withstand a drop in that company's quarterly earnings. That would accord the company's executives greater scope for longer-term thinking. They could make decisions that have a long-term payoff and a short-term cost.

The plan sounds intuitively reasonable. But a lower tax rate for capital gains will only impel *some* stockholders to trade less often. Stock will still trade; stock prices will still rise and fall. Hence, executives who overly worry about their company's stock price and their next quarter's result will *still* worry about quarterly results and stock price.

---

[25] Related to quarterly reports: Many firms give investors quarterly guidance—executives' *expectations* of earnings. Executives feel pressured to meet or beat their guidance numbers, even if only by pennies. But guidance is not required by law or regulation, so it could be changed at will. However, those worried about stock market short-termism should not get their hopes up that the ending of guidance would unlock previously suppressed long-term investment. Guidance is a minor business aspect that has gained much attention. And some firms that stop announcing their own earnings estimates will still feel compelled to meet or beat analysts' consensus estimates.

[26] One prominent proposal during the 2016 presidential election: Neera Tanden & Blair Effron, How to Foster Long-Term Innovation Investment (Center for American Progress, June 30, 2015), www.americanprogress.org/issues/economy/report/2015/06/30/116294/how-to-foster-long-term-innovation-investment/, which propelled candidate Hillary Clinton's platform on the subject. Their basis for the tax incentive begins with the belief that the average holding period is now only six months. (It's probably longer, as we saw earlier, but still many stockholders buy and sell over less than a year.) But these less-than-a-year stockholders are *already* insensitive to the timing phase embedded in today's capital gains tax. For contemporary critical commentary, see James Surowiecki, *The Short-Termism Myth*, THE NEW YORKER, Aug. 24, 2015.

[27] James B. Stewart, *One Beneficiary of Clinton's Complex Tax Plan: Tax Lawyers*, N.Y. TIMES, Sept. 15, 2016.

Focus on that last point; the anti-trading concept is that a volatile stock price worries managers, who then make short-term operating decisions. But reducing trading by changing tax incentives *will not eliminate trading*; the stock will still have a price that can move every day. Hence, volatility will persist and continue to affect management. If the stock price truly represents long-term value, the stock price will continue to do so. If the stock price is erratic, it will continue to be erratic. Worse, price movements if trading volume falls could be *more* erratic because less frequent trading could make prices jump more when a new trade happens—an effect opposite to what short-term reformers would want.

While curtailing trading will not dampen short-termism, it could have other effects, some of them good. If too much brainpower is now devoted to profiting from finding a slight mispricing of stock (as I believe to be the case), then taxing trades would make this activity less profitable, pushing some of these people and resources elsewhere. If frenzied trading is pernicious, or valueless, taxing trading will reduce its incidence.

Tax rate manipulations to dampen trading will not change key shareholders' incentives. Pension funds, foundations, and charitable endowments do not pay taxes anyway.[28] Many taxable stockholders, such as high frequency program traders that account for much of the recent decades' increased trading, *already* regularly buy and sell within a year, even though they then pay the higher tax rate on their profits.[29]

For the purpose of curing purported short-time problems, the tax rate manipulation is a waste of time and energy. Reducing trading does not unlink the executive's incentives to keep an eye on stock price. The tax arrow here would miss its target.

* * *

A further word about trading.

Heavy trading is said to encourage short-termism. The image of Wall Street traders frantically buying and selling does have a short-termist aura. But the means by which heavy trading induces corporate short-termism is more obscure.

Its best case is (1) that the traders trade on short-term information, such as the most recent quarter's earnings, (2) that trading leads to the stock market undervaluing long-term companies and long-term investments, and (3) that the executives and boards care about this undervaluation and manage their companies accordingly.

---

[28] Steven M. Rosenthal & Lydia S. Austin, *The Dwindling Taxable Share of U.S. Corporate Stock*, 151 Tax Notes 923 (May 16, 2016).

[29] True, the tax rate could be raised high enough, even to 100%, to stop taxable shareholders' trading cold, if that is desired.

This is all plausible, but that does not mean that it is universally true or deeply important. Consider for (1) that there's reason to think that trading is often integrating *long-term* information,[30] about which the buyers and sellers disagree. What counts more than the duration of ownership is the buyer's evaluation horizon. For (2), traders do not hurt the most long-term companies, viz. Amazon, Apple, and Google, as we've seen. And on (3), boards could pay executives appropriately and over the long-term to look out for the company's long-term and to ignore pressure from trading.

D. Tax Financial Transactions

If trading is the problem, why not discourage trading by taxing it directly, an idea endorsed by the Aspen Institute, a respected think tank?[31] By taxing every sale (instead of the profit from the sale), a transaction tax discourages trading, even if there's no profit in the sale, and even if the trader does not pay a tax on stock profits. Michael Bloomberg had it as a major policy proposal in his 2020 presidential campaign—a 0.1% tax on every sale of a stock, bond, or derivatives contract.[32] The tax is a favorite of those who see short-termism as a serious problem and who see traders as distracting executives from a focus on the long-term;[33] it gets policymakers' attention in Europe.[34] Sometimes it's called a "Tobin tax," for the Nobel Prize winner who promoted the idea (but promoted it to restrict destabilizing international money flows, not to lengthen corporate time horizons).

---

[30] *Cf.* Alex Edmans, *Blockholder Trading, Market Efficiency, and Managerial Myopia*, 644 J. FIN. 2481, 2486, 2501 (2009) (block traders are often well-informed of firm's prospects).

[31] *See* ASPEN INSTITUTE, OVERCOMING SHORT-TERMISM: A CALL FOR A MORE RESPONSIBLE APPROACH TO INVESTMENT AND BUSINESS MANAGEMENT 1–2 (2009). Prominent economists like Joseph Stiglitz and Lawrence Summers have suggested a financial transaction tax to reduce detrimental capital market speculation. *See* Joseph E. Stiglitz, *Using Tax Policy to Curb Speculative Short-Term Trading*, 3 J. FIN. SERV. RSCH. 101, 109 (1989); Lawrence H. Summers & Victoria Summers, *When Financial Markets Work Too Well: A Cautious Case For a Securities Transactions Tax*, 3 J. FIN. SERV. RSCH. 261, 272-73 (1989). *But see* G. William Schwert & Paul J. Seguin, *Securities Transaction Taxes: An Overview of Costs, Benefits and Unresolved Questions*, 49 FIN. ANAL. J., Sept.–Oct. 1993, at 27.

[32] Thomas Franck, *Mike Bloomberg's Proposed Wall Street Transaction Tax Explained*, CNBC, Feb. 18, 2020, https://www.cnbc.com/2020/02/18/mike-bloombergs-transaction-tax-would-levy-0point1percent-from-stocks-trades.html.

[33] *See* Editorial, *The Need for a Tax on Financial Trading*, N.Y. TIMES, Jan. 28, 2016, at A24; Shelley Marshall, *Shifting Responsibility: How the Burden of the European Financial Crisis Shifted Away from the Financial Sector and onto Labor*, 35 COMP. LAB. L. & POL'Y J. 449, 472 (2014) ("support across much of Europe [for a] financial transaction tax . . .").

[34] The European Union has considered a uniform financial transaction tax. *See* Taxation of the Financial Sector, Taxation and Customs Union, European Comm'n, www.ec.europa.eu/taxation_customs/taxation-financial-sector_en. France started taxing the purchase of shares of companies headquartered in France with a market capitalization of at least €1 billion at 0.2% in August 2012.

Perhaps such a tax will reduce trading that induces the destabilizing of rapid international currency flows.[35] Perhaps financial firm trading facilitates excessive financial risk-taking.[36] Or, perhaps trading wastes the talents of high IQ traders who, if trading were rendered unprofitable, would more directly contribute to our economic well-being.[37]

Whatever the tax's other advantages, it will not much affect purported short-termism. If the problem to address is stock-price-dependent executive compensation, that channel will persist unless it's changed through other means. If executives check their stock's price daily without a Tobin tax, they will still check it daily if there is one.

Second, the traders whom a financial transactions tax would hit hardest are inactive in corporate governance. Those who trade rapidly based on micromovements of stock price—the so-called program traders—do not try to influence their portfolio firms. They are not corporate activists; they may not even vote in corporate annual elections. Boards and executives can ignore them when deciding whether to build the long-term factory.

And the financial transactions tax is hard to implement. When tried, it has been easy to avoid. The trading parties, or their broker, need only move the locus of the trade to a jurisdiction without the tax. (True, that raises trading costs, which should diminish trading.) Several European nations enacted Tobin taxes, but gathered little revenue, because trading went abroad.[38] Yet the effort to construct an effective Tobin tax persists.[39]

* * *

[35] James Tobin originally sought a tax on inter-currency financial transactions to reduce short-term, speculative trades that he thought worsened volatility and undermined domestic financial systems. *See* James Tobin, *A Proposal for International Monetary Reform*, 3 EASTERN ECON. J. 153, 155–56 (1978). Critics of the Tobin tax argue that it can worsen volatility, because lower liquidity and trading volume means large orders risk even more drastic price changes. *See* Randall Dodd, *Lessons for Tobin Tax Advocates: The Politics of Policy and the Economics of Market Micro-Structure*, *in* DEBATING THE TOBIN TAX (James Weaver et al. eds., 2003).

[36] But this idea also misanalyzes the impact of a trading tax. Banks can take on large risks without trading. A risky loan portfolio, which need not trade at all, is all it takes. Mark J. Roe & Michael Troege, *Containing Systemic Risk by Taxing Banks Properly*, 35 YALE J. ON REG. 181 (2018).

[37] Jeremy C. Stein, Presidential Address: Sophisticated Investors and Market Efficiency, 64 J. FIN. 1517, 1543 (2009); Kenneth A. Froot, David S. Scharfstein & Jeremy C. Stein, *Herd on the Street: Informational Inefficiencies in a Market with Short-Term Speculation*, 47 J. FIN. 1461, 1463 (1992). Anti-tax proponents warn that burdening trading harms better pricing, reduces liquidity, and raises volatility because it makes for more price leaps and tumbles. Anna Pomeranets & Daniel G. Weaver, *Securities Transaction Taxes and Market Quality*, 53 J. FIN & QUANT. ANAL. 455 (2018).

[38] *Do Tobin Taxes Actually Work?* THE ECONOMIST, Sept. 10, 2013. For a review of the academic literature, see Gunther Capelle-Blanchard & Olena Havrylchyk, *The Impact of the French Securities Transaction Tax on Market Liquidity and Volatility*, 47 INT'L REV. FIN. ANAL. 166 (2016). *Cf.* Steven M. Davidoff, *Tax on Trades Is a Simple Idea With Unintended Outcomes*, N.Y. TIMES, Feb. 27, 2013, at B5; James Fontanella-Khan & Chris Giles, *Britain Challenges EU over 'Tobin Tax'*, FIN. TIMES, Apr. 19, 2013, at 3.

[39] *See* Council of the European Union Interinstitutional File 2013/0045 (June 3, 2016), www.data.consilium.europa.eu/doc/document/ST-9602-2016-INIT/en/pdf.

Since the program traders leave executives alone, they are not a high-value target for time-horizon purposes. Yes, hyper-trading activity will not be missed if dampened by a tax—its contribution to financial efficiency, if it contributes at all, is not weighty. But making hyper-trading disappear will affect companies' time horizons little, if at all.

E. Promote Loyalty Shares

Loyalty shares are thought to reduce short-termism. Corporate governance reformers in the United States have been considering the concept and pushing the Securities and Exchange Commission to approve its wider use. The development and implementation of this concept are farthest along in Europe.

The concept. Those shareholders who hold their stock for a specified period, two years in the most common formulation, get more votes—two per share instead of one, again in the most common formulation. The intuition is that long-horizon shareholders will want a long-horizon corporation and that with their extra votes, long-termers will defeat short-termers.

On the surface, this proposition seems to be a can't-lose idea: entice longer holdings with more votes and give more voting power to longer-term shareholders, and thereby foster longer-term thinking and make the long-term owners more powerful.[40] Academics and Silicon Valley lawyers—David Berger, Steven Davidoff Solomon, and Aaron Benjamin—have promoted the idea and analyzed how to get it going.

Caveats. But implementation could backfire in getting time horizons to lengthen, as Federico Cenzi Venezze and I analyze in depth elsewhere.[41] First, it will surely protect insider-controllers, who will have more votes in their companies than before. Controller entrenchment could be long-term or could just be controller entrenchment. In Europe, where loyalty shares are more widespread than in the United States, the evidence is that entrenchment has been the primary effect.[42]

Second, loyalty shares resemble dual class stock, which typically gives controlling insiders extra votes. Some think dual class stock reduces

---

[40] David J. Berger, Steven Davidoff Solomon & Aaron J. Benjamin, *Tenure Voting and the U.S. Public Company*, 72 Bus. Law. 295 (2017).

[41] Mark J. Roe & Federico Cenzi Venezze, *Will Loyalty Shares Do Much for Corporate Short-Termism?* 76 Bus. Law. 467 (2021).

[42] Marco Becht, Yuliya Kamisarenka & Anete Pajuste, *Loyalty Shares with Tenure Voting—Does the Default Rule Matter? Evidence from the Loi Florange Experiment*, 63 J. L. Econ. 473 (2020); Roe & Venezze, *supra* note 41.

short-termism. Perhaps it does, but if so then loyalty shares would not be a new departure but a variation of what's already out there. Hence, don't expect much that's new.

Third, new stockholders who want to shake up a somnolent company with loyalty shares will be handicapped, because they cannot get the extra votes for two years, while the insiders already have their voting boost. That weakness would make a potential new investor hesitate. New investors would have to sit on their hands for two years while incumbent investors have more votes and more power. The incumbents, with more voting power, could continue pursuing goals that the new investor seeks to change. The net result would favor the status quo over change and adaptability. (Indeed, entrenchment of founders and controllers is part of what some executive-allied proponents of loyalty shares seek. That could be considered long-term, in a sense, but not a particularly desirable long-term.)

And, fourth, will it really make institutional investors with extra votes think more long-term? Maybe not. A time horizon problem attributed to institutional investors is that their managers tilt toward the short-term to pump up their own short-term bonuses each year.[43] But loyalty shares will not help here and might hurt. The voting boost would enhance the voting power of investment funds that owned the stock for two years or more. These managers would still have whatever incentives they are thought to have to pump up short-term stock price. Worse, with loyalty shares, they would have *more* votes to do so.

Who gets the loyalty voting boosts? Indexers and public pension funds, not activists. Two categories of institutional shareholders would qualify for much of the voting boost: indexed pension funds and indexed mutual funds. (Recall: indexers buy and hold the stock of every company in the stock market or of a relevant index.) But these indexed investors are generally so passive that the question of whether they should be allowed to vote at all has been raised.[44] More votes will not motivate passive investors to hold their stock for longer because for them the vote is not meaningful.

The period needed for a loyalty share boost in typical loyalty plans thus far is two years. Yet that's only somewhat longer than investors' average holding period for stock nowadays. Shareholders getting ready to sell just after the

---

[43] Edward B. Rock, *The Logic and (Uncertain) Significance of Institutional Shareholder Activism*, 79 Geo. L. J. 445, 473–74 (1991); Zohar Goshen & Richard Squire, *Principal Costs: A New Theory for Corporate Law and Governance*, 117 Colum. L. Rev. 767, 804–05 (2017); Lynne L. Dallas & Jordan M. Barry, *Long-Term Shareholders and Time-Phased Voting*, 40 Del. J. Corp. L. 541 (2016).

[44] Dorothy Shapiro Lund, *The Case Against Passive Shareholder Voting*, 43 J. Corp. L. 493 (2018).

two-year mark would get more votes. But more votes just before selling is not what the long-termists would want.

Alternative loyalty share formats. Loyalty-share designers have devised lures that they think are better than a voting boost. Patrick Bolton and Frederic Samama proposed to compensate longer-term shareholders with a bigger cash dividend or warrants to buy the firm's stock at a favorable price.[45] Former Vice President Al Gore and Nobel Prize winner Joseph Stiglitz endorsed the concept.[46] Yet, this proposal has had no traction in real-world proposals in the United States, which anticipate extra votes, not extra cash.

A hypothesis why it has little traction: promoters of loyalty shares seek mostly to preserve the control of firm founders and insiders, with long-termism a (sincere) justification for founders keeping control. Extra votes can preserve control. Extra cash does not.

* * *

Loyalty shares may have other benefits. The economy might benefit from controllers' views not being homogenized by the prevailing investment sentiment.[47] And company founders often value continued control more than money, it's said.[48] If we get more startups because loyalty shares lock in founders' control, that would be valuable, but that's not a time horizon benefit.

F. Encourage Blockholding

One source of short-termism is said to come from corporate managers being unable to communicate complex technological information to diffuse, inexpert stockholders. We saw this earlier. If this is indeed a primary problem, facilitating blockholders in the large US corporation could help, as

---

[45] Patrick Bolton & Frederic Samama, *Loyalty-Shares: Rewarding Long-Term Investors*, 25 J. Applied Corp. Fin. 86, 86–97 (2013). A dividend boost would favor index funds, by getting them a better return. Longer-term holding need not mean more long-term engagement, as passive holders may take the dividend but continue to be passive, as proponents recognize. *Id.* at 96.

[46] Al Gore & David Blood, *A Manifesto for Sustainable Capitalism*, Wall. St. J., Dec. 14, 2011; Joseph Stiglitz, Rewriting the Rules of American Economy 8, 69 (2015), https://rooseveltinstitute.org/publicati ons/rewriting-the-rules-of-the-american-economy/.

[47] Zohar Goshen & Assaf Hamdani, *Corporate Control and Idiosyncratic Vision*, 125 Yale L.J. 588 (2016).

[48] Noam Wasserman, The Founder's Dilemmas 284–88 (2012); Bernard S. Black & Ronald J. Gilson, *Venture Capital and the Structure of Capital Markets: Banks versus Stock Markets*, 47 J. Fin. Econ. 243, 258–59 (1998); Roe & Venezze, *supra* note 41. While they value control, many do not get to keep it. The founder is often no longer the CEO when a start-up goes public. Brian J. Broughman & Jesse M. Fried, *Do Founders Control Start-Up Firms that Go Public?* 10 Harv. Bus. L. Rev. 49 (2020).

several—myself, Albert Choi, and Alex Edmans, among others—have emphasized.[49] With their larger investment, blockholders' incentives to understand the nuances of their companies would be greater, the costs of understanding would be spread over larger blocks of stock, the larger blocks of stock would give them more authority to be heard in corporate councils, and their presence and acquiescence to insiders' plans would signal to outsiders that those plans seem sound.[50]

But while this proposal has support from some academic thinkers, it lacks support in the corporate world. There, the most common cures proposed are *not* to facilitate blockholding but to *impede* it. It's plausible that this emanates in part from a view that what makes the corporation run well for the long-term is maximum managerial discretion. Its absence from the most prominent reform proposals also matches some executives' and boards' self-interest.

G. Big Problem or Small Problem, Reduce It Anyway

One might rebut the likelihood that short-termism is a minor problem with the idea that whether it's small or big, we should reduce it. Policies to reduce short-termism are valuable in this view—the only question is the magnitude of their value. True, if short-termism is only a local and not a severe economy-wide problem, as this book's author says it probably is, then the benefit is minor and local. But it's still a benefit, short-term theorists could argue. And, for all we know, pernicious short-termism might be a bigger problem than this book indicates.

A first answer to this "reduce short-termism anyway" view is that we should prioritize our problems and work on resolving bigger problems first. That is correct but will satisfy few. A second answer to a "reduce it anyway" objection is that solutions have costs that can be quite substantial. If we over-deter short-termism, we will gum up adaptability in the business sector. If we further insulate executives from markets, and if they then pursue their own agenda, that will slow the economy if their firms are run less well. These would

[49] MARK J. ROE, STRONG MANAGERS, WEAK OWNERS: THE POLITICAL ROOTS OF AMERICAN CORPORATE FINANCE 240 et seq. (1994); Alex Edmans, *The Answer to Short-Termism Isn't Asking Investors to be Patient*, HARV. BUS. REV., July 18, 2017, https://hbr.org/2017/07/the-answer-to-short-termism-isnt-asking-invest ors-to-be-patient; Albert H. Choi, *Concentrated Ownership and Long-Term Shareholder Value*, 8 HARV. BUS. L. REV. 53 (2018).
[50] This is the view I offered in Roe, *supra* note 49, at 240–47. For similar analysis, *see also* Choi, *supra* note 49; Edmans, *supra* note 49.

be poor outcomes, especially since the time horizon problem is not severe to begin with.

Since we face no deep and pernicious short-termism problem, we shouldn't pay to try to solve one.

If it ain't broke, don't fix it.

PART IV
THE POLITICS OF THE CORPORATE SHORT-TERMISM CONTROVERSY

10

Confusing Short-Termism with Accelerating Technological Change

Why did the short-termism problem burst out from corporate governance circles when the evidence for its advertised economy-wide impact is so weak?

I showed in Chapter 3 that many corporate wrongs thought to emanate from a misshapen time horizon instead come from corporations externalizing costs to society. I examine a parallel conflation in this chapter: Accelerating change is disrupting the workplace, the large public firm, and the economy overall. Disruptive change is often confused with pernicious short-termism. Anxiety about the economy and resentment of Wall Street are articulated as hostility to dysfunctional short-termism. But Wall Street is mainly the messenger for accelerating technological change—not its core cause.[1]

A. Accelerating Change

Technological change is greater than ever. Unruly technologies smash through the economy every five years instead of every five decades, government policy changes are more frequent, more consequential, and deeper than ever, and global markets push those changes into firms and the workplace more quickly than many people find comfortable.

---

[1] I expand here on an earlier discussion on how accelerating technological, economic, and political change can be conflated with stock-market-driven short-termism. Mark J. Roe, *Corporate Short-Termism—In the Boardroom and in the Courtroom*, 68 Bus. Law. 977, 1001–03 (2013).

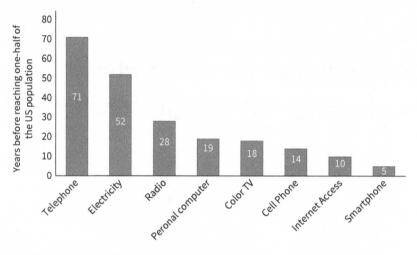

Figure 10.1.   The Rate of Diffusion of New Technologies

Source: For smartphones, *Number of Smartphones in Active Use in the United States from 2009 to 2019*, Statista, www.statista.com/statistics/800990/smartphones-in-active-use-in-the-united-states/ (accessed April 9, 2021). For the rest, Adam Thierer & Grant Eskelsen, *Media Metrics: The True State of the Modern Media Marketplace*, The Progress & Freedom Foundation, Summer 2008, at 18, as reproduced in Michael J. Mauboussin & Dan Callahan, Credit Suisse, *A Long Look at Short-Termism: Questioning the Premise*, 27 J. Applied Corp. Fin. 70, 72 (2015).

Previous technology breakthroughs took far longer to permeate society than those of today. Consider the time needed before new technologies like the telephone, the radio, the personal computer, the internet, and the smartphone reached half of the US population: nearly three-quarters of a century for the telephone, a quarter-century for the radio, nearly 20 years for the personal computer, only a decade for the internet, and five years for the smartphone. Figure 10.1 illustrates.

The trend in patent frequency and CEO sentiment corroborate this. The number of patents has tripled in the past 25 years, as Figure 10.2 shows. And 94% of the responding Fortune 500 CEOs agreed with the statement: "My company will change more in the next five years than it has in the last five years," with three-fourths seeing the rapid pace of technological innovation as one of the biggest challenges facing the company.[2]

A well-known modern management book states:

Coping with the relentless onslaught of technology change [is] akin to trying to climb a mudslide raging down a hill. You have to scramble with everything you've

[2] Fortune, 2015 Fortune 500 CEO Survey, www.fortune.com/2015/06/04/fortune-500-ceo-survey/.

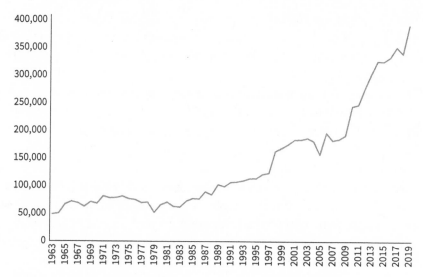

Figure 10.2. Rising Number of Patents Awarded Annually, 1963–2019
Source: U.S. Patent and Trademark Office, U.S. Patent Statistics Chart, 1963–2019, www.
uspto.gov/web/offices/ac/ido/oeip/taf/us_stat.htm (last visited May 30, 2020).

got to stay on top of it, and if you ever once stop to catch your breath, you get
buried.[3]

This disruptive pressure creates conflict. Even if the change is beneficial
overall, too many lose out.[4] *If* that conflict and disruption can be managed,
better economic returns could result. But if it cannot be managed well, then
the economy has a political and social problem, expressed in part as hostility
to stock market short-termism.

B. Corporate Turnover

Corporate turnover is also accelerating. The number of new firms is rising.[5]
And "public companies are perishing sooner than ever before. Since 1970, the
life span of companies, as measured by the length of time that their shares
are publicly traded, has significantly decreased. . . . [B]usinesses are dying at

---

[3] Clayton M. Christensen, The Innovator's Dilemma: When New Technologies Cause Great
Firms to Fail 98 (1997).
[4] I elaborate on this in Chapter 13 and the Conclusion.
[5] Bureau of Labor Statistics, Entrepreneurship and the U.S. Economy, Business Establishment Age, www.
bls.gov/bdm/entrepreneurship/entrepreneurship.htm (last visited, June 30, 2020). More precisely, the
number rose until the 2008–2009 financial crisis, dipped sharply, then began rising again.

a much younger age than the people who run them."[6] Some of these companies are not boarding their windows to close up but are being bought and reconfigured by other companies. Still, this too represents disruptive change for those affected.

The average life span of stock-exchange corporations was about six decades in 1970. By 2010 it had halved to three decades.[7] "[B]usinesses move through their life cycles twice as quickly as they did 30 years ago."[8] In 1958, the average duration of a firm in Standard & Poor's list of the 500 largest firms was 61 years. It was down to 18 years by 2012.[9]

Creative destruction is central to market capitalism, in Joseph Schumpeter's classical formulation.[10] But the emphasis here is not just on it being "creative." It is also, well, destructive. Lives are disrupted, careers ended, workers are thrown out of jobs. The rate of destruction can, even if it's creative, be too fast and too severe for the polity to absorb.[11] Change that adapts firms and markets to new realities is not much fun for the executives and employees made redundant.

C. Employment Uncertainty

Accelerating corporate turnover can make the average person feel less secure. Not only is the job insecure, but a person's career and skills have an ever-shortening half-life. A job lost decades ago might have meant an inconvenient relocation; but today it's thought more likely to mean a sharp drop in wages. Consider this statement from Senator Ben Sasse (once a historian before becoming a conservative US Senator):

> In the 1970s, it was common for a primary breadwinner to spend his career at one company, but now workers switch jobs and industries at a more rapid pace. We are entering an era in which we're going to have to create a society of lifelong learners.

---

[6] Martin Reeves & Lisanne Püschel, *Die Another Day: What Leaders Can Do About the Shrinking Life Expectancy of Corporations*, BCG HENDERSON INST. (Dec. 2, 2015), www.bcgperspectives.com/content/articles/strategic-planning-growth-die-another-day/.

[7] *Id.*

[8] *Id.*

[9] *Creative Destruction Whips through Corporate America*, INNOSIGHT, Feb. 2012, www.innosight.com/wp-content/uploads/2016/08/creative-destruction-whips-through-corporate-america_final2015.pdf. *But cf.* Dane Stangler & Sam Arbesman, What Does Fortune 500 Turnover Mean? 6, 10 (Kauffman Foundation Report, June 2012), www.kauffman.org/what-we-do/research/2012/06/what-does-fortune-500-turnover-mean (indicating that although Fortune 500 firms are turning over more rapidly, there have been similar turnover periods historically).

[10] JOSEPH SCHUMPETER, CAPITALISM, SOCIALISM AND DEMOCRACY 82–83 (1942, Routledge 1994 ed.).

[11] *See generally* Mark J. Roe, *Backlash*, 98 COLUM. L. REV. 217 (1998).

We're going to have to create a culture in which people in their 40s and 50s, who see their industry disintermediated and their jobs evaporate, get retrained and have the will and the chutzpah and the tools and the social network to get another job. Right now that doesn't happen enough.[12]

Whether or not the senator got the rates of job switching right, he captured a widespread sensibility. People do not always take disruption of their own jobs in stride. Some react by criticizing the agents of change as short-termist and some seek to slow things down.

This view of employment uncertainty fits the common understanding. I should, however, be more circumspect with this part of the rapid-change thesis, because the data does not irrefutably support it. The total separation rate (the sum of new unemployment, new dropouts from the labor force, and movement to a new job) *decreased* slightly in the 1994 to 2004 decade[13] and was stable thereafter, with the exception of obvious crises (financial in 2009 and health in 2020).[14]

What then explains the widespread sense that dislocation is today more common and disorienting? One possibility is that the conventional wisdom is incorrect; we've always felt this way and the pushback previously came in ways other than castigating short-term stock markets. A second is that the increasing insecurity of recent decades did not occur across the economy but in visible sectors (such as autos or steel) that previously were secure, powerful, and salient.[15] Manufacturing jobs have disappeared and service work has grown; the shift presumably induced insecurity, particularly in those with manufacturing but not service skills. A third is that there was once a core of stable jobs disproportionately held by white males, or by the politically central, and it was these jobs that became unstable. A fourth is that perceptions of insecurity have grown even if turnover has not. Media plays a role; slower economic growth plays a role. A fifth is that the consequences of losing one's job have become more severe.[16] For many workers, their next best job is much less well paid.

---

[12] Ben Sasse, *The Challenge of Our Disruptive Era*, WALL ST. J., Apr. 21, 2017.

[13] Robert E. Hall, *Job Loss, Job Finding, and Unemployment in the U.S. Economy over the Past Fifty Years*, 20 NBER MACROECONOMICS ANNUAL 101, 110 (2005).

[14] U.S. Bureau of Labor Statistics, Job Openings, Hires, and Separations Rates, Seasonally Adjusted, www.bls.gov/charts/job-openings-and-labor-turnover/opening-hire-seps-rates.htm (last accessed April 23, 2021) (4.3% separation rate in February 2006; 4.2% in Feb. 2021, with substantial stability through the interim).

[15] Susan B. Carter, *The Changing Importance of Lifetime Jobs, 1892–1978*, 27 IND. RELATIONS 287, 287–88 (1988).

[16] Hall, *supra* note 13, at 105, 111 (separation declines little during a recession but the time needed for separated workers to obtain a new job lengthens).

D. Policy Uncertainty

Policy uncertainty, a bête noire of conservatives, should not be ignored. From nearly a decade ago, we have the following from finance on policy uncertainty: "At Vanguard, [the large mutual fund complex,] we estimate that policy uncertainty has created a $261 billion drag on the U.S. economy."[17] As former Federal Reserve chair and economist Ben Bernanke said, higher uncertainty induces firms to postpone investing and hiring for projects that, once started, are costly to slow or stop.[18] Stanford's center on the subject sees policy-based economic uncertainty as rising (sharply during crises, moderately otherwise), climbing to a level of about 15–40% higher in the 2010 decade than in the 1980s and 1990s.[19] Spikes in policy uncertainty have a long-lasting negative economic impact.[20]

Policy uncertainty's source is not the stock market, but electoral uncertainty, political partisanship, and political polarization.[21] And the 2008–2009 financial crisis, the possibility of sovereign defaults on their debt, and political disruptions like Brexit all bolster global uncertainty, undermining companies' capacity to plan for the long-term. Uncertain whether the domestic partisan polity will break left or right, businesses, investors, and workers are wary about what to do for the long run. The chance of sharp political change is significant. Deadlock and partisanship, businesses could fear, are or will be punctuated by sharp changes.

---

[17] Bill McNabb, *Uncertainty Is the Enemy of Recovery*, WALL ST. J., Apr. 28, 2013, at A17. *Cf.* Kevin A. Hassett & Joseph W. Sullivan, Policy Uncertainty and the Economy (Am. Enterprise Inst., Aug. 2016), www.ssrn.com/abstract=2818624.

[18] Ben S. Bernanke, *Irreversibility, Uncertainty and Cyclical Investment*, 98 Q.J. ECON. 85 (1983).

[19] ECONOMIC POLICY UNCERTAINTY, US MONTHLY INDEX, http://policyuncertainty.com/us_monthly. html (last visited July 2, 2020); ECONOMIC POLICY UNCERTAINTY, INDEX, http://policyuncertainty.com/ index.html (last visited July 1, 2020). The Federal Reserve uses policy uncertainty measures from the Stanford group. Fed. Res. Bank of St. Louis, Economic Policy Uncertainty Index for United States, https:// fred.stlouisfed.org/series/USEPUINDXD#0 (last visited July 1, 2020). Huseyin Gulen & Mihai Ion, *Policy Uncertainty and Corporate Investment*, 29 REV. FIN. STUD. 523, 523 (2016), state:
> Policy-related uncertainty is negatively related to firm and industry level investment, and the economic magnitude of the effect is substantial. Our estimates indicate that approximately two thirds of the 32% drop in corporate investments observed during the 2007–2009 crisis period can be attributed to policy related uncertainty.

[20] Andrew Foerster, *The Asymmetric Effect of Uncertainty*, Fed. Res. Bank Kansas City, ECON. REV., 3d Q. 2014, at 1, 2.

[21] The best single explanation for increased polarization is increased inequality. And this—inequality—is a liberal commentator's favorite. *See* John V. Duca & Jason L. Saving, *Income Inequality, Media Fragmentation, and Increased Political Polarization*, 35 CONTEMPORARY ECON. POL'Y 392 (2017); John Voorheis, Nolan McCarty & Boris Shor, Unequal Incomes, Ideology and Gridlock: How Rising Inequality Increases Political Polarization 37–38 (Aug. 21, 2015), https://ssrn.com/abstract=2649215. *See also* NOLAN McCARTY, KEITH T. POOLE & HOWARD ROSENTHAL, POLARIZED AMERICA: THE DANCE OF IDEOLOGY AND UNEQUAL RICHES 75–117 (2d ed. 2016).

Short-term planning makes sense in such environments. If executives fear a major change in policy over the life of a 10-year investment—a change that could make the investment worthless—then they have reason to shorten the term of the investment to only a few years.

E. Speeding Technology, Greater Globalization, Changing Government Policies

Whether or not stock markets are moving faster, the world is. Technological change is faster, the internet is destroying old distribution systems, computers are changing how business is done, and modern telecommunications are making global markets local. International trade more quickly hits local businesses that were once isolated from world markets. Viruses that once shut down a locality and ravaged a nation now infect the world and destroy economic well-being.

* * *

Critics who believe that stock markets are excessively short-term focused need to rethink their premises. If adaptability is becoming more important than ever, and if technological change is going through phase shifts more quickly than an employee's or executive's commitment to the firm, then there should be a rising utility for the right kinds of pressures that push more firms to adapt to change. Some evidence supports this proposition: short-term pressure to adapt has been valuable for firms in some industries, sometimes leading "firms with more short-term institutional ownership [to] achieve better long-term performance than other firms in the new competitive environment."[22]

Accelerating technological, business, and economic change hence can make the activism and pressure of stock markets potentially *more* valuable today, not less. An economy that *facilitates* agents of change creates overall value for its population as long as most of the stock market pressure on management and firms is to adapt to new conditions. But the price for that adaptation is dislocation, and the costs of that dislocation fall unevenly. It dislodges some people from what once were good jobs. Jobs and skills that once were secure for decades are now only good for years. The disruptions of modern life, the cacophony of change, and the insecurities of the twenty-first century

---

[22] Mariassunta Giannetti & Xiaoyun Yu, *Adapting to Radical Change: The Benefits of Short-Horizon Investors*, 67 Mgmt. Sci. 4032 (2021).

can all be misanalyzed as arising in the pernicious short-termism of the stock market but are in fact a new reality of too much moving too fast.

Channeling these pressures to induce *better* adaptation is the challenge—to soften the blow to those disabled by disruption. We today face more destabilizing economic change with which we must cope. True, a functional stock market transmits these changes through the economy more effectively—more quickly—than a dysfunctional one. It is one of the means by which technological and other change pushes forward. But blaming the stock market for underlying technological pressure itself and seeking to slow it down are wrong ways to cope—unless there's just no other way to handle the boiling social pressure.

11

Short-Termism as Popular Narrative

Connotation, Category Confusion, and Confirmation

Short-termism's connotations help to explain why it's perceived to be more pernicious in the popular and political mind than the evidence in Chapters 2, 5, 6, and 7 shows it to be. It is seen as a scourge in people's minds even before it is analyzed, because short-termism connotes unreliability and instability, while long-termism connotes loyalty and consistency. Surely the first is to be avoided and the second promoted. Shifting the vocabulary can rehabilitate short-termism as flexibility and adaptability, two positives—and vocabulary shifting can also transform long-termism to stubbornly sticking with a bad business plan. But those post-shift connotations are not most people's initial reactions.

Short-termism seems more vivid, more powerful, and more widespread than the underlying data indicates it is because a strong narrative supports it. The image of traders with limited commitment to a company fits naturally with an image of hamstrung executives unable to invest for the long run. A powerful narrative is more convincing to most people than data, such as the data that I presented in Chapter 2 and evaluated in Chapters 5, 6, and 7—and Roy Shapira and I go deeper elsewhere to link the short-term narrative in this chapter to the behavioral economics literature.[1]

---

[1] Mark J. Roe & Roy Shapira, *The Power of the Narrative in Corporate Lawmaking*, 11 Harv. Bus. L. Rev. 233 (2021).

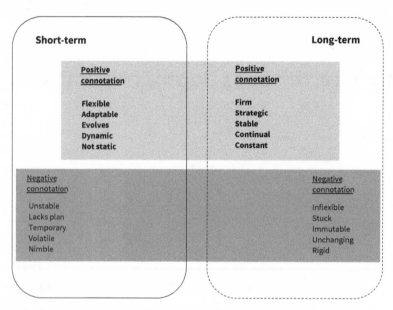

Figure 11.1. Contrasting the Negative and Positive Connotations of Long-Termism and Short-Termism

A. Connotation

Connotations count: long-term players are loyal, short-term players are flighty and lack a plan. The typical observer, in my experience, is immediately positive about the long-term and skeptical of the short-term. Short-termism is an epithet, long-termism a compliment.

The words themselves. Business basics again: short-termism need not be bad, nor long-termism good. A company's short-term decision to raise production because of skyrocketing demand is good. Long-term investment in a factory whose product has no future because its technology will soon be displaced is not. The words' immediate connotations fail to bring that business indeterminacy to the fore of the speaker's or listener's consciousness.

Long-termism connotes positive qualities of reliability, steadiness, and consistency, an examination of dictionaries and conversations indicates. Yet short-term players, rather than being fickle and disloyal, are sometimes just adaptable. They are adjusting. Analogously, long-term players could be loyal and steadfast, or bullheaded and stubborn. Figure 11.1 captures what seem to be the usual and dominant connotations and lists similar time-horizon words—near-synonyms—that, if they were more vividly associated with short- and long-termism, would reverse the baseline connotations.

B. Category Confusion

We saw in Chapter 3 that objectionable corporate phenomena that are not distorted time horizons are mislabeled as short-term in common parlance: environmental degradation, financial risk-taking, and employee mistreatment, for example. A poorly socialized firm, *even if it thinks solely in the long-term*, can and will pollute, degrade the environment, and warm the planet if it only considers its selfish benefits and not the social costs.[2] These degradations are objectionable in both the short- and the long-run. But because they are mistakenly mixed in the popular and political mind with true time horizon failures, *we perceive much more stock-market-driven short-termism than there is.*

C. Confirmation

Repetition reinforces belief. The idea of stock-market-driven short-termism is easy to understand, easy to state, and easy to repeat. It is persuasive. It can provide a bulletproof excuse: "I'd love to go ahead," says the company's CEO, who doesn't want to go ahead. "But it'll hit this quarter's profits at a bad time. Can't do it."

Confirmation from miscategorization. Confirmation comes from the miscategorization described in the prior section and in Chapter 3. Many negatives are seen to emanate from stock market short-termism but are really due to selfishness. As a consequence, executives, journalists, and policymakers constantly see many corporate actions that they (1) view as pernicious and (2) label as short-term. The idea that stock-market-driven short-termism is rampant is thus reinforced every time we read of an oil pipeline leak or a corporate fraud.

Confirmation by ease of repetition. Repetition of the wide extent of pernicious short-termism comes from the media, intermittently from political leaders, and regularly from those with an interest in promoting a wide belief in stock-market-driven short-termism. An echo chamber of major law firms, consulting companies, and the press promulgate and repeat the thesis in the corporate world. Professional memoranda, newsletters, and managerial journals repeat regularly that short-termism is a serious economic problem.

---

[2] Time horizon distortion would be relevant if corporate actions that lead to employee dissatisfaction, global warming, and financial risk-taking are usually to the firm's short-term benefit and its long-term detriment. However, if low wages are profitable over the long-term, or noxious emissions are profitable over the long-run, then we have a social problem, but one that's more than merely short-term.

They are more certain than the evidence we saw in Chapters 2, 5, 6, and 7 should lead them to be.

Publicly-distributed memos of prominent law firms confirm executives' beliefs and show solidarity with executives perceiving short-term pressures.[3] The memos buck up the executives' resolve to fight off shareholder activists and to condemn traders—all of whom are seen to be short-term.

In management consulting, McKinsey—the major managerial consulting company—regularly writes about how corporate short-termism, especially that originating with shareholders and the stock market, must be handled well by boards and executives, and supports research groups' efforts aiming to show wide stock market short-termism.

Confirmation from executives' perceptual distortions. Successful executives are optimistic about the future, as is well-documented.[4] If less optimistic (but more realistic?) shareholders, activists, and hedge funds oppose executives' optimistic expansion and investment, the executives can interpret their opponents' mistaken strategies as stemming not just from differences of opinion on the right corporate strategy but as stemming from the stock market's short-termism. It becomes easier for executives interacting with difficult, sometimes abrasive, stock analysts or activists to dismiss them as deleteriously too short-term; executives repeat their stories to other executives, reinforcing their own and others' beliefs.[5]

* * *

Connotation, category confusion, and confirmation make the stock-market-driven short-termism narrative more vividly convincing to executives, attentive citizens, journalists, and policymakers than the underlying data, analysis, and reality show.

Connotation makes the long-term something to prefer over the short-term, when business sense tells us that's frequently not the case. The basic connotations prompt people to be wary of unreliable short-termers and supportive of steady and stable long-termers. It takes reflection to see that

---

[3] *See* the Appendix to Roe & Shapira, *supra* note 1.

[4] J.B. Heaton, *Corporate Governance and the Cult of Agency*, 64 VILL. L. REV. 201, 218–19 & n.87 (2019); Ulrike Malmendier & Geoffrey Tate, *CEO Overconfidence and Corporate Investment*, 60 J. FIN. 2661 (2005); Richard Roll, *The Hubris Hypothesis of Corporate Takeovers*, 59 J. BUS. 197 (1986); J.B. Heaton, *Managerial Optimism and Corporate Finance*, 31 FIN. MGMT. 33 (2002).

[5] This conflict does not in itself, however, logically preclude executives from being the side that's systematically correct and financiers being systematically wrong. It only shows systematic disagreement. However, the evidence in Chapter 7 has the executives as sincere but incorrect.

long-termers are sometimes stubborn and obstinate while short-termers are sometimes nimble and adaptive.

Confusion leads people to see much unattractive corporate behavior as being short-term and stemming from the stock market's purported short-termism, even when not fundamentally coming from time horizon problems. The actions are often due instead to the corporation's capacity to off-load costs and problems onto society.

Confirmation comes from repetition that etches the idea into the public's and policymakers' consciousness. The stock market short-termism narrative is clear and simple. Those with an interest in promoting it can repeat it convincingly—and sincerely believe it themselves. Politicians and policymakers can identify short-termism as prominent and pressing, and vivid enough to use in the media.

12

Political Support from Inside the Corporation

Executives and Employees

Why is stock market short-termism one of the few corporate problems that emerges in politics and that grabs much media attention when, as we've seen, the supporting evidence is so weak? Chapter 11 highlighted the idea that it's easy to see short-termism as widespread and pernicious due to its connotation, to category confusion, and to its easy repetition and retention. And Chapter 10 showed how disruption from accelerating change, which occurs everywhere now, can be misunderstood as emanating from stock market time-horizon short-termism.

Political economy forces strengthen these impacts. Business interests benefit by weakening shareholder influence. Executives benefit, of course, as we've seen. But so do employees fearing job disruption. Politicians champion their cause. Stock market short-termism is the rhetorical cudgel.

The political problem posed by short-termism at one level is simple interest group pressure. At another level it is a more complex popular disaffection with work, with social arrangements, and with Wall Street.

A. Immediate Corporate Interests: Boards and Executives

For many executives and directors, it seems obvious that traders and shareholders—and especially activist shareholders—are just looking for a short-term profit while responsible executives and directors such as themselves have their companies' long-term health at heart.

Here are two examples of centralized, influential players. One, the powerful Business Roundtable—the association of the executives of the largest, most powerful US firms—regularly excoriates short-termism.[1] The *Wall Street Journal* provides their representatives with access to broadcast their message. After all, these are the country's most respected businesspeople, and they deserve to be heard. They inveigh against stock market short-termism; other businesspeople read their criticisms and are further persuaded of short-termism's perniciousness. Two, important legal actors broadcast the evidence favoring short-termism in ways that are well-absorbed in the legal community, quite plausibly even affecting the Delaware judges who are crucial to much day-to-day corporate lawmaking.[2] Newsletters and media spread the word.

This does not mean that those promoting the perniciousness of the financial short-termist view are insincere or that there's no consistent evidence. People often deeply and sincerely believe ideas that protect their own interests. Sometimes those ideas are correct; sometimes they are exaggerated.

B. Boardroom Ideology

Most well-socialized people need a non-selfish justification when pursuing their self-interest. For economic and business actors, it's satisfying to believe that their pursuit of self-interest is also good for the economy. Adam Smith helped them greatly in this regard, at least if they are self-interested butchers and bakers—the butcher's and baker's pursuit of self-interest, Smith promised, enriches the community and puts meat and bread on dinner tables.[3]

Wide belief in short-termism helps executives and board directors further by justifying their autonomy. Convinced that shareholder actions are pernicious and short-term, they can more confidently and sincerely believe that shielding executives and boards from shareholders is not self-interested

---

[1] *Business Roundtable Supports Move Away from Short-Term Guidance*, BUSINESS ROUNDTABLE (June 7, 2018), www.businessroundtable.org/media/news-releases/business-roundtable-supports-move-away-short-term-guidance ("short-termism is unhealthy for America's public companies").

[2] *E.g.*, Martin Lipton, *Empiricism and Experience; Activism and Short-Termism; the Real World of Business*, HARV. LAW SCHOOL FORUM ON CORP. GOVERNANCE, Oct 28, 2013, https://corpgov.law.harvard.edu/2013/10/28/empiricism-and-experience-activism-and-short-termism-the-real-world-of-business/.

[3] ADAM SMITH, AN INQUIRY INTO THE NATURE AND CAUSES OF THE WEALTH OF NATIONS bk. 1, ch. 2 (1776).

self-entrenchment but is instead the best way to counter shareholders' debilities, which damage the whole economy.[4]

T. Boone Pickens, who during the 1980s' takeover wars was a prominent corporate raider—the type of activist of that time who sought to buy stock in companies whose direction the activist wanted to change—captured this idea when he wrote for the *Harvard Business Review* about short-termism:

> When confronted with a perceived threat to their sovereignty, managers have learned to portray themselves as long-term visionaries and their dissident stockholders as short-term opportunists.
>
> Increasing acceptance of the short-term theory has freed executives to scorn any shareholders they choose to identify as short-termers.[5]

Pickens thought executives' belief to be manipulative and insincere, but his assessment *under*estimates the belief's importance. It is *more* powerful if sincerely held. Confidence in the legitimacy of one's own position is itself a source of power. That confidence makes it easier for executives, boards, and their allies to seek judicial determinations and regulation that bolsters executives' and boards' autonomy and power to fight off activists, makes it easier to deny activists' legitimacy, and makes it easier for them to stick to corporate plans even when outsiders and new technologies are telling the executives to adapt and change. It's not only right, as they perceive it, to resist the short-term pressure for the target firm's health, but doing so is not just self-interested: executive autonomy is best for the economy and the country overall.

C. Broad-Based Interests: Employees

Employees whose jobs would be made obsolete or whose workplace would be made more demanding also benefit from slowing down change. Their political allies advocate against short-termism on their behalf. Real short-termism is worth stopping, but this effort could go well beyond real short-termism to also seek to slow even basic change. We saw one such instance in the Introduction. A Wausau, Wisconsin paper company was slow to change its product line as email, the internet, and electronic files shifted demand away from fine-quality office papers to household paper products. When activists

---

[4] Jamie Dimon & Warren E. Buffett, *Short-Termism Is Harming the Economy*, WALL ST. J., June 6, 2018 (supporting the Business Roundtable anti-short-termism initiative).

[5] T. Boone Pickens, Jr., *Professions of a Short-Termer*, HARV. BUS. REV., May 1986.

pressed the company, senators swung into action to attack the activists' short-termism—even though the company's product shift was inevitable.[6]

The political combination of executives and employees aiming for the same result can be powerful. Executives have influence, status, and money for political campaigns. Employees have votes. Employees displaced by change—whether the change comes from pernicious short-termism or efficient adaptation—complain and the rhetoric of short-termism justifies their complaints to political decisionmakers. And if stock markets are believed to be too short-term, then these players need not see themselves as diminishing one of capitalism's strengths—adaptability to changing markets—but correcting one of its weaknesses.

Short-termist rhetoric obscures the possibility that incumbents—executives, directors, and employees with solid jobs at above-market wages—sometimes just want to slow down change. A loose protectionist coalition unites under the banner of short-termism.[7] One reason the short-termism idea came alive in the media and in policy discourse was that it unites executives and employees, and the politicians who serve them.

---

[6] *See supra* Introduction, pp. 3–5.

[7] Henrik Cronqvist, Fredrik Heyman, Mattias Nilsson, Helena Svaleryd & Jonas Vlachos, *Do Entrenched Managers Pay Their Workers More?* 464 J. Fin. 309 (2009). *Cf.* Marianne Bertrand & Sendhil Mullainathan, *Enjoying the Quiet Life? Corporate Governance and Managerial Preferences*, 111 J. Pol. Econ. 1043 (2003) (when managers are insulated from takeovers, employees receive higher wages); Marianne Bertrand & Sendhil Mullainathan, *Is There Discretion in Wage Setting? A Test Using Takeover Legislation*, 30 Rand J. Econ. 535, 545 (1999) (finding that antitakeover statutes reduce management's incentives to minimize labor costs, with firms in antitakeover states having wages "rise by 1 or 2% or about $500 per year"). The two last inquiries (but not Cronqvist et al., which does not use US data) use takeover statutes as indicators of managerial entrenchment. Such statutes are not strong indicators because, since the 1980s, antitakeover legislation is unimportant. By 1990 or thereabouts, boards could impede activists without protective legislation. *See generally* Emiliano M. Catan & Marcel Kahan, *The Law and Finance of Antitakeover Statutes*, 68 Stan. L. Rev. 629, 648–50 (2016). Some of the US data, however, is from the 1980s, which is more useful because it was collected before boards were clearly free to stymie takeovers without protective legislation.

13

Political Support from Outside the Corporation

Popular Opinion vs. Wall Street

There are other reasons why anti-short-termism is rhetorically popular with politicians. It provides the "right" targets for politicians seeking votes—Wall Street not Main Street. It provides a plausible solution while better solutions are harder to implement, more difficult to communicate, or blocked by influential groups. It obscures political failure—like the decades-long decline in governmental support for basic research. It conflates self-seeking private interests—executives and employees with good jobs in a declining industry—with the public interest in developing more long-term companies.

Some of the power of anti-stock-market short-termism's popular appeal comes from a backlash to disruptive change. In this chapter I look further at this intersection between disruption, legitimate political rhetoric, and the various interests.

A. Public Opinion

Material interest can drive ideas and outcomes, of course. But more is in play. Many citizens find the concept of short-termism intuitively likely, and the concept also resonates with many citizens' aversion to Wall Street. Across the political spectrum, 58% of US citizens think that Wall Street harms the economy more than it helps it.[1] For those who dislike Wall Street, it is convenient to reinforce their revulsion with the belief that its drawbacks include a short-termism that punishes the entire economy.

B. The Rhetoric of Criticizing Capitalism

The modern economy has left many behind, while many of those with good jobs fear losing those jobs as their industry changes or as technology makes their skills redundant. To many voters, it looks like Wall Street financiers pull down heavy rewards for destabilizing the corporation and putting innocent employees out of work.

The legitimate vocabulary for criticizing the economy and capitalism is limited in the United States. Most political players and media pundits do not want to be seen as fringe malcontents. Even with the increasing acceptance of democratic socialism in political circles—viz. Bernie Sanders and Alexandria Ocasio-Cortez—the rhetorical rejection of capitalism for socialism is unpersuasive politically in the United States. But *condemning the stock market as short-term* is legitimate. For populists, doing so allows the speaker to reject the current capitalist arrangement *without rejecting capitalism overall.*

Critics of Wall Street can affirm their respect for long-term, steadfast capitalist investors, while rejecting short-term players who close down factories. "Long-term investors represent true, venerable US capitalism," they can say and believe. "But we reject the illegitimate skullduggery of traders and activists, who lack coherence and commitment. We do not accept what they do to their companies, to their managers, to their factories, and to their employees. They are unreliable. They are short-term. They are not true capitalists, but leech-like, unreliable, ephemeral traders." Political leaders can take over business leaders' anti-short-term rhetoric and thereby avoid taking a fringe position.

Opposing Wall Street in general can be politically dicey but opposing Wall Street short-termism is not. A political player who wants to criticize Wall Street profoundly can pick up anti-short-termism rhetoric from businesspeople and then attribute the negative quality that the populist is criticizing (like low wages for some, poor working conditions for others, climate degradation for all) to Wall Street's short-termism, not competitive capitalism. The political actor then is not so easily marginalized as an anti-capitalist outcast.

---

[1] Philip Bump, *Shock Poll: Everyone Hates Wall Street*, WASH. POST, June 30, 2016. *Cf.* Jim Lardner, *Americans Agree on Regulating Wall Street*, U.S. NEWS & WORLD REP'T, Sept. 16, 2013.

After all, the political leader is attacking short-term behavior as a deviation from good capitalism—even if time horizons have nothing or little to do with the criticized behavior. Pretexts are valuable.

The vocabulary of short-termism provides a rhetorically acceptable way, in some circles, to reject the basic economic arrangements in US society that cannot otherwise readily be legitimately rejected.

C. Undermining the Rhetoric of Shareholder Primacy

Similarly, diffuse political issues like a generalized angst about business and economic life often lack traction. Short-termism, however, can give such issues more politically viable traction.

Consider the current corporate purpose debate. A stance against short-termism partly corresponds to a position on shareholder primacy versus stakeholder respect. That is, a central corporate dispute today is whether shareholder primacy provides the utilitarian greatest-good-for-the-greatest-number or surreptitiously bolsters the wealthiest sectors in the United States, at the expense of employees, the environment, communities, and stakeholders in general.

So, imagine a colloquy between X, a stakeholder supporter, and Y, a shareholder primacy supporter and modern-day, market-respecting disciple of Adam Smith. Y argues that in the end shareholder primacy provides the most value for all, including stakeholders. It grows the biggest economic pie and then government can redistribute that pie in the fairest way.

X, the stakeholder supporter, undermines Y with the argument that even basic shareholder wealth maximization is incoherent. Shareholders cannot get their firms to maximize shareholder value (much less stakeholder value) for the long-term because the stock market is so short-term oriented that it induces public firms to be mismanaged.[2] Since shareholder primacy cannot even protect shareholders' long-term interests, how can one expect it to protect society's long-term interests? Even if it bakes a good pie for today, it starves even the corporation itself tomorrow.

In this rhetoric of short-termism and stakeholders, capitalism deserves respect, but deviants from good capitalism—like short-term shareholders—do not deserve that respect.

---

[2] *E.g.*, David Ciepley, *Beyond Public and Private: Toward a Political Theory of the Corporation*, 107 Am. Pol. Sci. Rev. 139, 153 (2013).

D. Efficient Short-Termism?

The profound political difficulty comes from the increasing likelihood that in the past two decades we're seeing rising *efficient* short-termism. Product cycles shorten. Technological change quickens. That shortening and quickening dislocates employees and executives. Some firms, executives, and employees adapt, some react. Some react by blaming the stock market or foreign trade or elites and vote for candidates who will slow down change and reduce Wall Street's capacity to influence business. Part of the reaction is to blame stock markets as perniciously short-term and aim to reduce their influence and capacity to disturb the status quo.

E. Those Displaced by Change

Change disrupts. People dislike the disruption, especially when it affects them. Hard-learned skills lose value. Communities shrink when the town's factory cannot produce efficiently anymore and its sales stagnate. Those who are displaced and suffer misfortune, through no fault of their own, often want to blame a malevolent force, not circumstances.

Scapegoating for one's loss is a well-known phenomenon:

> Frustration generates aggressive tendencies, which cannot be directed against the actual thwarting agent because this agent is not visible, or is capable of retaliating with severely punitive action. A needed outlet is then found for the pent-up aggressive "energy" through attacks upon some innocent minority group. The displaced aggression is rationalized by blaming the minority for the frustrations the aggressor has experienced and/or attributing undesirable characteristics to this group.[3]

Transfer the scapegoating concept from its typical environment to short-termism. The disruption of modern economic change is the thwarting agent from the quotation above, one that leaves too many people behind. But general economic change is a little abstract and not vividly visible to many people, even those who lose out from that change. Much more sharply visible and therefore more readily blamed are Wall Street traders and activists—short-termers

---

[3] Leonard Berkowitz & James A. Green, *The Stimulus Qualities of the Scapegoat*, 64 J. ABNORMAL & SOC. PSYCHOL. 293, 293 (1962); Eugene Toker, *The Scapegoat as an Essential Group Phenomenon*, 22 INT'L J. GROUP PSYCHOTHERAPY 320, 321 (1972).

all—who purportedly profit from the economy being perniciously short-term. In some ways, Wall Street is an agent for that change, by financing new technologies and withdrawing from fading ones. In most ways, though, it is no more than the messenger.

This tension is not new and indeed is a fundamental aspect of capitalism. A thick strand of twentieth century social analysis, exemplified by Karl Polanyi's *Great Transformation*, has shown how markets can, and often do, destabilize the polity, because too much of a democratic polity dislikes the disruptive results that markets bring.[4] The rhetoric of short-termism is in no small part an appeal to people's sense that markets are moving too fast.

---

[4] KARL POLANYI, THE GREAT TRANSFORMATION: THE POLITICAL AND ECONOMIC ORIGINS OF OUR TIME 75–80, 136–39, 151–55, 164–65, 185–86, 210–12, 260 (1944). *Cf.* Mark J. Roe, *Backlash*, 98 COLUM. L. REV. 217 (1998).

Conclusion

"The finance world's short-termism will destroy our communities, economies and the planet,"[1] we are told. But the evidence does not support the popular view that toxic short-term pressures from stock markets are severely harming the US economy.

* * *

The short-termism inquiry became a vital part of corporate law and governance in recent decades, engaging academics, judges, and lawyers; it has been one of the few corporate law issues that spills over into national politics and the nonbusiness media. It engages presidents and presidential candidates—Hillary Clinton, Joe Biden, Barack Obama, and Donald Trump. Media and political commentators regularly see stock-market-driven short-termism as widespread and pernicious for the economy.

One class of damage is said to come from corporate America cutting R&D, crippling itself by wasting cash in huge stock buybacks, and eating away at its own foundations by failing to invest in new capital and equipment. Worse yet, a second class of damage from short-termism induces financial crises, global warming, and employee mistreatment. Today there is much public discussion seeking to widen corporate purpose, expand corporate social responsibility, and heighten corporate sensitivity to the risks of catastrophic climate change.

But the problems in the second class are not primarily due to warped corporate time horizons. Financial crises, global warming, and stakeholder mistreatment come from the profitability of firms (and the rest of us, when driving cars and heating homes) selfishly polluting while others bear the brunt of that pollution and from financiers selfishly taking risks that create profit

---

[1] Sasja Beslik, *The Finance World's Short-termism Will Destroy Our Communities, Economies, and the Planet*, WORLD ECON. FORUM (May 17, 2017) (position pushed forward for the World Economic Forum by the then Head of Sustainable Finance of Nordea Group, the largest financial group in northern Europe), www.weforum.org/agenda/2017/03/the-finance-world-s-short-termism-will-destroy-our-communities-economies-and-the-planet/. Cf. *The Compact for Responsive and Responsible Leadership: A Roadmap for Sustainable Long-Term, Growth and Opportunity*, WORLD ECON. FORUM (Nov. 30, 2016), www3.weforum.org/docs/Media/AM17/The_Compact_for_Responsive_and_Responsible_Leadership_09.01.2017.pdf.

in good times and that governments cover in bad times—when Washington bails them out. Corporate selfishness is the root of this class of problems, not distorted corporate time horizons. Manipulating stock market time horizons will miss these targets because these problems are not at their core short-term.

It's the first set of problems that relates to short-termism, at least potentially. If R&D falls nationwide, if buybacks starve firms for cash, and if capital spending is slashed across corporate America, the nation's economy will suffer. The problem here is that the evidence does not support the conclusion that any of these problems are severe, or even that the shortfalls that we see are due to stock-market-driven short-termism.

In Part II, I evaluated the evidence and pushed forward three ideas that are not part of current thinking. First, the public consensus outruns the evidence. The firm-level studies that use the best statistical techniques are roughly equally divided, and I showed why the studies finding short-termism not problematic are stronger, with some of the iconic studies of short-termism not showing as severe a problem as they're regularly interpreted as showing. Moreover, second, I showed that these studies cannot readily tell us whether a local problem (if there is one) is offset by other firms picking up enough of the profit opportunities when a public firm misses a long-term opportunity. There's reason to think that broad sectors in the US economy can and do take up many such lost opportunities: the largest US public firms are future-oriented technology firms, many private firms that go public are tech firms selling not their short-term capabilities but selling their future, and strong private firms, of which there are many, do not directly depend on the stock market. There's an ecosystem quality to the US economy; not every firm must be good at everything for the economy to function well enough.

Third, I showed, primarily in Chapter 2, that the economy-wide data is not helpful to the short-termist idea. R&D is not declining in the US economy. Public firms dependent on the stock market are spending more than ever on R&D. Perhaps corporate R&D spending should be rising even more, but this has not been shown. Stock buybacks are indeed up, yes. But so are new stock sales and so is corporate borrowing, with the cash inflow from stock sales and borrowing, on the one hand, and the outflow from buybacks, on the other, approximately netting out. While buybacks are up in the larger firms, capital raising is up by about the same amount in smaller firms, i.e., capital is moving out from bigger and older firms and into smaller ones. That's what one should want from a well-functioning stock market.

Capital spending is down since the 2008–2009 recession—just as short-term critics say. But it is also down all around the developed world, both in nations that use stock markets heavily and in those that do not. And it's actually down less in the United States than elsewhere. Changing economies and shifting technologies—intangibles and R&D becoming more important and investment in hard manufacturing assets becoming less so—could explain the trend as well as or better than short-term stock market debilities.

* * *

A short-termist critic could respond that, whether stock-market-driven short-termism is a big or a small problem, we should reduce it. Anti-short-term policies are valuable and, for all we know, stock market short-termism might be a much bigger problem than this book indicates it to be.

But such policies would have costs that could be substantial. If we overly deter short-termism, we could gum up business adaptability. If we further enhance the authority of executives to pursue their vision of the correct corporate direction—in the belief that they are more long-term than the stock market—they may overly favor themselves and still neglect long-term economic goals. Evidence supports this concern as potentially important. This problem of executive self-favoring and corporate sluggishness has historically been serious and could become serious again. Worse, it can exacerbate economic inequality and further insulate one of our elites—the corporate elite—which is hardly good for today's polity. If we cannot on balance see good evidence that there is a deep, pernicious, and economy-wide short-termism problem—and I showed in Chapters 2, 5, 6, and 7 why the evidentiary case for it is weak or to the contrary—we should not seek to solve a problem that has not yet been shown to be severely detrimental to the economy overall.

Moreover, we will miss targets needing reform if we waste time aiming our policy arrows at a weak problem or a non-problem. Take R&D. Government R&D spending *has* dropped precipitously; corporate R&D spending has steadily gone *up*. Maybe we need more of both. But if we had to choose which to fix first, the place to start is with government R&D—which has long been a foundation for US economic success. That's the R&D funding channel that's been moving in the wrong direction—the victim of misplaced economizing on government spending. That's the high value target. If we mistakenly think stock market short-termism is the primary cause of reduced R&D and it is not, then we will aim at the wrong target and make policy errors.

* * *

Nor should we underestimate how the wide belief in stock market short-termism bolsters private interests. Lawmakers who are unsure of whether to give executives more autonomy from stockholders—a recurrent corporate and securities regulation controversy—presumably are more comfortable doing so when they believe that stock markets are too short-term and directors are not. While substantial executive autonomy is necessary for big firms to be run well, short-termism should have no weight in the balance between autonomy and accountability—because it has not been shown to be serious (and doesn't seem to be) and because more power for executives could in the abstract just as well increase short-termism as decrease it.

Believing in severe stock market short-termism gives executives an empowering, coherent world view. When they seek more autonomy from financial markets, they need not see themselves as selfishly seeking power; they are doing the right thing not just for their own company but also for the economy and society. It is not self-aggrandizement. Ideological coherence—the banishment of self-doubt—delivers its own source of managerial power.

* * *

Some basics: Long-termism is not necessarily good, nor short-termism automatically bad. The first can perpetuate a failed business, the second could allow the business to adapt to new technological and market realities.

But the short-termism idea in and of itself carries negative connotations—we want steady long-term growth, not short-term instability. Condemning short-termism too quickly and too broadly could readily undercut flexibility and nimble adaptability, because flexibility and adaptability can easily be mistaken as being short-term. Those who see stock market short-termism as profound have captured the rhetorical high ground: short-term instability's connotations are negative—flighty, unreliable, undisciplined; long-term's connotations are positive—reliability, steadfastness, sticking-to-plan.

* * *

Technological and global change has accelerated. The resulting disruption means executives and employees find their business models and job expectations overturned more often and more quickly now than before. These disruptions generate pushback from those affected—executives and employees. And that may be the deep structure underlying the popular animus against short-termism. Politics tends here to favor incumbents over markets; anti-short-termism rhetoric is a way that incumbents express their discomfort with the pressure.

This acceleration leads to an insidious and destabilizing political thesis. Stock markets could have become *efficiently* more short-term because product cycles are shortening, technology is changing faster than ever, and the impact of that technological change is wider, deeper, and more disruptive. These market forces are channeled into and through the stock market and the corporation, which cannot or at least does not provide security for its stakeholders. But even if this efficiency dynamic is true—and to be transparent, I believe it to be substantially so—its truth does not make everyone accept the results but instead induces many of the affected to react, irrespective of whether markets were efficiently or inefficiently short-term. Those who lose out—displaced workers, their families, and their political champions—respond politically and blame their plight on stock markets and those markets' purported short-termism. The polity needs to take care of these people and, if it doesn't, they and their political and media protectors will blame the corporation and the stock market.

Contrasting Joseph Schumpeter's and Karl Polanyi's thinking on these social conflicts brings out the conundrum. Creative destruction, said Schumpeter, is key to making market capitalism work:

> Capitalism . . . never can be stationary. . . . The fundamental impulse that sets and keeps the capitalist engine in motion comes from the new consumers' goods, the new methods of production or transportation, the new markets, the new forms of industrial organization that capitalist enterprise creates.
>
> The opening up of new markets, foreign or domestic, and the organizational development from the craft shop and factory to such concerns as U.S. Steel illustrate the same process of industrial mutation—if I may use that biological term—that incessantly revolutionizes the economic structure from within, incessantly destroying the old one, incessantly creating a new one.[2]

Much of what is taken to be short-termism is a 21st century variety of Schumpeterian creative destruction. The United States more than any other major economy has long let the forces of economic creation and destruction operate. But there comes a pace of destruction, creative or not, that is too fast and too severe for the body politic to absorb.

And that is where Polanyi comes in. Even if the pressure is largely (even if not entirely) toward efficiency and adaptability, the political backlash can be harsh, perhaps enough to undermine political stability. Markets can gnaw at and disrupt the polity when a democratic polity abhors market results. So, in

---

[2] Joseph Schumpeter, Capitalism, Socialism and Democracy 82–83 (1942, Routledge 1994 ed.).

Karl Polanyi's formulation, marketplace outcomes and changes need taming, because otherwise political instability will ensue: "Polanyi got . . . the big picture right. Democracy cannot survive an excessively free market."[3] "[W]hen markets . . . create severe social dislocations, people eventually revolt."[4] Polanyi's revolt against the market parallels this view I advance here: populist anti-short-termism is less a disciplined analysis concluding from the evidence that the stock market has a defective time horizon than a reaction to disorienting and disruptive change.[5]

Consider the possibility that the pace of change has become so fast and so complete that it disrupts more people's lives than ever before. They acquire skills, get themselves good jobs, and then poof, those jobs are gone and their skills are rendered valueless.

They rebel. They rebel against disruption and instability, latching on to short-termism as a unifying, underlying cause. They would hardly be dissuaded if they were convinced that much of what they see as *short-term is efficient adaptation.* Nor would it make much difference, I assert, if it were shown that their factory's closing was due not to short-termism but to long-term technological change that will bring more jobs, but bring them later on and for other people. Efficient or not, those people whose working lives, personal lives, and sense of self are disrupted often blame markets, financial and otherwise, for their problems. They react politically. They demand that change slow down and not disrupt their work as much as it has. Political and media leaders who blame financial market short-termism find a sympathetic audience.

This conflict—between pressure to change and pushback from those who would be displaced—is real. Production cannot proceed without sufficient political peace. If unresolved, social consensus fractures and political stability subsides.

Consider the consequence of this last possibility. Whether the stock-market-driven short-termist idea is on the evidence truly severe—and the analysis in Chapters 2, 5, 6, and 7 says the evidence for that is not there—would become politically and socially irrelevant. Even if change brings about economic progress for most of us, that progress fails to comfort those who lose out. The polity turns away from the better policy targets (or is captured by

---

[3] Robert Kuttner, *The Man from Red Vienna,* N.Y. REV. BOOKS, Dec. 21, 2017, at 55, 57.

[4] *Id.* And "[i]n many countries, populist parties are the only ones to argue that there exists a real alternative." Bojan Bugaric, *The Two Faces of Populism: Between Authoritarian and Democratic Populism,* 20 GERMAN L.J. 390 (2019).

[5] *Cf.* Mark J. Roe, *Backlash,* 98 COLUM. L. REV. 217 (1998); MARK J. ROE, POLITICAL DETERMINANTS OF CORPORATE GOVERNANCE 116–41 (2003); Jeffrey N. Gordon, *Corporations, Markets, and Courts,* 91 COLUM. L. REV. 1931, 1972–74 (1991).

interests) because the short-termism rhetoric expresses the underlying anxiety well, even if it aims at the wrong target.

If we only had a technical problem (is the stock market's time horizon off kilter?), we would look only at whether the evidence supports the idea that stock-market-driven short-termism is perniciously severe—and we'd see that it does not. But what underlies much of the public controversy is not so much disagreement over the actual evidence but social conflict due to social disruption. The short-termism controversy in public rhetoric is a rejection of the stock market not so much for its time horizon but because of widespread economic anxiety. And that underlying conflict will not soon abate.

Acknowledgements

The book had its origins in the run-up to the 2016 presidential election, when the short-termism issue was prominent in the Hillary Clinton campaign and the never-formally-started 2016 Biden campaign. I considered then, outlined, and did preliminary work on why pursuing anti-stock-market short-termism would not implement the core of the anticipated Clinton administration agenda—why it would miss the target and how it misjudged the importance of short-termism for the liberal political agenda. A Clinton administration did not come to pass, so I put aside the larger project, and turned core aspects of the ideas into separate academic articles, such as "Stock Market Short-Termism's Impact."

Short-termism has been a staple of corporate governance thinking and public rhetoric for a half-century, waxing and waning in prominence, but always important. It appeared in the 1970s and 1980s as central to the debate over corporate takeovers and became central once again in the early 21st century as hedge fund shareholder activism became prominent. The public short-termist rhetoric in the past few years became intertwined with, and sometimes subservient to, climate change, corporate purpose, and corporate social responsibility. That tangle made this a good time in my view to study, examine, and assess short-termism's importance, so that we're more ready than otherwise to understand how, and to what degree, stock-market-generated short-termism interacts with pollution, climate, purpose, and responsibility.

That reemergence of short-termism in a new milieu, and the regular tagging of climate and responsibility issues as rooted in stock-market-driven short-termism, led me to turn back to the original short-termism project with this book. The message is the same as it originally was: stock-market-driven short-termism is not much of a problem, the evidence for it is weak or inconclusive, and the principles of how businesses work make it unlikely to be powerfully debilitating. Of the consequences attributed to stock market short-termism issue itself, like diminished R&D, the better policy response would be to bolster government-sponsored research first. The public corporate issues of the day—corporate responsibility and purpose—are only tangentially and weakly connected to corporate time horizons. And there still persists the not small chance that the short-termism issue can be and sometimes is captured by corporate interests who, acting quite sincerely—because they believe short-termism is not intermittent and occasional, but pernicious and ubiquitous—bolster their own corporate agendas in ways that would not always be good for the economy.

* * *

I've had the good fortune over the years to have had excellent students and colleagues with whom to discuss, analyze, and at times disagree with on the issues in this book. The students were those in seminars on corporate short-termism, corporate governance, and corporate purpose that I taught in one form or another annually for several years, those who did independent research projects, and the several who helped as research assistants.

Alex Edmans, Jesse Fried, Jeffrey Gordon, Tom Gosling, Charles Nathan, Robert Pozen, Roy Shapira, Holger Spamann, and Michael Troege all read a draft of the book, and the book is much better for their having done so. Other colleagues read parts or drafts of several articles I wrote on the subject when working on parts of the book. Drafts of several of the articles listed below circulated and were the subject of academic seminars across the United States and in Europe, in which lively discussion honed the thinking. At my home institution, Harvard Law School, colleagues commented on these articles or discussed them in our regular business law group lunches at the law school. Lucian Bebchuk, Bob Clark, John Coates, Bala Dharan, Allen Ferrell, Howell Jackson, Mark Ramseyer, and Guhan Subramanian were regulars at such events and discussions. Louis Kaplow, Steven Shavell, Charlie Wang, and I discussed several of the key issues. Lisa Rydin and Arevik Avedian from the law school's library regularly uncovered critical sources and focused with their staff on how to assemble some of the underlying data. Anastasia Tolu and Joanne Wyckoff maneuvered the manuscript into presentable form.

I've been lucky to have excellent research assistance for this book and its constituent prior articles. For work on the book in its near-final form, I thank Denise Han, Jessica Ljustina, Harold Schaff, Zach Singer, and Amy Zeng.

Work on four academic articles built out a big part of the book's foundation:

1. *The Power of the Corporate Narrative*, 11 Harvard Business Law Review 233 (2021) (with Roy Shapira).
2. *Will Loyalty Shares Do Much for Corporate Short-Termism?* 76 Business Lawyer 467 (2021) (with Federico Cenzi Venezze).

3. *Stock Market Short-Termism's Impact*, 167 UNIVERSITY OF PENNSYLVANIA LAW REVIEW 71 (2018).
4. *Corporate Short-Termism—In the Boardroom and in the Courtroom*, 68 BUSINESS LAWYER 977 (2013).

Mark Roe
Cambridge, Massachusetts
October 1, 2021

Index

For the benefit of digital users, indexed terms that span two pages (e.g., 52–53) may, on occasion, appear on only one of those pages.